Old Lines, New Forces

Old Lines, New Forces

Essays on the Contemporary British Novel, 1960–1970

Edited by Robert K. Morris

Rutherford • Madison • Teaneck
Fairleigh Dickinson University Press
London: Associated University Presses

©1976 by Associated University Presses, Inc.

Associated University Presses, Inc.
Cranbury, New Jersey 08512

Associated University Presses
108 New Bond Street
London W1Y OQX, England

Library of Congress Cataloging in Publication Data
Main entry under title:

Old lines, new forces.

  Bibliography: p.
  1. English fiction—20th century—History and criticism—
Addresses, essays, lectures. I. Morris, Robert K.
PR883.04   823'.9'1409   75-18243
ISBN 0-8386-1771-9

PRINTED IN THE UNITED STATES OF AMERICA

For
Tina and Peter,
and for John – readers still

Contents

vii

Contents

Acknowledgments

The editor wishes to thank authors, publishers, and agents for permission to quote the following excerpts:

Kingsley Amis, excerpts from *The Anti-Death League.* Copyright © 1966 by Kingsley Amis. Reprinted by permission of Victor Gollancz Ltd, Harcourt Brace Jovanovich, Inc., and the author.

Malcolm Bradbury, excerpts from *Stepping Westward.* Copyright © 1965, 1966 by Malcolm Bradbury. Reprinted by permission of Martin Secker & Warburg Limited and Houghton Mifflin Company.

Anthony Burgess, excerpts from *A Clockwork Orange.* Copyright © 1962, 1963 by Anthony Burgess. Reprinted by permission of William Heinemann Ltd. and W. W. Norton & Company, Inc.

Margaret Drabble, excerpts from *The Millstone.* Copyright © 1965, 1966 by Margaret Drabble. Reprinted by permission of George Weidenfeld and Nicolson Limited and William Morrow and Company, Inc.

Michel Foucault, excerpts from *Madness and Civilization: A History of Insanity in the Age of Reason,* translated by Richard Howard. Copyright © 1965 by Random House, Inc. Reprinted by permission of Fairstock Publications Ltd. and Pantheon Books, a Division of Random House, Inc.

Eden Gray, excerpts from *A Complete Guide to the Tarot*. Copyright © 1970 by Eden Gray. Reprinted by permission of Crown Publishers, Inc.

Doris Lessing, excerpts from *The Golden Notebook*. Copyright © 1962 by Doris Lessing. Reprinted by permission of Michael Joseph Ltd., and Simon and Schuster, Inc. Also for excerpts from *The Four-Gated City*. Copyright © 1969 by Doris Lessing Productions Ltd. Reprinted by permission of Curtis Brown Ltd, Alfred A. Knopf, Inc., and the author.

Robert K. Morris, excerpts from *Paradoxes Order: Some Perspectives on the Fiction of V. S. Naipaul*. Copyright © 1975 by The Curators of the University of Missouri. Reprinted by permission of The University of Missouri Press.

V. S. Naipaul, excerpts from *An Area of Darkness*. Copyright © 1964, 1965 by V. S. Naipaul. Reprinted by permission of Andre Deutsch Limited and Curtis Brown, Ltd. Also for excerpts from *The Mimic Men*. Copyright © 1967 by V. S. Naipaul. Reprinted by permission of Andre Deutsch Limited and Macmillan Publishing Co., Inc.

Andrew Sinclair, excerpts from *Gog*. Copyright © 1967 by Andrew Sinclair. Reprinted by permission of George Weidenfeld and Nicolson Limited, Elaine Greene Ltd., and the author. Also for excerpts from *Magog*. Copyright © 1972 by Andrew Sinclair. Reprinted by permission of George Weidenfeld and Nicolson Limited and Harper & Row, Publishers, Inc.

A. E. Waite, excerpts from *The Pictorial Key to the Tarot*. Copyright © 1971 by A. E. Waite. Reprinted by permission of Rider & Co. and Steinerbooks.

Angus Wilson, excerpts from *The Old Men at the Zoo*. Copyright © 1961 by Angus Wilson. Reprinted by permission of Martin Secker & Warburg Limited and The Viking Press Inc.

Introduction

Ours is a productive and sophisticated age of criticism, though one danger it has continually run has been the temptation to yoke the writing of literary history with the utterances of prophecies about literature. To give substance to this generalization it is not necessary to consider much beyond the strange case of the contemporary British novel, which by general consensus dates from shortly before the Second World War to the present. Wars, however disruptive of social and intellectual life, provide natural demarcations for literary periods. So far as British literature is concerned, World War II was something of a symbolic demarcation as well. James Joyce and Virginia Woolf had died in 1941, and D. H. Lawrence, whose posthumous *Apocalypse* all but envisioned the oncoming holocaust, ten years earlier. In a little over a decade, the English-speaking world had buried three of its novelistic giants (the fourth, E. M. Forster, had not written a novel since 1924). It remained for the second war to end the "modern" period that the first had begun, and after that for the interpreters-cum-prophets, already forecasting the choke, sob, and death rattle of the novel, to get on with the real business of burying the corpse.

More out of concern and industry than chauvinism or insularity, the prophesying game began. The successful British novelist Rose Macaulay wrote as early as 1946, when the bitter fruits of war had not been fully gathered at "closing time in the gardens of the West,"[1] and before reconstruction had begun its

---

1. Cyril Connolly's phrase in the last issue of *Horizon* 20 (1950): 17.

pruning of despair and confusion:

> A kind of miasma, a dullness still obscures the imaginative
> life of many. . . . No new style is even faintly to be seen on
> the horizon. . . . There has been in fact a flight from style
> . . . the novel of the future will be in plain, uncolored En-
> glish, with no frills. . . . Those who write mannered English
> are all of older generations; the future of the novel is not with
> them.[2]

Even accounting for the temporary postwar depression of the
young men and women who had become toughened or desen-
sitized by the experience, or that of the preceding generation
who (after their second major war) had become inured to it,
Macaulay's realization that the driving force once called the
British novel had reached an impasse seemed just. Thirties'
writers like Henry Green, Ivy Compton-Burnett, Christopher
Isherwood (one of the greatest disappointments in British fiction), and writers like Aldous Huxley and Evelyn Waugh,
whose work hovered between the twenties and thirties, became more concerned with evoking remembrances of things
past than engaging things present or to come; or when involved
with the latter created fanciful fictions to offset or corroborate
the general horrors perpetrated on their world and their sensibilities.

Rose Macaulay's piece seemed to set the tone, if not always
the direction for explaining novelistic paralysis. Writing in that
same year for the middlebrow *Atlantic*, Jacques Barzun departed from mental to dwell on mettle fatigue:

> Perhaps we come too late to expect any novel experiences
> from the novel. The genre may be exhausted, though it is
> always pointless to prophesy artistic negatives of this sort.
> The only thing to say is that for a good while now, the alert
> reader has only had his memories stirred by new novels, not
> his sense of life and of life's endless translatability. Instead,
> looking back over a "new" work just read he could say:—

---

2. In "The Future of Fiction" in *New Writing and Daylight* 7 (1946): 69.

"Hardy country. A Jamesian young man, whose father is a Dickens' character, steps out of a Galsworthy house just as a Jane Austen girl goes by. Thackeray suspicions are in order. Ah, the Meredith ahead! But no, the girl's father is a Trollope clergyman. Early a widower, he brought up his baby Austen as a Charlotte Yonge lady. . . . Flaubert! Flaubert!"[3]

The truth of Barzun's academic jest was of doubtful help to the working novelist trying to sort out his dilemma. It contained in fact two things that make novelists loathe critics. For one, Barzun's cast back into the eighteenth and nineteenth centuries—when the novel could hardly have been anything but fresh and vital—was both superfluous and astigmatic: his comparisons were (only the cliché will do) odious. Wound up on this ratchet of "influence," even the major talents could scarcely angle for a fair evaluation. For another, it refused to single out the extraordinary or exceptional. Graham Greene, at high watermark and with a great career still to come, had almost nothing in common with the best on Barzun's list, and was cuts above Galsworthy and Yonge, and perhaps Trollope.

But Barzun's central and responsible truth remained. Even the almost-established younger novelists responded to the dirge that now had taken on the overtones of a requiem, though the responses took the form of criticism rather than fiction. In a little book called *The Novel in Our Time* (1948), Alex Comfort noted that the trouble with the novel was not (as Macaulay and Barzun seemed to think) a matter of too little too late, but of too much too soon:

> The modern novel is patently not succeeding in coping with the material which is presented to it, because like everyone else, the novelist is becoming saturated, both in his sense of tragedy and in his capacity for indignation or for analysis.[4]

On the whole one could not have asked for a more level-

3. "Non-Fiction Novelists," *Atlantic* 178 (1946): 129–32.
4. *The Novel in Our Time* (London, 1948), p. 75.

headed insight, but in failing to reconcile means and ends, it was also slightly evasive. The idea of saturation was a poor rationalization for not getting the job done. Lawrence provided the best example of a novelist who had become, first as a Victorian, then as an Edwardian, and finally as a "modern," saturated by these very things: not merely saturated, but exposed to overkill. The real question was not why the younger novelists were parroting the techniques, subjects, and often sensibilities of Dickens, Meredith, Bennett, and Galsworthy, but why they were reluctant to be "influenced" by already acknowledged titans like Joyce and Lawrence and even the Bloomsbury crowd.

In the accelerated debate over the death of the British novel, the British (typically) remained cool while the Americans grew fevered, and in places hysterical. In a 1949 article Herschell Brickell flogged practicing novelists with Dostoevski and Tolstoy, as well as with Conrad and James, to illustrate the lack of moral and metaphysical elevation in contemporary life and letters:

> Perhaps *the* principal reason why so many of us find a minimum of nourishment in current fiction is that characters seem to have bodies, very active bodies, which perform their natural functions successfully enough, but no minds to speak of, and certainly no souls. . . . Plainly, man without his mind and soul has lost the dignity that has made him worthy of serious consideration as a subject for art . . . if the movement continues unabated we may quite well find fiction abandoned as an art form, leaving it to entertain but not to delight, to stir, to arouse, nor to do any of the other jobs for which art was so obviously created in the beginning.[5]

The alternative to Comfort's not squaring up to the question seemed to be Brickell's begging it. As an "art" form, the novel was at best a latecomer on the scene, and its genesis was never lofty to begin with. Richardson, one remembers, wrote *Pamela*

---

5. "The Present State of Fiction," *Virginia Quarterly Review* 25 (1949): 92–98.

while working on a manual of letter-writing that two booksell-
ers had asked him to prepare; and Fielding wrote *Shamela* and
Joseph Andrews to parody Richardson. What Jane Austen did
after them, and what Dickens and George Eliot and Thackeray
did after her, were dictated less by considerations of art than by
the demands of the times and their responses to them.

The point I mean to make here is that the form and function
of the novel—particularly the British novel—seemed always
more closely allied with the spirit of time and place than with
any categorical aesthetic. And it was surely quixotic of critics
to seek amidst the flux and ruins of a postwar world for the
vitality, audacity, and energy of the great "peacetime" Victo-
rians and Edwardians when the war had so clearly sapped these
qualities not only from writers but from everyone. Man had not
almost wholesale lost mind and soul and dignity; he was tired
and confused.

"The world," wrote Storm Jameson in 1951, "was more than
the novelist could manage."[6] The grim litany of such names as
Buchenwald, Hiroshima, and Nagasaki, Dresden, and Nurem-
berg bore witness to this. As great as the disgust and loathing
might have been after the first war, the "lost generation" writers had never been so totally disoriented; they had found themselves, in a sense, even in their lostness. It was possible that
the chaos within the post-World War II novelist inhibited
flights to greatness, but more probable that the chaos without
did. Such order is necessary before experimentation and inno-
vation can begin. And certainly the world lacked order; its
horrors had grown immense and man had dwindled. Ironically,
this very theme seemed to impose limitations on the one writer
continually promising to write the "big" novel. Graham
Greene, according to Jameson, wrote about "the sense of man's
littleness in the face of the terrible forces which try to possess

---

6. "British Literature," *Saturday Review* 34 (1951): 24–26. I realize that Jameson's
currency does not stand particularly high in academic or critical circles, but she was
indeed one of the first to voice in a respected "slick magazine" an analysis of the
novel's situation in the fifties, and for that reason alone her comments deserve more
than passing attention.

him."[7] The response of the novelist, again to his ethos and not
to the demands of art, seemed to produce small gems from a
great mass of bedrock.

In retrospect, Jameson's piece is notable for moving the debate over the death of the novel away from speculations as to
why the times were not turning out "great" novelists, to why
they were turning out many interesting and accomplished ones.
This, of course, scarcely generated much cheer.

> The virtues of the better novelists have been intelligence,
> powers of subtle analysis, an anxiety to make the finest pos-
> sible discrimination between motives, an equal anxiety for
> precision and language . . . but their cleverness has outrun
> their spiritual and emotional grasp. Even when one of our
> writers tries to grasp what is really happening in the world,
> the merely intellectual effort he has to make takes all his
> energy, and you get a novel full of clear and sometimes
> profound ideas and no depth of feeling. . . . The best writ-
> ers prefer to work integrity, care, subtlety on themes they
> can explore without attending much to the approach of a
> Dark Age.[8]

The last phrase is the significant one. For it was exactly this
myopia that made Jameson's "better novelists"—that is,
Graham Greene, Elizabeth Bowen, L. P. Hartley, William
Sansom, Nigel Balchin, P. H. Newby, Ivy Compton-Burnett
and Henry Green—too soon anachronisms, but heralds, too, of
a new and exciting decade in British fiction.

The cases of L. P. Hartley and P. H. Newby, to take two of
the most polar writers on Jameson's list, are symptomatic of the
British novelist's failure to take and keep hold after the war.
Hartley's *Eustace and Hilda* trilogy—his most sustained and
artistic fiction, though by no means as popular as *The Boat* and
The Go-Between—for all its aesthetic perfection and mythic architectonics, becomes in the end a frustrating farewell to a

7. "British Literature," pp. 24–26.
8. *Ibid.*

period whose temper and tempo never caught up with the modern age. Newby's forties' novels, and those in the very early fifties—quests aimed at arresting confusion in a confused time—leave his protagonists high and dry, straddling crises and sensibilities, and refusing to make the demanding gesture that will carry them outside the limited range set by the novel itself. To account for the relative failure of Hartley and Newby to make more than a stir on the postwar scene, I would say that despite their vivid foregrounds they never managed enough depth of field to focus on those greater blocks of action and change taking place behind. They did not light up the coming Dark Age.

If the accuracy of Jameson's criticism, of her *self*-criticism (for unlike their American counterparts who were academics or journalists, the British critics were novelists themselves), could dampen the spirits of these best writers, two other things gave still colder comfort. One of these was British poetry. Given the continuity of Eliot and Masefield of the older generation, Auden and Spender of the middle, and Thomas of the younger, it continued to be regarded as highly as before the war. The other was the American novel. It was impossible, at the opening of the fifties, to find in England any single postwar novel to rival Norman Mailer's *The Naked and the Dead,* whose title alone evoked the human condition and divisions of that terrible period in history; to find, again, other works reflecting the disillusionment, pessimism, alienation caught so perfectly by J. D. Salinger in his *Catcher in the Rye* or Ralph Ellison in his *Invisible Man;* or along quite different lines, opening out to a rare direction in contemporary American fiction, to find a novel so filled with compassion, discovery, wonder, and optimism as Saul Bellow's *The Adventures of Augie March.* To be sure, Anthony Powell and C. P. Snow had published several volumes in their formidable sequences, but neither pattern nor scope had yet emerged, and anyway they seemed not so much to be speaking to the confusion and restlessness of the present age as to reviving the order of a past one. Outside America, only the maverick Canadian and expatriate Malcolm Lowry was able in the early fifties to hold the line on the critical popularity shown American novelists and to gain some notoriety. Lowry's *Under the Volcano* was an eruptive book, freeing good and evil from their ethical entrapment in the works of Greene and Hartley and Newby, and pointing out man's fallible, brutal, willful, inchoate, chaotic posture as destroyer and self-destroyer. But this was hardly the sort of novel one would have classed in F. R. Leavis's great tradition.

The breakthrough that came in 1953 with the publication of Kingsley Amis's *Lucky Jim* and John Wain's *Hurry on Down* (*Born in Captivity* in the English edition), or that the more discerning date several years earlier with William Cooper's *Scenes from Provincial Life,* threw into relief isolated novels like Angus Wilson's *Hemlock and After,* Iris Murdoch's *Under the Net,* and the early volumes of Doris Lessing's Martha Quest series, "Children of Violence." Gauged objectively, none of these novels created at international, literary ground zero the critical impact of Truman Capote's *Other Voices, Other Rooms* and *The Grass Harp,* William Styron's *Lie Down in Darkness,* Flannery O'Connor's *Wise Blood,* or James Baldwin's *Go Tell It on the Mountain.* Yet something had been shaken loose. Where only a year before critics had been hinting at the death of the novel, some were now at least intimating a renaissance. What only remained was for British fiction to prove itself, through quality and quantity, beyond the mere hope.

Which in part it did. Whether through accident, charisma, or the time spirit at last taking hold, the singular link among the writers of the fifties—their "dissentience," as Kenneth Allsop calls it in *The Angry Decade*—had succeeded in revitalizing a tired culture and the novel along with it. The British novelists around thirty, as opposed to the novelists of the thirties, no longer withdrew to recollect in tranquility the prewar or the interwar years, but to confront in rebellion their own decade. These were the "Angry Young Men." And all were galvanized into responding: some to England's shrinking political, social, and economic importance in the world; some to the galloping *Angst* of nuclear tests and the race for armaments; some to the

Welfare State and its anesthetizing socialism; some to
Americanism; some to the "shiny barbarism" of the new mass
culture; some to the insular "I'm all right, Jack" ideology;
some, simply, to postwar hangover. But all were responding.
No one has outlined the overtones of the phrase *Angry Young
Man* better than Kenneth Allsop, and since I will be returning
to them in my comparison of the novelists of the fifties and
sixties I think that I should set out here nothing less than the
entire quotation. The overtones were

> irreverence, stridency, impatience with tradition, vigour,
> vulgarity, sulky resentment against the cultivated and a
> hard-boiled muscling-in on culture, adventurousness, self-
> pity, deliberate disengagement from politics, fascist ambi-
> tions, schizophrenia, rude dislike of anything phoney or fey,
> a broad sense of humour but low on wit, a general in-
> tellectual nihilism, honesty, a neurotic discontent and a de-
> feated, reconciled acquiescence that is the last flimsy shelter
> against complete despondency.[9]

Though this was a gallimaufry of credos eclectic in design
and without any visible coherence, a movement more in theory
and feeling than in fact and technique, *Angry* became the universal label slapped or pasted at random on all of the new
writers. The differences in aims, methods, and directions un-
avoidably concealed beneath the label were not at once apparent. Few of the Establishment critics were anything but indifferent or callous or hostile to the lifeline being thrown the novel
or the attempt at pumping new blood into tired veins. Those
who only a few years before had been disheartened because the
novel did not seem to be going anywhere were now disap-
pointed at the strong direction it had suddenly taken. Stephen
Spender wrote in 1953: "There is one good reason for doubting
whether university teachers will bring life to literature: they
might confuse literature with lecturing about literature."[10] A

---

9. *The Angry Decade* (London, 1958), pp. 37–38.
10. *Encounter* 1 (1953): 66.

year later, J. B. Priestly eschewed Spender's fiat, but with a
nostaligic look at the stability and responsibility demanded by
the older sort of novel, and a lament for the anarchy and anti-
heroism pervading the new ones, couldn't prophecy for them
much beyond a transient vogue.[11] And shortly after this Somerset Maugham capped any ill will and reservations about the
younger breed of "Angries" with his vehement and now
notorious pronouncement on their heroes: "They are mean,
malicious and envious. They are scum."[12]

It was Shaw, I believe, who somewhere raised the point that
the curious thing about scum is that, like cream, it rises to the
top. Nothing could have proved truer. However cool the ancient regime was to the "Angries," its criticism over the novel's
life and death had taken on a much different cast from the
previous debates, moving away from the perplexity and melancholy tone to outright challenge and engagement. The energy
of the novelists had reenergized the debate itself. The old shell
game of trying to spot the "great" British novel through shop-
worn critical manipulation gave way to the more free-wheeling
critical roulette, which, of course, still left the outcome in
doubt, but allowed more numbers to play. The shift in attention away from what the older novelists had not done toward
what the newer might do was at first desultory. As of 1954, for
example, Anthony Powell, who had completed but two volumes in "The Music of Time" series, was the only postwar
novelist given a long, scholarly analysis in a leading American
quarterly, and that essay was an examination of the novels he
had written in the thirties.[13] It was an odd reversal to have
revaluation precede evaluation, but the significant point was
that criticism on contemporary works had taken hold.

The dramatic shift came in 1958. Analytic articles (not mere
journalistic puffs or pieces in slicks) began appearing on Kingsley Amis, Lawrence Durrell, William Golding, Iris Murdoch,

---

11. "New Novelists," *New Statesman and Nation* 47 (1954): 824.
12. Letter to *The London Times*, 1955, August 25, p. 4.
13. R. J. Voorhees, "Anthony Powell: The First Phase," *Prairie Schooner* 28
(1954): 337–44.

John Wain, Angus Wilson, Alan Sillitoe, and Doris Lessing. Allsop's book (still the best one on the period) and William Van O'Connor's *The New University Wits* were both published in that year. Allsop's witty and scrupulous analyses of the "dissentients" and O'Connors more general survey of many of the same writers (Wain, Murdoch, Amis, Dennis, etc.) ostensibly gave the lie to David Daiches's *The Present Age in British Literature* (also 1958), which hardly concerned itself with the present age at all. Despite the brouhaha over the new writers, Daiches could obtusely suggest: "At the moment of writing, in the mid-50's the English novel seems on the whole to be in the hands of *competent but unexciting* professionals"[14] (italics added). Coming from a tyro critic rather than an arbiter of taste, the italicized epithet, I am certain, would have been editorially challenged. On the contrary, most of the scholars and critics had already conceded the quality of excitement and newness in these novels and occupied themselves with mining any substance that might lay beneath them.

If it had taken a decade for the novelist to catch up with the *Zeitgeist*, it took longer for the critic to catch up with the novelist. And almost as soon as he had done so, the "anger" had passed. It was a vociferous, vital, shattering, and consequential movement and phenomenon, this "angry decade," but a groping as much as a rebellion. Its chief virtue was to renew the awareness of the novel as a living form. Whether critics quibbled with these new novelists' concern for mere technical competence as opposed to depth, inveighed against their negativeness, canted about their self-advertisement, the very fact of response showed that the novel was neither stultifying nor dead. Ingenuous but questionable predictions had surrendered to more substantial analyses. Perhaps the only bit of latter-day auguring that seemed sensible rather than self-fulfilling came from O'Connor, who pointed out in the conclusion to his book that the mood and movement of the "Angries" was already being reshaped by a new spirit in fiction. Some-

---

14. (Bloomington, Indiana, and London, 1958), p. 118.

thing more, then, than a mere affirmation in the viability of the
postwar British novel had emerged in the late fifties. On the
threshold of another decade, charged by the vitality of the last
one and by the momentum through time itself, it had moved
out along new lines to reveal talents and forces that challenged
the earliest prophecies of Rose Macaulay and Alex Comfort,
and probably pleased them in doing so.

I must apologize at this point for an introduction that has not
yet directly touched upon the subject it is intended to introduce. Yet one must, I think, have well in mind these above
reactions to the direction of British fiction in the first fifteen
years after the war in order to see how in the next ten it so
effectively changed course. Without plunging into *post hoc ergo
propter hoc* pitfalls, I would nevertheless suggest that criticism
seemed partly responsible for the change. Only the most insen-
sitive of novelists could have been, at that time, unaware of the
continual buzzing of critical gadflies. Persistent appeals by
writers like Walter Allen, Frank Swinnerton, and Jack Lindsay
to overhaul the novel so that it became something more than a
vehicle of reportage rolling unmerrily on its iconoclastic, nihilistic, anti-intellectual, insular, and sociological way, and to refur-
bish it with imagination and poetry, were perhaps overharsh;
but their shock value was undeniable.[15] By 1960 the Jim Dix-
ons and Charles Lumleys and Jake Donahughs and Arthur
Seatons had ended their short, fascinating, prototypical careers.
As though to a man (and woman) the younger and older
novelists had read the cautionary symposium on the new novel
in John Lehmann's *London Magazine,* he/she seemed suddenly
to abandon concern with man as a "social being" and to turn to
the "idea of the novel as a whole world, an image of life that
engages all the faculties of mind and feeling."[16]

---

15. In, respectively: *The English Novel: A Short Critical History* (London, 1954), p.
7; "Eclipse of the Novel," *Contemporary Review* 189 (1956): 336; *After the Thirties: The
Novel in Britain and Its Future* (London, 1956), p. 101.
16. Frank Kermode's phrase in his contribution to "New Novelists," *London
Magazine* 5 (1958): 13–31.

Of course it was not as sudden as all that; and the novelists, not the critics, were responsible for the turn. However far criticism had gone to giving the novel an inferiority complex, it never became so vulnerable as to surrender its centuries-old tradition of perdurability and continuity. The British tyro novelist of the angry decade, whether angry or not, had kept on writing novels throughout. A substantial but flexible base for the novel of the sixties was built during the fifties, a time of variety and prolificness. Even more important, a new feeling as to what one should expect from novelists and they from themselves was becoming current. No longer urged to compete with the Americans (who oddly enough had turned to journalism and para-journalism) or with Lawrence and Joyce, they began to see that this "whole world," this "image of life" need not necessarily be crammed into any single book. This may account for the phenomenal interest in series novels; it certainly made the novelist freer and less prone to whip himself into a competing frenzy.

The sixties became singular for this new feeling; it was as though a new tradition, too, had gotten underway that canceled previous conceptions, perhaps misconceptions about what the novel had or needed to do. The feeling was first communicated, I believe, by Anthony Burgess in his own critique of the contemporary novel, a retrospective view written in 1967:

> We can no longer expect the one big book, the single achievement, to be an author's claim to posterity's regard. We shall be more inclined to assess the stature of a novelist by his ability to create what the French call an *oeuvre*, to present fragments of an individual vision in book after book, to build, if not a *War and Peace* or *Ulysses*, at least a shelf.[17]

Some of the best critics of the sixties—James Gindin, Frederick Karl, Walter Allen, Bernard Bergonzi, Frank Kermode, and Paul West—anticipated or intuited Burgess's method of

17. *The Novel Now* (New York, 1970), p. 117.

assessment.[18] But none, surprisingly, was able to see beyond those "fragments of an individual vision" the loomings of what I would call the collective vision. The incredible number of good novels published without interruption by the fifties' novelists, and the emergence in the sixties of the new, younger novelists' works, had by 1968 or 1969 already produced an impressive, imaginative, and diversified literature. The largest of its fragments had not contributed much to changing England's picture of itself; but the total effect was stimulating and undeniable. Out of the ethos a shaping spirit had emerged—in the novels and in some cases perhaps because of them.

The natural question that arises from all this is how *did* this spirit differ from that of the fifties? Most important, it was no longer dissentience or anger. Allsop's lengthy catalogue of the personal and cultural overtones sounded in the "angry decade" had shrunk by the sixties to the odd item here and there. I have in mind things like "honesty," "schizophrenia," "vigour," and "adventurousness," which continued to operate in the sixties' novels. Indeed, all of them could be found in *The Golden Notebook;* but these had always been the subjects and attitudes of novelists and hardly the monopoly of one or two periods. Writers, too, were still manifesting "neurotic discontent"; but American novelists like John Barth and Thomas Pynchon had come up with a superlative case for paranoia, before which neuroses seemed almost innocent and pleasurable deviations. The disorder seemed to attract at least one significant novelist—Iris Murdoch, who became partial in her later books to the paranoid type.

On other counts, too, the major bulk of Allsop's list had shifted or settled. The iconoclasm encompassing "irreverence, stridency . . . vulgarity, sulky resentment against the cultivated and a hard-boiled muscling-in on culture" was finally taken to be no more than a heresy of petulance. The search

---

18. In, respectively: *Post-War British Fiction* (Berkeley, Calif., 1962); *The Contemporary English Novel* (New York, 1964); *The Modern Novel* (New York, 1967); *Situation of the Novel* (Pittsburgh, Pa., 1971), and many reviews in the sixties; *Puzzles and Epiphanies* (London, 1962); *The Modern Novel* (London, 1967).

turned toward authenticity, toward finding whatever of value or truth in the culture might yet remain. The sixties' novelists stopped writing satire and began writing comedy. It had been much too easy "to make the worst of a bad job"; the difficulty—reflected in books like Burgess's *The Right to an Answer* and Olivia Manning's Balkan Trilogy—was to try to make, failing radical change, the best of it. The continuing sequences of Powell and Snow, Andrew Sinclair's *Gog*, John Fowles's *The French Lieutenant's Woman*, so different in technique and intention, all nevertheless showed a strong reliance on "tradition"; and, in fact, most of Doris Lessing's "Children of Violence" series is a painstaking reconstruction of traditions that go furthest to explaining both heroine and author's desire for change.

This dissent from dissentience on the part of the sixties' novelists was capped by their most glaring rejection of what seemed the ruling passion of the fifties: its "intellectual nihilism." Allsop's phrase strangely enough squinted in two directions at once. For many of the novelists were not simply occupied with the denial of all traditional and existing principles, institutions, and values, but with the annihilation of whatever value intellect itself had. The new novel's departure from this finally specious and self-defeating line was timely. And without it I doubt very much whether the sixties' writers in England—and, I believe, the same holds true for the American novelists as well—would have become as unique and forceful as they did.

The radical shift back to "intellectualism" is easy to see; how to account for it is more difficult. Perhaps the new novelists of the sixties, and those of the fifties who propagated anti-intellectualism when not actually originating it, wearied of the pose of the capable intellectual hiding behind the mask of the rough-hewn—Colin Wilson being the most notorious example—and insouciantly casting his cultural pearls before swine; perhaps they finally experienced proper disgust or boredom at using as whipping boy the very processes of intellect by which art is formed and through which it survives; perhaps the

growing presence in world literature of Vladimir Nabokov and
the advent of Jorge Luis Borges accounted for more of the
change; and the happy accident of novels from polymaths like
Burgess, Fowles, and Sinclair for the rest of it. A collective faith
in the intellect had been reaffirmed, often because the writer
was actually not ashamed of being an elite in a world leveling
all to mediocrity, often because he believed that intellect might
ultimately achieve what mere anarchy and anger had failed to. I
would place V. S. Naipaul, along with the three other British
novelists I have just mentioned, in the first category. Naipaul's
crystalline prose, his focus on the subtlest shadings of the colonial and expatriate mind, and his extraordinary sensitivity to
the backgrounds that have formed it suggest a feeling for the
novelist's role as a maker of a world. The panoramas of Fowles
and Sinclair are given an added immensity by being populated
with countless literary allusions, anthropological arcana,
pyrotechnics of language, and outrageous devices, as well as by
treating themes ranging from the personal to the universal;
without imitating the letter of Joyce, they have revived the
spirit of his symphonic anatomies. Burgess, a linguist, a
Shakespearean and Joycean scholar, and an outspoken critic of
sloppiness and dullness in writing, is one of the more remarkable innovators of language in the decade. With the qualification that "intellect" for Doris Lessing also relates to feeling as
much as to politics, art, and psychology, I would place her in
the second category; and certainly the philosophic
constructs—what are indeed fables—of Nigel Dennis and
Angus Wilson would place them there, too.

So far my case for the novelists' rejection of "intellectual
nihilism" has considered but one face of Allsop's Janus-like
epithet. I have talked about their recovery of intellectualism
through form, and clearly not all the novelists writing in the last
ten years were experimenters in style. Indeed William Golding
and Lawrence Durrell, who matured in the previous decade
and who never for a moment relinquished the function of
novelist-as-intellectual, are still considered most experimental.
Yet both were at least partially hypnotized by the fifties' nihilistic spell. Durrell's Alexandria, stripped of its bizarreness, mys-

tery, and opulence, stands at the end of the quartet revealed in all its tarnished, shoddy reality; and Golding's best novels, those depicting and bewailing "the end of innocence," profess unsatisfactory encounters with experience and often the profoundest pessimism.

One must look then beyond the novel's form to find the spirit of the sixties reified in its content. And it is here that the new force creates its most sustained impact, creates a unified and unambiguous sense of what an age meant to its representative novelists. "Intellectual nihilism" has been discarded and replaced by what I would call intellectual positivism. Even at its most violent or apocalyptic, the novel has become a means for voicing determination rather than resignation, for reshaping overblown declarations into substantive questions,[18] and for asserting the primacy of the creative over the destructive principle. The picaresque evasion and nihilism of the fifties, provoked by society's failure to establish some permanent framework to enclose personal values, were recast by the sixties into encounter and engagement: the search for permanent values within a personal framework. Search is the dominating spirit of the sixties. Not with all passions numbed or spent, but with them renewed, a decade of quest transcended a decade of anger.

One might say that this distinction does not go very far in offsetting the uniqueness of an age, and up to a point I would agree. The kinds of quests common to the British novel of the sixties—quests after identity, experience, freedom, paradise, love, avatars, fulfillment, salvation, fathers, mothers, et cetera, et cetera—are scarcely uncommon. And the quest motif itself, as Northrop Frye has theorized, is the archetype central to all literatures and consequently its grandest cliché. Where the sixties has proved itself singular and curiously persistent is in its transvaluation of the archetype. Because the novelist's concern with his hero's personal determination, dynamics, drives, and achievements independent of existing systems has inspired an almost universal solipsism, the quest as object is of only slight interest. Since man's fate is to be absorbed, thwarted, ruined, corrupted, deadened, even annihilated by society—the ulti-

mate system—ends become as immaterial as they are deter-
ministic. It is now the origins of the quest and the gesture to
embark upon it that are of importance: the act, not the goal,
defines the hero.

What makes the sixties unique, too, is how its novels have
revealed this cohesive vision by an enlarged focus on similar
themes. Despite their disparate cultural and intellectual
backgrounds,[19] their very different sense of style and structure,
their contrasting philosophic orientation, the novelists seem to
make up a community of identical sensibilities when responding to the paradoxes and dilemmas of the decade, and to the
raw abstractions that set the quest in motion.

Were I to single out from these the one that goes furthest to
being the prime mover behind the questing spirit, it would be
the psychogenetic conflict between claustrophobia and
agoraphobia that began manifesting itself in the last half of the
fifties, but was not articulated until five or six years later. The
most complete and complex treatment of the enclosure-
freedom theme is to be found in Lessing's *Golden Notebook* and
Four-Gated City; but the elaborate zoo metaphor in Wilson's *Old
Men at the Zoo*, the symbolic greenhouse in *A House in Order*,
Alex's stereo womb in *A Clockwork Orange*, the Isabella and
London of *The Mimic Men*, and the alternately safe and dangerous rooms Rosamund inhabits in *The Millstone* are more concise
reductions of the same idea. In a somewhat different vein,
Sinclair's gigantism in *Gog* and *Magog* is an attempt to abort
England's shrinkage to insularity and isolation, while Bradbury's *Stepping Westward* is concerned with the personal expansion and expansiveness of an English writer within the large-
ness, openness, if finally unsatisfactory freedom of America.

To find this freedom-enclosure opposition dominating so
many of the novels of the sixties is at best unusual; but I find
even more so their almost universal concern for determining its

---

19. This is borne out, I think, by the present collection of essays, which em-
phasizes the reconstructive over the apocalyptic. Also see Kermode's *The Sense of an
Ending* (New York, 1968).

genesis and tracing its consequences. I take *genesis* as the crucial term here, for behind both the fear of confinement and the fear of escape lies an amoral force, creative but finally destructive. It is the machine; or, when not quite that literal, a mechanistic principle in opposition to the organic or life principle. No one has provided a better metaphor for this dichotomy than Burgess. Man is in danger of becoming, if he has not already become, "a clockwork orange." A human being created to "ooze sweetness" can too easily be programmed, conditioned, cyberneticized, if he allows himself, into a willess tool of a mechanistic god—a god, as Lawrence wrote about in *Women in Love*, that crushes, saps, destroys our organic vitalism. With his "Ludovico technique" Burgess pushes the idea of the machine to its limits, but hardly to absurdity. It is no more a *reductio ad absurdum* than the Welfare State that has started much of the trouble, something that Margaret Drabble also ponders in *The Millstone*, though the problem there is her heroine's resistance to allowing her body to become a machine. If "the millstone" is, on the one hand, her child, it is also the impersonal forces of the system grinding out stereotypes of human beings. On too many levels to discuss here, the dehumanizing mechanics engineered by the fifties and sixties become primary themes in Lessing's novels. Dennis's novel opposes to the mechanistic principle a spiritual one, Fowles's novel opposes to it what the author calls "the heart," and the quest in Sillitoe's unfinished trilogy is to authenticate being by overriding the deadness of an automatic life.

However concerted the novelists' belief that man's *Non serviam* in the face of the mechanistic principle is necessary, they recognize too that its consequences can be disastrous. Certainly not to submit always places a fearful burden on the individual; and freedom, if and when achieved, can be terrible. It can lead to the Manichaeism in Burgess and Amis, the sense of inferiority in Bradbury, the loneliness in Drabble, the frozen mimicry in Naipaul, the madness in Lessing. But it is precisely at this ebb tide of emotions or personality or relationships that awareness and action are renewed. The new forces in the sixties so seldom resonate against society because such a response would vitiate the private vision. The social being lives monistically, according to norms, rules, regulations, systems, gaining identity through a reflection of others, never through himself. This is why the so-called rebels of the fifties discovered so much about society and so little else. Place Lucky Jim's pranks alongside Alex's rapes and murder, Charles Lumley's (*Hurry on Down*) gratuitous rise alongside Ralph Singh's (*The Mimic Men*) fated spiral to the top, Jimmy Porter's funks alongside Martha Quest's bouts with schizophrenia and it becomes at once clear why the sniping at or undermining of society as a wholehearted gesture can never really reveal the truth about oneself. The resonance in the sixties is always within. And what the decade has given us in this transfiguring introversion is a greater knowledge of the inward duality necessary for individual growth and discovery. Anthony Burgess has best named this duality "conflict and confluence,"[20] the ego's application (if I understand it correctly) of the philosophic and aesthetic elements of yin and yang. Thus to know freedom we must experience enclosure, to sense our organic vitalism we must confront and conquer the machine, to discover wholeness we must suffer fragmentation, and, perhaps most consequential of all, to arrive at order within we must become inured, even callous to the chaos without.

That such chaos is inevitable, if not already a *fait accompli*, seems to be the conviction of all the novelists represented here, though they are much less hysterical in presenting it than American writers like John Barth, Thomas Pynchon, and Norman Mailer, and certainly more convinced that it may well be in the eschatological scheme of things. The chaos that can lead to "ultra-violence" in *A Clockwork Orange*, anarchy in *The Old Men at the Zoo*, war in *A House in Order*, potential holocaust in *The Anti-Death League*, and even apocalypse in *Gog* and *Magog* and *The Four-Gated City* sees also the ultimate establishment of order. The reason for this, I think, is that this overpowering

---

20. In *Urgent Copy* (New York, 1968), p. 183.

dichotomy of chaos and order are the cyclical children of flux and change, which themselves are offsprings of history and myth. And it is in the contexts of history and myth that these novelists order their heroes' quests. I would say further that there is no novel here without myth or history importantly at its center, expanding as much as explaining the novelist's world, and carrying it beyond the limits of fiction to universal statements on our past and present and, if we are really fortunate enough to survive, our future. This concern alone would make the British novel of the sixties substantial and viable enough to justify scholarly and critical appraisal, though I hope my extended comments above have suggested a viability and orginality far and beyond.

In the twenty-five years since the earliest published reflections on the death of the contemporary British novel, prophecies have come almost full circle. A recent article by Frank Kermode was entitled "The British Novel Lives"; one not long afterward by Walter Allen carried as its theme "The novel is not dead."[21] The unwritten premise of both these similar conclusions is that the novel *is* alive because it has become progressively charged with a new feeling, vitality, and direction. I have tried to sketch in the introduction what these "new forces" (as I choose to call them) are, and how they have in part emerged from older lines of the novel, though the weight of any assertion I have made can be felt only by reading the novels themselves, as well as the critical essays about them.

The aims of these essays are two: to assess the viability of the contemporary British novel by indicating the universality of its range; and ultimately to chart that range through readings in depth of fourteen very distinctive novels from the sixties. I realize, of course, that the first of these reasons for bringing such a collection together may be damned as a tautology; too, that the second presumes a certain measure of folly, if not

21. In, respectively: *Atlantic* 230 (1972): 85–88; *Contemporary Novelists* (New York, 1972), pp. vii–xii.

arrogance in hoping to classify a rather complex whole—that is, *the* contemporary British novel—through the sum of only some of its parts. But I realize, finally, how such objections are answered by the inspiration of the novelists and the concern and care of those writing about them. The fact that such extended, forceful criticism has distilled from the novels what is quintessential as well as essential, has detected their rich substances and mined their techniques, themes, characters, symbols, and contexts illustrates beyond theory or debate their essential value. The nature of the novels and the quality of analyses do, hopefully, prove the universality of contemporary British fiction and do reveal the whole through its parts.

This, I think, should be the most satisfying and profound result of such a collection, though I believe too that readers will continue to find many other things as well. Indeed, what all of us writing here hope to make clear is that these representative—and to our minds among the best—novels of the sixties show that decade, both in output and execution, as one of the most exciting periods for the contemporary novel. To see that the older line of writers who became prominent in the fifties sought, in the sixties, new directions for the novel, departed from the security of the sort of novel that made them famous—and I am speaking here of writers like Amis, Dennis, Sillitoe, Wilson—should indicate how renewable the spirit of this literature is. Add to this the words of the younger writers who began flourishing in the sixties, who found new vistas for exploration, new techniques for experiment, new visions, and the spirit carries us beyond simple appreciation or admiration to something like wonder.

Robert K. Morris

Editor's Note

With the exception of Andrew Sinclair's *Magog*—included here as a mandatory complement to *Gog*—all the novels dealt with in this collection were published in the sixties.

My decision to publish essays on two of Doris Lessing's novels was prompted by my purely prejudiced belief that *The Golden Notebook* and *The Four-Gated City* are indisputably two of the greatest books of the postwar period.

Since this collection is exclusively a critique on the contemporary British novel, I have listed only novels under the bibliographical section of the authors' biobibliography.

R. K. M.

Old Lines, New Forces

Metaphors of Enclosure: Angus Wilson's
The Old Men at the Zoo (1961)

IRVING MALIN

The Old Men at the Zoo begins brilliantly: "I opened the large central window of my office room to its full on that fine May morning. Then I stood for a few moments breathing in the soft warm air that was charged with the scent of white lilacs below. The graceful flamingos, shaded from flushed white to a robust tinned salmon, humped and coiled on their long stilts; a Florida pelican picked and nuzzled comically with its orange pouched bill among its drab brownish wing feathers; the herring gulls surprised me, as they did every day by their size and their viciously hooked beaks." The narrator, we can see, is enclosed; he wants to breathe freely. There is an opposition between the room (business, restriction) and the natural scene. But this opposition is subtly developed—it is not black and white—and it continually offers the element of *surprise*. The narrator is a keen observer, noting subtle tints (shades) and refusing to let go completely. He is an ironist. He recognizes the comedy of the pelican—and of his situation in the middle of things.

Simon Carter, the narrator, is an administrator—as we would

judge from his carefully ordered, qualified rhythms—but he is also a "naturalist." He yearns for "order" *and* "disorder." Thus when he finds that a giraffe in the Zoo (where he works) has killed a young guard, he is greatly disturbed. What went wrong? Did the giraffe have too much freedom? Was the guard careless? Simon's questions are related to the personal definitions (and problems) he has never mastered. At thirty-five he is still *unformed*. Perhaps these reasons explain why he feels "furious with the shapeless, purposeless emotions that so meaningless an accident could bring." He recognizes that he is desperately involved—in order to banish morbid thoughts, to be "trapped," he thinks of his wife's thighs: "living bodies to banish the dead. . . ." He is unsuccessful.

Simon is, perhaps, more upset than the other administrators, Dr. Leacock, Lord Godmanchester, and Sir Robert Falcon, who can simply call the accident "unfortunate" and let it disappear (or use it for their different political ends). He is less political than they—this characteristic almost kills him later—and he refuses to accept all things as *means*. He is an idealist; he worries about law and order. He feels enclosed by abstractions and by personal needs (which have not been thoroughly explored). When he thinks of going to the window again, he recognizes that he cannot view the natural scene in the same way as he did once. He knows more than the animals; he cannot be a free, unthinking beast: "I went to the window but the long legged grace of the flamingos seemed grace no longer, only stilted absurdity; and the pelicans' comicality, mere swollen folly."

Simon discusses the accident with Leacock and Falcon. Both men use it as a convenient excuse. (Simon also does, but his ultimate goal is self-knowledge.) Leacock insists that the "antiquated enclosures mean danger to life." He wants "limited liberty"—a reserve in which animals can roam within larger limits than a Zoo—and he maintains that the giraffe acted out of fear of—or anger at—imprisonment. Falcon, on the other hand, believes in the old ways. He accepts the enclosures as "natural," helpful and necessary. There are several ironies that shade the matter. Leacock, as we shall learn, pursues the idea of "limited liberty," but he has never defined *correct* limits. His daughter, Harriet, is a violent, nymphomaniacal believer in complete freedom—perhaps as a result of his obsessive views of liberty. Leacock cannot administer; he has not ordered himself (or his daughter) in any meaningful pattern. Falcon goes against his own "understated" beliefs. He constantly goes on expeditions, choosing openness rather than enclosure. He is a dandy. He is arrogant. One description captures his willful freedom: "The exhibitionist quality of his defiantly asserted archaism was thrown into highlight as he stood near the exit. His small, curly brimmed bowler hat, his broadly checked tweeds, his umbrella, gloves and vivid chestnut suede shoes seemed such a ridiculous challenge to the open necked shirts and billowing trousers of the ordinary summer visitors around him."

Simon is an alien, a strange "animal," in this setting of political deceit and corruption. He tries to follow his ideals, but he cannot get through the masks of Falcon and Leacock. He is prone to anxiety. It is, in fact, exaggerated when he confronts "old men"—self-deluded opportunists—and war: "Then the print swam in front of me, the letters diving and blurring and fading only to shape themselves into the one word—War. The stab of terror was sharp. It was also familiar. It carried memories of similar apprehensions right back into my childhood." He recognizes that somehow the accident, the muddled feelings he has, and the threatening war (which will be fought about ideas of restriction—should England remain independent or join Uni-Europe?) are bound together in one "tall story."

Simon continues to feel hostile toward the "old men." When he enters the Lion House, he believes that he "is a prisoner of the caged beasts." No longer can he delight in their sensual freedom: "I was in the wrong place. . . ." And he sees in the various Declarations of Political Powers—at one point America and Russia warn England and Uni-Europe to refrain from war—more symbols of his self-imprisonment. He even fades away from Martha, who does not share his ironic, occasionally priggish views of life.

"Wars, Domestic and Foreign"—a chapter title—begin to accelerate. Rumors move rapidly; sides are defined and re-defined. I stress the shifting alliances because their erratic movements are constantly contrasted to metaphors of enclosure. The metaphors, indeed, *battle* each other. Simon, for example, hopes to "find the end to the bifurcation of his life" in the "deciduous woods." He yearns for natural freedom, un-limited liberty—he embraces the open air of the first chapter—but he cannot surrender completely to the "chance flow" of things. He must make patterns and shape movements. In the most powerful scene so far Simon searches for badgers in their natural setting—the Zoo has been given some of Lord Godmanchester's land as a reserve—and he hopes to capture their innocent beauty. Thus the details function metaphorically when he tells us: "A light breeze blew dead against me. The bracken's scent brought serial memories stretching far back into my childhood. . . . The situation was ideal." He is "free" at last; he has recovered the pleasures of childhood; he has found some fresh air. But even here Simon must make order—he waits for the proper light to study the badgers; he notes care-fully shades and angles. The important thing is that he is not tortured by details (as he is at the Zoo), that he is not enclosed by duties of administration.

There are several ironies. Simon discovers in the midst of "anticipated glory" that he is exactly where he told Harriet, Leacock's daughter, he would be. By chance he has situated himself in a *fixed* position. (Wilson is shrewd here in suggesting the tangle of chance, fate, and free will in human experience). Therefore he is not so liberated as he imagined. Suddenly Harriet approaches and touches him. He finds that he is as trapped by her advances as by designs of mad "old men." Although no sexual event of great importance occurs, Simon admits that he cannot be a naturalist: "The setts by the sandy bank would yield nothing again for some nights."

He continues to be an administrator: "I got through my work, got through it competently but it was only with the surface of my mind, my body and my spirit were smothered in a fog of unhappiness. . . ." He is caged; he dislikes the "muddling, maddening, blundering" others who come near him. Because of his rigidity—he is more "limited" as a result of his sexual frustration since Martha has left him—he cannot function freely *even as administrator*. He does not know how to define substantial duties and limits. It is appropriate that he identifies with a lynx that is shot. The lynx has asserted its freedom in the reserve by threatening someone. It has overstepped the bounds—even in the open air!—and it is a shadow of himself: "It seemed so little ferocious, more like a poor house cat dazed from a glancing blow of a bicycle wheel."

More animals rebel and are punished. Often the punishment (as in the case of the lynx) is unjust. But Simon is unable to fight the growing madness of Leacock; he is on the edge himself. When Harriet is found dead—she has been attacked by her pet (her sexual object)—he almost goes over the edge. It is ironic that the incident occurs near Simon's favorite badger setts. The incident is an extreme one; it not only calls into question Leacock's judgment—he suddenly gives up his Directorship—it forces Simon to decide about his future plans, and to take a step.

Simon acts after his wife returns from America. (The war scare has lifted for the time being; she feels that she can safely live in England once more, although she does leave their children with her sister in California.) He gains new faith in the ability to balance things; he believes his hope "of blending town and country, the Zoo's office life of human contact and the Reserve's peace of heightened sight and sound was not an absurdity." He appreciates "secret unity." He need not be torn apart by "pleasure and duty." (*Tearing* is an interesting choice of word; it links the destructive accident involving the giraffe, the attack of Harriet's dog, and his own inner tensions.)

Martha functions here as support. Her approval of his decision to remain at the Zoo is crucial. She becomes a foil, as it were, to the "old men" because she is able to express things clearly. She is honest, intelligent, and forthright. This is not to say that she is a believable creation; she is too shadowy to compel our belief in the midst of administrative battles.

The British Day approaches. Falcon wants it to be a celebration of old virtues. The "quaintness" of Victorian Zoos will be shown to the public; the "antiquated enclosures," now slightly open, will be made attractive. But Simon realizes that the exotic past is not enough; odd displays and "manic-depressive" preparations by Falcon are as imprisoning to the spirit as unlimited liberty. The Zoo becomes a variety show, trapping people into comic roles and not allowing them to breathe freely. Simon tells us that Falcon "enrolled them somehow in his happy absurd antics and mixed them in with the staff and the contractors' extinction." Unlike Falcon he holds on to his sanity, as shaky as it may be. He does not let go, perverting his senses. His irony remains. The metaphors of enclosure and freedom are used again. Simon informs us that "many people at that time ran away from London, but only the foolish thought that there was anywhere to run to." He goes about his business; he stays in one place (even though it is stifling.) *He battles triviality and apocalypse.*

It is characteristic of Simon to think of the animals' survival. Despite all the talk of war and the accompanying frenzy of "old men," he believes that he must take measures in case *the world does not end.* When he proposes "safety measures" for the public and for "the animals in our care"—a sacred duty—he is attacked by Falcon: "He gave a roar like a lion and came for me. Youth tells and I had sprung aside before he reached me." Simon sees the arrival of the "age of violence," the age in which "old men" become wild beasts. He looks at Falcon on the ground and feels a "strange and unfriendly sense of power." But he will not exert unlimited liberty; instead of shooting him (even if it would help the public), he places a cushion under his head and locks him in the room. (Falcon must be "caged" for public safety.)

The Day arrives. The Zoo is brightly illuminated; the

"whole Gardens seemed to be flooded with light of every colour—blue, rose, green, amber, purple"—and this lighting is in marked contrast to the natural shades Simon saw in the first chapter. Everything is garish, undisciplined, and dangerous. The "pantomime transformation" demonstrates the reckless and unthinking Falcon. Although Simon would like to submit to the "prettiness' and die, he cannot waver in his duty. (Wilson shows us how that duty increases as others pursue unlimited liberty.)

There is a joke. Just as the ceremony is about to reach a climax (there is a sexual aura about the festivity) the sirens wail: "And then came the crackling, whistling thudding sound of the universe." Simon describes chaos in a precise, thoughtful way and his comments, although superficially calm, ironically oppose the effect of the explosion. The technique is powerful. We do not know how to respond. Should we yield to apocalypse and consider only the bombs? Should we hopefully note Simon's administrative power? I believe that Wilson wants us to be caught in the middle and, finally, to admire his hero's real sense of duty.

In the next few hours Simon (and the others) work "like beavers to repair our dam against a tide that any minute would engulf us and all our works forever." The animal simile is important—men have been likened to animals throughout the novel (more in "wildness" than in work)—but the dam is even more so. Simon recognizes the need for *shelter*, shelter that does not inhibit freedom but, on the contrary, contributes to it, and this shelter is in marked contrast to the claustrophobic office setting in which we initially met him. The dam reminds us of his beloved badgers' habitat. Occasionally there are natural, comforting enclosures!

It is, of course, comic to see Falcon hanging "over the bronze lion." He has become the wild animal; his instincts have exploded, and his movements are in ironic opposition to Simon's work. He must be hosed by the firemen.

In the next chapter, "Massacre of the Innocents," the violent movements grow until they dominate the rest of the novel.

(Thus we have moved from *threat* to *actuality;* the pace has accelerated.) Patterns are broken; old ways are outmoded. Simon informs us that we "lived an improvised, all-hands-on-deck, air raid shelter, darts and sandwiches sort of life. . . ." Public disorders abound. And as the wilderness increases, it influences private arrangements. Simon and Martha battle about safety and fidelity—she relates her past feelings toward Falcon as possible lover—and their quarrels add to the general confusion.

It is during such confusion that Simon finds greater happiness in his work. He likes to repair things; he loses his identity in group tasks: "The closer the threat of general devastation, the harder we worked to preserve. Against a background of ruins and stench we banded together to save the collections. . . ." He resembles a beaver once more. But even now his pleasures are interrupted by "old men" who insist that their priorities come first. Thus Beard commands him to save the anatomical specimens and place them in cold storage. The refrigeration plant, which is in the country, functions as the most claustrophobic enclosure we have yet encountered. (I have not mentioned Beard's family life—he comes from "a family of lunatics, cardiacs, spastics and hysterics"—but it distinguishes his mad activities at this point. The family is, indeed, a "refrigeration plant" in his case, causing him to function coldly.)

Before the expedition to the plant (notice how carefully Wilson uses expeditions throughout the novel; most end in disaster!) there is another crisis at the Zoo. Simon is at work sorting out minutes that are "essential for future historians. After all history had as high a claim as anatomy." He rushes to the window—as he did in the first chapter—when he hears explosive noises outside. He sees a wild crowd intent upon capturing and devouring the animals. The slogans reverberate: "Men not Beasts." Simon notes the "ugly sound" because he refuses to separate men and beasts (except within disciplined limits). By not accepting the natural innocence of beasts, men become bestial. *They break the bonds of living creatures.*

Simon runs down into the crowd, but he is too late to save Matthew Price. With the "holocaust of witches" at hand, he longs to return home — to Martha; nevertheless, he stands firm: "to give up now would be to make nonsense of all proper order, of anything I believed in. . . ." He yields to Beard's request to save specimens.

The expedition begins. Simon wants desperately to talk to Beard, but he realizes that the other man is so enclosed in his private nightmare that communication is impossible — they do not share the same ideas of "all proper order." When he begins to have stomach pains, Beard insists upon the priority of saving his specimens. There is a blur of violent pain — wild, starving people attack them — and then Simon finds himself near "long used entrances to badger setts." Shelter at last! Wilson does not spare the irony. Soon Simon is so weak that he — as do the other townspeople — kills and eats his beloved animals: "Nausea fought with hunger in me." His ambivalence is so great that he passes out and his last words in this "massacre of innocents" are "The room span round. My head fell back on the cushions and everything became dark, became nothing."

The next chapter opens with sharp contrasts. Time has passed; the political order has changed; "nothing" has become "everything." Simon and Martha sit and enjoy a rich meal at the Englanders (who, ironically, are loyal Uni-Europeans). But he feels guilty; he is aware that this comfortable room is even more enclosed than his former office. And his guilt increases when he agrees to work at the "new" Zoo, which will now be made up totally of European collections.

There will be a new ceremony to celebrate the reopening of the Zoo. Although Simon seems not to remember (or at least mention) the previous celebrations, especially the Great Day, we grow fearful. (Ceremonies are for Wilson necessary but wild; they subvert "all proper order" if not "enclosed" properly.) He brings together fauna "of every kind, grouped geographically, upon migration, breeding, general demography, adaptation to human environments, relation to human economy." But as he begins to note, he is so enclosed by his work that he does not see "the changing world outside." He is in a "cocoon of busyness." He is not ready for the final ceremony.

The weather is beautiful—there are "soft" breezes; lilacs fill the air with perfume. The crowds are controlled. Everything is peaceful (in marked opposition to the preceding chapters). A verse is recited to honor the occasion: "Peace shall come to this house/When the hoopoe lies down with the grouse." Simon is at ease in the "house."

We expect the change. Suddenly crowds march in—they are made of "all who [are] too obstinately individual to fit in, yet too weakly individual to make their mark"—and they clash with the fashionable observers. The old political battles of England and Uni-Europe resume; it is the Uni-Europeans who have the day. Blanchard-White, an enemy of England and Simon's temporary superior, reveals a display: "There in a pit dug seven or eight feet below the ground level was an old mangy brown Siberian bear." The bear is treated as a political symbol: "The Russian Bear in Difficulties." (We remember how at the beginning the giraffe was used by Leacock and Falcon for symbolic, political reasons.) Simon laughs at the idiocy, thinking "things would soon come right." But his laughter is hollow; he is again in an "untenable position" because his sense of proper order has been violated. He cannot lie down (or work) with his enemies.

It is fitting that the final chapter (and the shortest) is entitled "Down and Up Again." Throughout the novel Simon has fallen and risen (as have the political alignments). Now we understand the metaphorical implications of this "tall story": *there are no set arrangements in human affairs—men are enclosed in never-ending cycles.* When they fail to move within the flow of things (either by attempted, obsessive "freedom" or willing imprisonment), they lose whatever capacities for creative expression they possess.

In this chapter Simon is seen drinking, then raping Martha (who has lost all respect for him), and breaking down. He is thoroughly down and out. (Work is pictured as a liberating force; Simon is at his best when he finds satisfaction in administrative order.) Time, however, moves rapidly. He finds himself (after his actual imprisonment in Enfield Camp) as Acting Director of the Zoo. The Uni-Europeans have been defeated; England is independent once again: "Stability of a kind had come to us. The last three years had given me a wealth of ideas for the Zoo's future and a corresponding wealth of caution and moderation in my belief in their possible application." There is the chance that he will be made permanent Director.

There can not be a happy ending. Simon remains unsure; he does not know (does anyone?) whether he is up or down in this "tall story." As soon as he learns of his future position, he returns home. He is "determined" (a play on determinism) to repair his relationship with Martha; he finds, however, that she treats him as a child and says: "If you get to be a nuisance, Mummy will send you away." When his children (who have finally returned to England from America), ask about the "strongest" animal—is it a giraffe?—he replies that he doesn't think a giraffe can kill people. Thus we are back at the beginning. At the end of all the changes that have occurred, Simon has learned true wisdom: there is no *complete freedom or enclosure;* all that he can know finally is that "I'm not sure yet."

2

Leaving the Safety of Myth: Doris Lessing's *The Golden Notebook* (1962)

BARBARA BELLOW WATSON

> *"And what is the next stage?"*
> *The next stage is, surely, that I leave the safety of*
> *myth and Anna Wulf walks forward alone."*[1]

The Golden Notebook contains multitudes, yet it is as claustrophobic as the 1950s, the decade it portrays. The protagonist is a woman whose education in disillusionment gives the novel its enormous scope, ranging as it does from international political movements to the fine nuances of bedroom politics, with anatomies of psychoanalysis, the private and performing arts, friendship, marriage, and other matters along the way. Yet the sense of constriction prevails, and with reason, for this woman on her pilgrimage through experience finds that each of the vaunted roads to salvation is ultimately a trap. Each one offers

---

1. Doris Lessing, *The Golden Notebook*, 2d ed. (1962; rpt. London: Michael Joseph, 1972), p. 403.

her a myth, an explanation, a guide for the perplexed, a way of life, a coherence. To each she submits against her better judgment, driven by her need for answers as large as her questions. By the end of the book she is ready to see all these systems as traps and to turn away from them, even though no new refuge is available to her.

Doris Lessing herself shows the same kind of courage, for she has left behind the established ways of dealing with subjects of this kind and has transformed the incipient clichés of the mid-century experience by evolving a form that precisely expresses the major themes. The most prominent of these is the theme of fragmentation, of breaking down and breaking up, psychologically, politically, socially. Second, and closely related, is the theme of the human struggle against original chaos, which *The Golden Notebook* studies in great detail just at its turning point, the point at which systems become as dangerous as the chaos they have been designed to conquer. Third, the theme that aroused the most comment when the book first appeared, is the theme of woman's experience as unique, as uncharted territory in the psychological universe, and certainly one of the great values of this book and of Doris Lessing's work as a whole is that with it half the human race moves a little more into daylight.

On the other hand, this treatment of women's experience and this presentation of a new kind of woman in fiction, together obscure the equally interesting connection between this theme and the two other themes, those of fragmentation and the slavery to system. Special as it may be, the woman's point of view is nonetheless a paradigm of the fragmentation in contemporary life and a paradigm also of the failure of sets and systems to respond helpfully to human questions. *The Golden Notebook* can be read as an encyclopedic survey of the major systems of our times and a rejection of them all. "Infallible Solutions for the Human Dilemma and How They All Failed" might be a subtitle. In her quest for an answer, Anna Wulf, like her predecessor, Martha Quest in the "Children of Violence" series, has made strenuous investments in all these systems. It has been harder for her than for any man to succeed in putting the pieces of her life together. When each closed system fails, there is nowhere to go but out—leaving the safety of myth, looking beyond myth to the dangerous solitary places of reality.

This concatenation of themes produces a novel that is new in kind, even though it falls into various familiar categories and probably contains no single element that is entirely new, no character quite without precedent, no technique without a parallel, no feeling unnamed before. There are interesting points of comparison with *The Way of All Flesh, Ulysses, The Magic Mountain, Point Counter Point, U.S.A., Man's Fate, Bread and Wine*, even with the writings of Colette. Doris Lessing herself has bravely said that she was trying to do for our time what Stendhal and Tolstoy had done for theirs, nothing less than the panoramic portrait of an age. In this case the technique of the portrait is as much a part of the reality as its subject. This technique has much in common with cubism in painting and with cinematic narrative style. The story itself dictates this treatment.

The story of Anna Wulf (Ella in the Yellow Notebook) is a prototypal story of our times. Born of conventionally bourgeois parents against whom she instinctively rebels, Anna has left home, has become a communist, has lived with a man and eventually married him in a rather loveless and sexless relationship, has borne a child and divorced her husband, and after the war has returned from Africa to England with her child. At the time when the book begins, in 1950, Anna is living in London with her child on the proceeds of her successful first novel, *Frontiers of War*, which deals with her experiences in Africa during the war years as part of a close-knit group active in Party work. She has shared an apartment for some time with Molly, a close friend, an actress, who is also divorced and bringing up a child on her own, and also a communist and sexually a "free woman." Both women have gone to the same analyst, Mrs. Marks, whom they call Mother Sugar. At some point (for the time schemes differ slightly in the different tellings of this basic story), Anna-Ella has been involved for five years in a serious love affair that absorbed this aspect of her personality completely. When this lover, the most shadowy, from the reader's point of view, of all the men in Anna's life, takes his departure, Anna finds that she has forgotten how to function without him.

> Sometimes when I, Anna, look back, I want to laugh out loud. It is the appalled, envious laughter of knowledge at innocence. I would be incapable now of such trust. I, Anna, would never begin an affair with Paul. Or Michael. Or rather, I would begin an affair just that, knowing exactly what would happen; I would begin a deliberately barren, limited relationship.
> *What Ella lost during those five years was the power to create through naivety.* (p. 183)

This is one of the deepest fragmentations of the self for Anna. Along with the other events of the 1950s, it has made her incapable of writing another novel. She has joined the Party and left it. She has refused to have her first novel turned into a movie script or a television series. She has moved into a flat of her own and lives there now with her child and her four notebooks. Men come and go in her life. Molly's son, torn between the values of his Bohemian mother and those of his rigidly conventional father, shoots himself. Her own daughter finally rejects Anna's way of life to the extent of insisting on going away to a perfectly conventional boarding school.

Inside her room Anna lives cut off but not insulated from the outside world. Her consciousness is under assault always by the events of the 1950s, the decade into which poured the enervation, the mangled idealism, the wounds, the mutilations, the survivors' psychoses of the end of the Second World War. Some of the most successful passages reach back to the experiences of the war years in Africa. The geography of the book includes England and Africa, with psychological sidetrips to the United States and the U.S.S.R. Politically, the dimension is Marxist and reaches out into the whole history and pathology of the Left, its international and its local manifestations, treating Marxism as a metaphor of all social and psychological movements. In historical terms, the setting is the seamed aftermath of the holocaust in Europe, a prelude to the annihilation forecast at Hiroshima. All this is more overpowering for Anna than for any of the other characters, and it is technically overpowering for the novelist to convey as an integral part of Anna's experience. In the conventional novel, public events form a background to experience, adding certain kinds of atmosphere or significance to the personal life. In the exceptions, certain genres like the war novel, the personal life becomes the background, helping to differentiate the characters and give an emotional resonance to events. Here the technical difficulty is that there is no valid separation between the personal and the public anguish. Another difficulty is the size of the world to be included. Doris Lessing's solution in *The Golden Notebook* is to expand the novel form itself and to build within that expanded form a structure so articulated that it can deal with outer-events-as-inner-life and also treat the division of Anna's consciousness within itself.

Essentially, *The Golden Notebook* is a novel about the wars between order and chaos. The many narratives contained in it can be read in a variety of ways, but the structure of the book insists on this theme, this obsession. Nothing could be more orderly, nothing could be more a response to chaos than this structure. There are five sections of an interior novel, *Free Women*, the first and last of which begin and end the book. Then there are four notebooks, black, red, yellow, and blue, each of which is again divided into four parts and symmetrically disposed within the five sections of *Free Women*. And the inner Golden Notebook, a symbol of unification and healing, comes between the final section of notebooks and the final section of *Free Women*. The squaring of the four, the enclosure of the four within the rounding-out five parts, the echo of the five in that fifth notebook that gives its name to the whole novel, all impose an order so precise that it points to its opposite. In the inner Golden Notebook, Anna is given, in a rare act of reciprocity by a man, the opening sentence for her new novel, which is the opening sentence also of *The Golden Notebook*. The circularity recalls *Finnegans Wake,* as the interplay of order and chaos recalls *Ulysses,* and the comparison is instructive. Joyce imposes order as a playful pattern laid down upon pure experience, an order supremely artful, proclaiming its own uselessness and the awesome detachment of the artist from the life so patterned. The life portrayed, however, emerges full-blooded from the pattern: childbirth, street brawls, baths, breakfasts, fornications, nightmares, disgust, meditation, anxiety, all blooming with reality. Lessing is also imposing order on the overwhelming chaos of modern life, but the pattern is so rigid with seriousness that it sometimes hampers the spontaneity of expression.

The seriousness of the narrative devices for the author is analogous to the seriousness of the notebooks for the protagonist. Anna is an artist and blocked, like so many of the central figures in modern fiction. The notebooks are to enable her to write again, to fulfill her obligations, among which self-fulfillment and service to society vie for first place. A novel, a better novel than her first, a novel that does justice to the full reality of her experience, would merge these two functions as one and satisfy both. By inventing the notebooks, Anna can begin to write again without waiting to digest the indigestible realities of the Rosenberg trial, political purges in the Soviet Union, the attempted suicide of Molly's child, her lover's defection, the Bomb, the dumb agony of the letters women write to women's magazines, and the novels Party members hide away in drawers. She can set down whatever has meaning for her, without having to discard parts that can't be worked into the form of a novel. She is responding to her own question about her first novel:

> Yet now what interests me is precisely this—why did I not write an account of what had happened, instead of shaping a "story" which had nothing to do with the material that fueled it. Of course, the straight, simple, formless account would not have been a "novel," and would not have got published, but I was genuinely not interested in "being a

writer" or even in making money . . . . Why a story at all—
not that it was a bad story, or untrue, or that it debased
anything. Why not, simply, the truth? (p. 61)

Anna knows that, in any profound sense, nothing is less simple,
less simply attainable, than "simply, the truth." But in
common-sense terms of the contrast between the form of the
novel and the formlessness of feeling and experience, the
notebooks do answer. Ultimately, her hope is to put ". . . all of
myself in one book" (p. 519), in the beautiful new notebook of
dull gold.

Structurally, *The Golden Notebook* has its complexities. Like
the author herself, Anna Wulf is a novelist and writes the four
notebooks as well as the novel *Free Woman*. Her own story,
obviously in its essentials another version of Lessing's story as
well, is given various degrees of aesthetic distancing. In *Free
Woman* Anna uses her own name and keeps the names of the
other characters in the frame story unchanged, although many
other details are changed enough to establish the inner novel as
a fictionalized reworking of the material. The inner novel is a
third-person narration of material that, in the notebooks, is
told, for the most part, by Anna as first-person narrator. Each of
the four notebooks has a title, but the titles appear only after
some random scribblings ". . . as if Anna had, almost automati-
cally, divided herself into four, and then, from the nature of
what she had written named these divisions" (p.55). Each
notebook has its own color, its own materials, often overlap-
ping, but where *Ulysses* associates each episode with an organ of
the body, here each notebook is associated with an aspect or
method of the mind.

The Black Notebook is entitled *THE DARK*. Its associations
are with darkness, terror, fear of being alone, fear of the city.
These immediately evoke their antitheses: light, heat, white,
red, Africa, a physicality of nature sensed blindly through
closed eyes by smell and touch. Sun and hot dry granite are one
reality. Set against that powerful reality, lunch with the agent
of a film company seems unreal. The pages of the notebook are

divided down the middle by a black line and the subdivisions headed "Source" and "Money." Anna's first novel, *Frontiers of War*, a best-seller so profitable that Anna is still living on the proceeds, is not reproduced here but is presented indirectly, under the heading "Source" in two very different ways. In one, Anna retells the events she used as subject matter for the novel, trying this time to tell "simply, the truth." These scenes of young people isolated in a backwater of the war and absorbed in communist activities and their own endogamous sexual relations, intrinsically bound with the social and the physical world of Africa, have narrative vividness that scarcely exists elsewhere in the book. By contrast, everything that takes place in the actual setting of the book, England in the 1950s, conveys a certain numbness. Anna is persuaded that her novel had somehow failed of this truth and presents it twice in parody, once in a tidy film script called "Forbidden Love" and once in a burlesqued pulp-fiction version called "Blood on the Banana Leaves." The "Money" side of the notebook deals with business transactions about the novel. Later the notebook becomes a series of newspaper clippings dealing with "violence, death, rioting, hatred" in Africa.

The Red Notebook follows, headed "The British Communist Party." Although its pages are not divided, they are full of doubt and conflict, and Anna says, ". . . there were always two personalities in me, the 'communist' and Anna, and Anna judged the communist all the time" (p. 66). This comment calls for a digression, because the two personalities will appear again in reference to the compartments Anna keeps for her child and her lover. The interest of this quotation is that it makes explicit the painfulness of the conflict, which is not merely the common experience of shifting from one role to another. The characteristic identity crisis for women involves more than an uncertainty or a multiplicity; it involves each self judging the other and finding the other wanting. The Red Notebook again involves parody, even more bitter. The stories sent in by comrades have a certain uniformity, but Anna is more disturbed by the fact that for so many she cannot decide whether they are straightforward and very bad, or parodies and quite perfect:

> When I first read it, I thought it was an exercise in irony. Then a very skillful parody of a certain attitude. Then I realised it was serious. . . . But what seemed to me important was that it could be read as parody, irony or seriously. It seems to me this fact is another expression of the fragmentation of everything, the painful disintegration of something that is linked with what I feel to be true about language, the thinning of language against the density of our experience. (p. 259)

The Red Notebook after 1956 is reduced to a series of newspaper clippings on which comment is obviously both redundant and unbearable.

The Yellow Notebook is introduced by the following bracketed comment: "The yellow notebook looked like the manuscript of a novel, for it was called *The Shadow of the Third*. It certainly began like a novel" (p. 148). In this, presumably the failed novel that is later replaced by the writing of *Free Women*, Anna becomes Ella, her friend Molly becomes Julia, her lover Michael becomes Paul, and her daughter Janet becomes a son named Michael. The implication would seem to be that the comparative artistic success of *Free Women* has to do with its being less fictionalized and more closely related to "simply, the truth." This narrative shows that there is another way of rendering in fictional form the same events that furnish material for *Free Women*. Once again, therefore, multiplicity and fragmentation are insisted on. There is one further complication. Ella, heroine of this inner novel, is also writing a novel. But here the echoes will stop, for the novel is about a man, the theme is suicide, and it is apparent that the fictive novel is not another way of turning the mirror on plot, but in this case is a resonating symbolic end to this particular corridor, serving the same purpose as Anna's dreams in the frame story, to reflect back from the character's unconscious the themes that haunt both outer and inner novels. It is also possible that, by making her protagonist a man and by leaving out all that is circumstantial in her own life, Ella is further evading the struggle with reality.

The Blue Notebook sets out to conquer this habit of evasion: "Why do I never write down, simply, what happens? Why don't I keep a diary? Obviously, my changing everything into fiction is simply a means of concealing something from myself" (p. 197). In this notebook the woman as woman emerges. The first sentence is: "Tommy appeared to be accusing his mother" (p. 197), establishing at once the two women's roles as mothers and the theme of guilt. Why guilt? Both seem to have been better mothers than any of the unfree women they know. Again because the self is divided, and one part judges the other. Also, the child has become another self and is passing judgment in incalculable ways of the mother, who is a person. The theme of guilt runs through the narration of the Blue Notebook, which focuses on the friendship of the two women, their children, the men in their lives, their relations with their analyst, Mrs. Marks, Anna's dreams, and—again—clippings. This time the clippings are cold war, but again all violence, cruelty, and threats of destruction, on a scale large enough to account for the fragmented structure of the novel, the cubist overlappings, double exposures, surrealities. Anna suffers from knowing too much, more than anyone can know without breaking down, falling apart, and yet she cannot know less. "After such knowledge, what forgiveness?"

All the refuges of irresponsibility are closed to her, except perhaps madness, which grazes her in the Golden Notebook, the notebook that is physically beautiful, one of the few objects after the African experience that is given a sensuous description. Here the leap toward *The Golden Notebook*, the complete work, is made. The physical golden notebook is abducted by a capricious male novelist who writes in it a typically masculine novel, the opening of which is presented to us with certain implications about the difference between a man's world and a women's, but quite without malice. The title *The Golden Notebook* is therefore both a sadness and a triumph. It points to the stolen unity of the artist and the women, the unity stolen from her by the male. In her golden notebook he writes his novel, a "successful" novel, a novel with a social conscience but perhaps without an artistic conscience, since it seems to be possible for him to contain all the enormities of his experience (and by implication ours) in a normal novel form. That moderate success would seem to be a sign of his failure. On the other hand, there is a certain reciprocity. As Anna provides Saul with an opening for his novel, he provides her with an equivalently feminine opening for hers. This sentence, the reader finds, has become the opening sentence of the book, so that its promise has already been fulfilled. That is the unstated triumph, especially since the whole golden thing has been written without the possession of the golden notebook itself.

The Golden Notebook, then, announces in every way that its theme is fragmentation, breakup, breakdown. The structure embodies this theme, the characters talk about it explicitly, being highly conscious, introspective, and communicative people. The events in the narrative, both fictional and historical, demonstrate how true this fragmentation is to the mid-century experience. It is evident now that the first response to the novel as a work primarily "about" a new kind of woman was inevitable and true and yet ultimately wrong. Anna does claim that her experience is ". . . a kind of experience women haven't had before. . . ," and insists on that interpretation although her analyst wants her to admit a continuity with ". . . a great line of women stretching out behind you into the past." Anna holds her ground on this point, and the force of the whole novel supports her. Even if one or another woman in the past may have done each separate thing she has done (her analyst mentions only independence and sexual freedom), none has shared the totality, and above all, none has shared the awareness. "They didn't look at themselves as I do. They didn't feel as I do. How could they?" (pp. 403, 404).

In her preface to the second edition, Doris Lessing says her novel was not read "in the right way" because of this emphasis on its concern with women and the war of the sexes (p. ix). To the extent that the theme of breakdown has been ignored as a result, that is true. But the two ways of reading the book, as a novel of fragmentation and as a novel of women's experience, are not at all contradictory and in fact are not even separable. Women in our time have become experts in fragmentation. Fragmentation is the essential theme of women's consciousness, and when a novel deals with the experience of being a self-directed woman and a woman trying to establish a unified sense of self, it is also dealing by analogy with the fragmentation of society as a whole. Certainly when the narrator of such a novel is explicitly aware of the social and intellectual breakdown that parallels her own psychological breakdown, the result must be, as it is in *The Golden Notebook*, a symbiotic relationship between the two themes. Therefore it is probably an understatement to say, as the author does, "Of course the attempt on my part assumed that the filter which is a woman's way of looking at life has the same validity as the filter which is a man's way. . ." (p. x). More likely, in these times and for so central and devasting a theme, a woman's point of view is more likely than a man's to bring out in strong relief the inconsistencies, the impossibilities, the incompatibilities of the way we live now and the way we think.

The woman's point of view may have relevance also at the next stage of the argument. At this stage, the form of the novel raises further questions. All these bits and pieces of narrative, symbolic of disunity as they may be, seem to have solved provisionally the question of how to present with integrity the kind of experience that most novels trim down, smooth out, oversimplify. In order to render the experience, the author has shown herself moving from neat and even facile renditions to renditions that seem laborious and even disjointed. Only so can the whole experience be rendered, and to render only part is to create a false unity, a mutilation. To arrive at unity by splitting things up, into notebooks or any other way, is paradoxical, to say the least. But there is nothing playful about this paradox. There it stands in a kind of naive sobriety, not very sporting in an age of outrageousness. So many games might have been played among these notebooks, calling them not-books and knot-books, as indeed they are; so many astounding stunts could have been instigated among these characters born of characters, these newsreels unwinding in the unreality we remember from their actuality. None of this is done. With the awful seriousness of the female, sometimes so tedious to the male mind, Doris Lessing deals soberly with her paradox. As Virginia Woolf points out in *Three Guineas*, women have had a different education from men, largely an education in doing without. Woolf cites the major subjects in this curriculum as poverty, chastity, derision, and freedom from unreal loyalties. Lessing seems to add breakdown. Both, in their irony, mean exactly what they say: these are valuable lessons, even more valuable than lessons in mathematics, marching, or medicine.

Nothing less is involved than a transvaluation of values. The reigning assumptions of our culture about unity or consistency or wholeness are questioned repeatedly in *The Golden Notebook*. Tommy, blind, is at one with himself for the first time. Marion, drunk, is ". . . a lush and a whole person . . ." (p. 340). Sober, she lisps girlishly and reverts to all the false mannerisms of her feminine training. Anna prefers to be divided in some ways: "The two personalities—Janet's mother, Michael's mistress, are happier separated. It is a strain having to be both at once" (p. 287). The Communist Party or any other group works on ". . . a self-dividing principle . . . exists and perhaps even flourishes by this process of discarding individuals or groups . . ." (p. 64). For the individual also the Party is divisive: ". . . somewhere at the back of my mind when I joined the Party was a need for wholeness, for an end to the split, divided, unsatisfactory way we all live. Yet joining the Party intensified the split . . ." (p. 142). To Mrs. Marks, near the end of her analysis, Anna maintains: "But the essence of living now, fully, not blocking off what goes on, is conflict. In fact I've reached the stage where I look at people and say—he or she, they are whole at all because they've chosen to block off at this stage or that. People stay sane by blocking off, by limiting themselves" (p. 402). And later in the same conversation the proposition is reversed: "But sometimes I meet people, and it seems to me the fact they are cracked across, they're split, means they are keeping themselves open for something" (p. 405). This statement may be the thematic core of the book. When Charlie Themba cracks up, it takes his friends a long time to recognize paranoia, just because, in the nature of politics in Africa, his delusions seem quite probable. In his case, the madness of the world merely serves to camouflage his disease, but in other cases the implication is that madness may open a door to salvation.

At this point, another kind of pattern begins to emerge. I said earlier that the essential conflict of the book is that between order and chaos. And whereas endless semantic volleys can go on between the achievement of unity by mutilation (by Tommy's blindness or the Party's purges) and the achievement of completeness by breaking apart (by keeping four separate notebooks or by letting go of sanity), that is a game so abstract that nobody wins. The war between order and chaos, on the other hand, is not so abstract as it sounds.

Form takes a number of forms in *The Golden Notebook*. In the Red Notebook it is Marxism, determinist, positive, dogmatic. In the Blue Notebook it is psychoanalysis, systematic, percipient, saving. The parallel is implied in the name of Anna's analyst, Mrs. Marks, who is as dogmatic in her way as Mr. Marx. The logical contradictions at the bases of both systems are probed by Anna, but when the dogmatists refuse to be moved by logic ("intellectualization"), Anna returns to submission. She feels the inconsistencies of both most painfully in relation to art, which may be significant, since art is another way of imposing order on the chaos of experience. In the Black Notebook, she deals with art as another temptation to submit to order for its own sake. Through art, multitudinous life is given a unitary form and is necessarily betrayed by that very act. The two columns, "Source" and "Money," in the Black Notebook indicate both a split and an indecently close connection between the human events that furnished material for the novel, and her exploitation of the experience for the sake of money and other worldly rewards. With less success and less

money the moral guilt might have been less obvious, but the
implication is clear that the facility of the novel was a betrayal
of the experience in any case. At the next remove from integrity are the projected movie version and television series. At the
last stage travesty takes over in Anna's mock script for the film.
But these are all matters of degree. Anna's experience is not so
grossly betrayed in her new novel as it was even in *Frontiers of
War*, but neither one is "simply, the truth." In that case, one
may assume that the writer's block, glibly so called, is the
artist's integrity fighting the facility of the novel as a form, an
exact parallel with her integrity as a woman, which she decides
is the cause of her "frigidity" with men who do not accept her
fully as a person. Hence Anna declares that she no longer
believes in art, rejecting that kind of order for reasons that,
beneath the surface, bear some resemblance to her reasons for
leaving the Party and ending her analysis. Each of these certainties is a temptation to suppress the fullness and complexity
of experience.

This theme of the rejection of forms may seem to leave out
of account one part of the novel, but its interest becomes even
greater when it is applied to that part, to Anna's personal life.
There is a first and enduring temptation for Anna here that is
functionally very much like the temptation of the psychoanalytic, political, and literary systems. Each offers the self a pattern
to impose on the formlessness of existence, something sure
that can be referred to and deferred to. In times of fear and
doubt the system lifts responsibility away from the self. The
system may be oppressive in other ways, but its oppressiveness
may even help it to serve this particular function. These
dynamics apply equally well to the traditional woman's system
of giving life a shape by transferring meaning to the custody of
other people—first to men, then perhaps (such is the
sociophysiology of the matter) to children. This has obviously
nothing to do with the origins of such a system, or its purposes,
but, as the system operates, its very oppressions reduce responsibility, or seem to, and give the formlessness of experience
varying degrees of form. The "free women," Molly and Anna,

have rejected a system that subordinates women in marriage and motherhood under rules as strict and as fundamentally illogical as a party line.

But here too the existential freedom of these independent women carries its component of nervousness, and there remains in them something that critics have called a dependence on men. The characters speak of it themselves. This need for men and loyalty to men seems highly suspect in the emancipated woman. Has she rejected the slavery of marriage only to enter the slavery of promiscuity or the slavery to a lover who owes her nothing in return, not even the rickety forms of marital obligation? In fact, this need that looks like a regression to the old feminine slave mentality has its genesis, like the other forms of dependence, on a need for rules, for a shape to life. When Anna's daughter goes off to boarding school after Anna's lover has left her, she is demoralized, being a person who has forgotten how to make her own choices. Life has no form—or at least all familiar forms are removed. Normally, form arrives with the first markings of consciousness on the wide mind of sleep. Janet must have breakfast and be ready for school at a stated time. Before leaving for the office, Anna must provide for the child's supper, early and wholesome, and the lover's supper, late and luxurious. "Housewife's disease," Anna calls it, and one way of reading the long, difficult day that is recounted in such detail, 17th September, 1954, a miniature Bloomsday for "free" women, is as a complaint about the exploitation of women, a valid reading. As "free" women learn to expect, everyone takes and no one gives. Her own resiliency will have to absorb the shock of every conflict of the day. Her child cannot be expected to defer supper for a day or two. Her lover if neglected will complain that she prefers the child to him. At the office she cannot plead problems at home. They will think, "Then you shouldn't have had a child." At home, if she pleads a hard day at the office, they will think, "Then you shouldn't have taken a job." And from all sides the chorus will chant, with some satisfaction, "Then you'll just have to do without the lover, won't you?" Anna knows all this, knows that a "free woman" is a member of an army under strict discipline, all volunteers who cannot expect sympathy. Eventually, the drain on her energies will tell.

But it is also possible to give the account of this day another reading, not necessarily contradictory. Among these timetables, among these menus, among these pure and impure beddings, Anna does exist and work and think. All her obligations set limits, and limits, however wide or baroque, create a form. To do without this form requires not simply strength, but a power of inner decision. The daring of Ibsen's Nora, of Mrs. Alving, is underestimated always. After Nora slams the door the ultimate terror is that decisions rest with her. From this point on, the way bristles with choices, and these will be all her own, not her husband's, not based on the welfare of the children—her own. This burden is understood in Lessing's ironic use of the term "free women."

In our society women are accustomed to depend on these limitations, and there is reason to think that that is what Molly and Anna are doing when they make men so important in their lives. A dependence on masculinity itself cannot be their weakness. Hardly ever do the men in this book give sexual pleasure or protection. They do not lend their prestige to the women. They are more inclined to insult than to flatter. Love is rare by any definition. And the women are so experienced that they scarcely even hope that the next man will be any different. But their men and children give these women's lives a shape like the shape that husbands and children give the lives of conventional women. In neither case does the system work. The "free" women are not so enviable as the wives spitefully believe. But the wives are worse off by far. They may console themselves with illusions of superiority, but they are uniformly miserable or obliterated. The prime example is Marion, driven to alcoholism by her marriage with Molly's ex-husband, but even among the lesser victims there is no exception to the rule that marriage is destructive for women. Significantly, in *The Shadow of the Third* in the Yellow Notebook, the identity of the third begins by being Paul's wife, becomes the younger Ella, then Paul, and ends by being Ella herself.

In other words, the subconscious identifies mistress with wife, and the free woman, in her humanity, is full of resentment at the man who will use his adventure with her to denigrate his wife. The conventional system dominated by marriage and the family works very badly, but it should not be surprising that it still holds its temptation. The other systems work badly too, but that does not prevent Anna from going into analysis and joining the Party. Mrs. Marks becomes Mother Sugar, a help in swallowing the bitter dose that is life, an undignified form of dependence. The British C.P. has faults so evident that Anna decides against joining even before she does join, and soon thereafter begins to decide to leave the Party. But these, like art, give life a form and unity that it lacks when ingested as raw experience, and Anna is faced with the impossibility of all of them and with her need for something to take their place. Again, system fails her, and she is thrown back on the resources of her own character.

Fragmentation, then, is not caused by flaws in the personality of the protagonist, as subjectivists might assume. The fragmentation expressed in the structure and substance of this novel surely comes from the irrefragability of brute outer events. Children of violence are broken by that violence. They can hardly be expected to bring any and all events, including the unthinkable, into some competent system of thought that tames the entire jungle. Michael, the lover, who is so seldom heard from, says one sensible thing:

> Michael came in, very late. I told him what I was trying to think out. After all, he's a witch-doctor, a soul-curer. He looked at me, very dry and ironic, and remarked: "My dear Anna, the human soul, sitting in a kitchen, or for that matter, in a double bed, is quite complicated enough, we don't understand the first thing about it. Yet you're sitting there worrying because you can't make sense of the human soul in the middle of a world revolution?" And so I left it, and I was glad to, but I was nevertheless feeling guilty because I was so happy not to think about it. (p. 142)

Yet, children of violence though they be, Anna and Molly are also surviving children of an earlier age, an age of order and law, an age in which responsibility seems to begin in a waking, rational comprehension of sequences—cause and effect, action and reaction. As grandchildren of the puritan conscience, these "free" women carry responsibility to a neurotic degree. In personal relations they are not only responsible for their children, whose fathers drop out of parenthood rather easily, but also, in varying degrees, for the friend's child, for the former husband, for the recent bedfellow, and for the former husband's new wife. The hungry are fed, the houseless taken in, the egomaniacs listened to, the children protected, the sick nursed, the drunken cozened, and a variety of complainants taken to bed. This mania for social service, for the most part ungraciously received, is one of the more puzzling elements in the characterization of the women, especially Anna. Whatever havoc these women may wreak, it is not through carelessness.

Surely this reflex of responsibility for any and every need is puritanical, just as Lessing has always noted that the C.P. is puritanical. The fact that Anna goes to bed with men on very short notice may camouflage this fundamental quality in her nature, but the fact remains that even these beddings are puritanical, having so little to do with pleasure and so much to do with a sense of duty. Like the homosexuals to whom she rents a room, the heterosexuals to whom she lends her bed are not expected to repay kindness except with spitefulness, and they do not. Incidentally, anyone who thinks the portrayal of this male couple, Ronnie and Ivor, displays prejudice, should consider how exactly like the "masculine" men in the story they are, in their self-absorption, their malice toward the female, their fears, and their belief in setting things right with a sop like a bunch of flowers. The fact that the woman goes on knowing what to expect and letting herself in for it anyway is baffling and revives the mutterings about female masochism. The reader may well lose patience with all these bowings to the inevitable. Martyrdom without sainthood has always been a female vocation. But it is uninspiring. This submissiveness, not her deviationist views on the highly political issue of the vaginal orgasm, makes Anna a questionable role model for the New Woman. Yet this submissiveness is not essentially sexual, being so much like her subjection of her own will and judgment in political matters.

In the public sphere this puritanism asserts itself in ways that are equally striking. And unless the "dependence on men" is recognized as being a similar system to rescue the self from its condition of floating free in chaos, the whole structure of the novel cannot hold together. Both Marxism and psychoanalysis are shown as cataleptic postures aping some ultimate salvation. Anna persists conscientiously in following both. Misplaced faith and the impossibility of dependence are themes stated with variations in the various notebooks. But a trace of genuine sainthood appears at the next stage.

The same sense of responsibility that has drawn Anna to these solutions of the insoluble also moves her beyond them, when obviously it would be restful to remain. Her intellectual courage is manifest here as it is in the ambitiousness of the notebook system. This woman's bravery in taking all experience for her province has much to do with her being a woman. As a woman, as the ultimate outsider, she has the advantages of her privations. She has had a rigorous training in disenchantment. Not all women are experts in this field. So much is obvious. But all women, even the cautious, get a number of lessons. And women like Anna, who will not follow the rules, get an expertise that is fully doctoral in the field Virginia Woolf called "freedom from unreal loyalties." No man in this novel has both the penetration and the courage to forgo all solutions. All take refuge somewhere, even if only, like the archetypal American novelist, Saul Green, in the bed of a sympathetic woman against whom he is able to protect his pride by the crafty expedient of ingratitude.

This sounds as if the cards were stacked against men, and they may be, but the reading of the novel does not give that impression. The texture of the book, the details of characterization, the tone of narration, the handling of the plot lines in relation to character all forbid the assumption that these male

figures have been unfairly manipulated to lead to a predeter-
mined answer. Above all, the restraint of comment and the
conscientious neutrality of tone, threatening dullness at many
points, show the author's determined honesty. Though the
details of these men's behavior and the things they say verge on
caricature, being pure realism, Lessing never yields to the
temptation of satire. There may be no other fiction ever written
that speaks so exactly of the painfulness of men to women, yet
speaks so entirely without cruelty or vengefulness. Witness has
been borne. That is enough.

It is woman, then, who steps out of all the systems men have
made to protect themselves against chaos. And *The Golden
Notebook* has been constructed with painstaking craft to be her
springboard into the unknown. The existing systems are constructed to account for all data and to protect themselves from
new, intrusive, and contradictory data. The logical games involved are notorious. System is the second oldest enemy of life.
Anna, a creator of a first child and first novel, has tried to
accommodate herself to system, even while rejecting *the* System, and is blocked. Her solution, in the form of the four
notebooks, symmetrical and, in a sense, cosmic, a symbol of
unity, is indeed a method of imposing some sort of order on
chaos, but it is an open system, not a closed one. The old
revolutionary systems, like the old conservative systems, are
deductive, imposing their own interpretations always. The
notebooks are inductive, open. Reality, extremely unmanage-
able, arrives and is admitted. There will be no conclusions until
the data are all in. When she is ready to leave her analysis, as
she has left the Party, Anna says, "The next stage is, surely,
that I leave the safety of myth and Anna Wulf walks forward
alone" (p. 403).

There is never a time, of course, when the data are all in.
And the data of experience are never finally assessed and inter-
preted in *The Golden Notebook*. The novel has no such end in
view, nor should it. One recent critique quarrels with Doris
Lessing over that lack, but this is only one example of the
touching faith some novelists are able to inspire, a reverence

resulting quite naturally from the reader's sense of the miraculous in the creation of the novel itself, and incidentally a testimony to the persuasiveness of the fictive life given by art.[2] In this novel the characters are struggling with life, with war, with politics, with betrayal, with insanity, with personal cruelty, with the holocaust. The author, as author, is not.

But though Lessing has not solved the problems of the world, she has solved the problem of her novel. The novel that Anna-Ella once could not begin has been begun and finished. It is, moreover, a novel superior in truth and artistry to her conventional and simple-minded first novel. But great as this advance is for Anna, it is far from satisfying the spectacular ambitions of Doris Lessing, or expressing her dissatisfaction with anything that even a "good" novel can do justice to. She has not rested content with writing *Free Women*. Reality is always beyond the novel, bigger, less comprehensible, infinitely seductive. That hunger for reality expressed in the long novels of the nineteenth century is here. And just as none of those earlier novelists ever walked away sated from the mad banquet of reality, so Lessing, on behalf of her heroine, remains as unsatisfied with *Free Women* as with *Frontiers of War*, even though not so ashamed of it. And as the old forms fail to hold the new reality, a new form must be found and has been found: the notebooks are a system to beat all systems. They are open to all experiences. Where the political, psychoanalytic, and conventional social systems shape experience to their own pattern, turning even private feelings into a lie, the notebooks let experience shape them. They do not even take on titles until the self has played about loosely and shown its untutored direction. The richness, crowding, and confusion are there. That is a triumph. But the triumph goes beyond even that. The invention of the notebooks makes it possible to express fragmentation in a way that implies the hopelessness of the search for unity and perhaps, by establishing the hopelessness of that

---

2. Nancy M. Porter, "A Way of Looking at Doris Lessing," *Female Studies VI* (Old Westbury, N. Y.: The Feminist Press, 1972).

search, makes possible the contemplation of a different goal, one that may be less maddening. The hint already given in *The Golden Notebook* is that the new goal may be, not a system accounting for all the fragments of experience, but an anti-system living by the unaccountability of its elements, the strangeness of all our parts to each other, the mysteriousness known to everyone but usually too fearful to acknowledge. It may be that Lessing's later work, notably "The Temptation of Jack Orkney," shows an accommodation being made in that direction. The temptations of religion are the only major systematization absent from *The Golden Notebook*.

> . . . There is, it seems to us,
> At best, only a limited value
> In the knowledge derived from experience.
> The knowledge imposes a pattern, and falsifies,
> For the pattern is new in every moment
> And every moment is a new and shocking
> Valuation of all we have been. . . .[3]

No endorsement of chaos is implied. That is clear in every tone and gesture of this novel that never stops thinking. If these orders rejected by Anna are false orders, illusions, they are worse than nothing, because they stop people from thinking, or at least set thinking in patterns that may mask a true order of reality. Anna, like Martha Quest, is on a long perilous voyage of discovery, and what is primarily required of the quester after any grail is to ask the right questions. The prevailing systems dictate questions, not just answers. To judge a book, a dream, or a decision, one must ask, "What is the archetype?" or "Does this spoil the shape of my novel?" or "Will it advance the revolution?" or "Will I risk losing Michael?" None of these questions leads to the castle.

   The sense in which Lessing's women illuminate the situation of humanity in general is a rather special sense. Their quarrel with the culture is essentially different from the quar-

---

3. T. S. Eliot, "East Coker," *Four Quartets* (New York: Harcourt Brace, 1943).

rels of women who speak only of their own oppression. The difference is not that they are more generous, although generosity is a great attribute of both Molly and Anna—and the term needs to be set firmly beside the term *masochism* and the two looked at together for a while. Lessing's women see that women's oppression is not only similar to other forms of oppression, but is, like all forms, a matter of the relations between the self and the pressures of society. They recognize that society is the necessary matrix of human life and that the self can never meaningfully define itself in isolation from that matrix. To pretend otherwise is frivolity. Literature in the past has shown women in relation to their cultures, some acting in complicity with the culture, some consciously or unconsciously in conflict with it. But even those consciously in conflict have not generalized or theorized their experience. Lessing's work is a full-scale consideration of the female self that recognizes and defines its own conflict with the culture.

In so doing, her women define the corruption of the men as another symptom of oppression. The men are split in their own way. "He leaves and she thinks for the hundredth time that in their emotional life all these intelligent men use a level so much lower than anything they use for work, that they might be different creatures" (p. 392). In England, "this frozen soil" (p. 17), sex becomes conscious and tormented, very much as Lawrence viewed it, and at Molly's rehearsals, "every man in the cast is a queer but one, and he's sixteen" (p. 45). The American man, as epitomized in Saul Green, has a different pattern:

> He stood lounging, his thumbs hitched through his belt, fingers loose, but pointing as it were to his genitals—the pose that always amuses me when I see it on the films, because it goes with the young, unused, boyish American face—the boyish, disarming face, and the he-man's pose. (p. 473)

But perhaps this is not so different: "Whenever I meet an American man I wait for the moment when his face really lights

up—it's when he's talking about the group of buddies"
(p. 535). With her he has sometimes "the face of a little murderer" (p. 517). But Anna has learned not to take these things
personally. At one point she speaks of "the wife 'back home'
whom he patronized with every word he said (but really he was
afraid of her—he was afraid not of her but of the obligations to
society she represented)" (p. 466). This is later taken one step
further:

> But I saw this not merely as denying Anna, but as denying
> life itself. I thought that somewhere here is a fearful trap for
> women, but I don't yet understand what it is. For there is no
> doubt of the new note women strike, the note of being
> betrayed. . . . It is in me, Anna betrayed, Anna unloved,
> Anna whose happiness is denied, and who says not: Why do
> you deny me, but why do you deny life? (p. 509)

Meanwhile, women are going mad, full of guilt they know is
irrational:

> Five lonely women going mad quietly by themselves, in
> spite of husband and children or rather because of them. The
> quality they all had: self-doubt. A guilt because they were
> not happy. The phrase they all used: "There must be some-
> thing wrong with me." (p. 146)

The men stay sane, at least by a masculine society's definition
of sanity, although the eternal "I, I, I, I, I" that Anna notes so
often in Saul's speech is as much a symptom as her stammering
when she finds herself giving an essentially false lecture. The
madness of the women, Anna's inability to function, stand as
an implicit criticism of the men's "sanity." In private life that
"sanity" is parasitic on the melancholy women who wait at
home. In public life, it permits the men to stay in the Party, to
publish novels, to corner aluminum saucepans, to drop bombs.
Sanity seems to be, like unity, a value that has lost its value.
    In a significant passage, the Black Notebook declares its
author's views on the novel:

—the interest with which I read these books had nothing to do with what I feel when I read—let's say Thomas Mann, the last of the writers in the old sense, who used the novel for philosophical statements about life. The point is that the function of the novel seems to be changing; it has become an outpost of journalism; we read novels for information about areas of life we don't know—an area of society, a type of person, not yet admitted to the general literate consciousness. . . . Inside this country, Britain, the middle-class have no knowledge of the lives of working-people, and vice-versa; and reports and articles and novels are sold across the frontiers, and read as if savage tribes were being investigated. . . . Yet I am incapable of writing the only kind of novel which interests me: a book powered with an intellectual or moral passion strong enough to create order, to create a new way of looking at life. (p. 59)

This is interesting because *The Golden Notebook* is, in a sense, this new kind of novel-report, bringing in data from "savage tribes" like authors, communists, "free women." Yet, in another sense, Anna's statement about her own writing obviously does not apply to Doris Lessing. She has written a novel that is as much philosophy as it is journalism, with intellectual or moral passion strong enough, if not to create order, then to survive beyond order, in the dangerous air of freedom.

3

Linguistics, Mechanics, and Metaphysics: Anthony Burgess's *A Clockwork Orange* (1962)

ESTHER PETIX

The second half of the twentieth century has passively acknow-ledged the emergence of its most controversial gadfly, John Anthony Burgess Wilson: philosopher, critic, theologian, lin-guist, musician, academician, and author. Yet the seemingly facile task of the Burgess critic is not so much a matter of ascribing priorities within Burgess's various spheres of exper-tise, but rather (and amazingly) in shouldering the onus of redressing the dearth of any critical attention. Serious and exhaustive research reveals that Burgess's tremendous energy and soaring imagination have netted only moderate acclaim, a modicum of intellectual authority, and a quasi-reputation as one of the century's comic artists. For too long Burgess's liter-ary precision and satire have been obscured beneath labels of precocious, light wit. While his contemporaries moved to the heights of fame and fortune, garnering critical attention, es-teem, and aggrandizement, the wealth of Burgess's knowledge and ingenuity within the form of the novel remained ignored.

Most certainly Burgess has his following, but his disciples' enthusiasm (at times almost hysteria) has not diverted attention to his themes, nor has it acquainted large numbers with the universality of his traditionalism and messages. Perhaps, then, he is in need of one fewer disciple and one more evangelist. For as any devotee of Burgess knows, this is an era that enjoys the dramatic sweep of technocracy. Today one must introduce status (of any sort) from the point of volume rather than quality or essence, and by contemporary standards, shibboleths, and axioms, Burgess's work is not established. In terms of sheer physical output, Burgess ranks high. Compared with the popularity of contemporaries, however, Burgess's sales offer only tepid comparison.

That Burgess is not a top seller has many implications. First, and obviously, there are distinct implications for Burgess himself. As a professional author, he is certainly aware of market returns to his own purse; aware, too, that what and how much he sells has a material effect upon his own life-style, if not his *raison d'être.* Unyieldingly, however, he tends toward remoteness and obscurity, holding out in effect for principle over capital. Ideally, Burgess's stand is consistent with his philosophy.

The implications for the reading public are another matter. Why, for example, is Burgess considered intellectually oʋ scure? Why, after nearly thirty books, must one still introduce him as "the author of *A Clockwork Orange,*" and that reference only recognizable because of the barely recognizable film version (call it rather, perversion) of the novel? An obvious problem exists when an author who has so much to say and is possessed of such profundities is not widely read; is, in fact, dismissed as a perpetrator of violence or as a comic. But then, Burgess criticism is at best confused. It is further obfuscated by the fact that he holds sway over a devoted following (which includes some first-rate critics), yet does not hold commensurate stature among scholars. It is my contention that the major force of Burgess has been siphoned off into static frenetics rather than into direct qualitative evaluation. That a clouding of Burgess's fiction has occurred is patent; how and why it has occurred requires a deeper analysis of Burgess's fiction and mind, both of which are labyrinthine. The labyrinth, a symbol often invoked by Burgess himself, is charted with the aid of various threads and clues running through his fiction. And pursuing these leads, these seeming difficulties, these ambiguities, these strata and substrata brings the reader to the inner core of Burgess's central satire: the Minotaur's Cave.

As a maze-maker, Burgess challenges not only Dedalus in the manner of construction, but God in the act of creation—a device and theory he learned from Joyce. Yet such creations and constructs demand a more formal system, and often an elusive one. Like the protagonist, the reader is drawn through threads of the literal plot into the maze, formed often as not below the author's own hilarious crust of ego. Yet, concurrently, Burgess as readily hides himself in the center of his creation, sequestered and insulated by its vastness as well as its intricacies. Readers thus are invited, nay dared, to master the maze, to pick up the various threads and wander the labyrinth; but the same reader always comes to the mystical center— volitionally, and only after much effort.

Imperfectly read, Burgess is necessarily open to charges of philosophical bantering; misread he is often missed entirely. It remains, then, to follow those distinct, definitive threads designed by the architect himself which lead to the mind of the maze-builder, the "God-rival." For at the center the reader may discover an entire universe in which the author attempts to contain the human colony. As with all artists who attempt to match wits with God, Burgess provides only a scale model. Yet it is a model unique in many vital, identifiable ways. Stated as a more classical apostrophe, Burgess constructs his cosmogony to explain—there is no longer in the modern world any need to justify or vindicate—the ways of man to man: to see hope through failure; to set a course while adrift; to seek certainty in ambiguity. In following the threads leading into the center of the labyrinth, we are able to spin from Burgess's fictions something of our own identities.

Midway in Burgess's decade of authorship, and bleakest

within his fictional cosmogony, are the years of the early sixties. It is a period marked by excessive concern with death (his own seeming imminent) and with protagonists only thinly disguised as alter-egos. Added to a medical diagnosis of (suspected) brain tumor were England's failures through socialism, her displacement as a world power in the aftermath of World War II, and her lack of character among the modern nations. All this greeted Burgess upon his return home from the Far East. In facing his own death, he also faced the demise of England. And the twofold bitterness is reflected in a twin-bladed satire so lacerating and abrasive that it goes beyond satire into black comedy.

In 1962 Burgess published his two dystopian novels, *The Wanting Seed* and *A Clockwork Orange*. Both are horrible visions of the future, predicated upon the present. In essence what Burgess does in the two novels is to project socialism and the excesses of the Welfare State (*A Clockwork Orange*) and historical behaviorism (*The Wanting Seed*) into a future that is at once nebulous and contemporary. Through such an extension in time he contends that socialism leads to a loss of the will and behaviorism leads to a loss of the soul. These companion novels consider the impact of original sin, abortion, cannibalism, violence, and free will on human beings who daily grow more will-less and more soulless.

However bleak the authorial outlook, however black the comedy, Burgess in his dystopian mood is Burgess at his most lucid. No longer are the protagonists culled from Establishment posts: Ennis of *A Vision of Battlements* was a soldier; Crabbe of "the Malayan Trilogy" was a civil servant; Howarth, of *The Worm and the Ring*, was a schoolteacher. Now the anti-hero of Burgess has become a full-blown rebel, and the quiescent, or slightly recalcitrant Minotaur is savage and obvious. One must keep this in mind in turning to *A Clockwork Orange*, for it is not only Burgess's best-known novel; it is Burgess at his most exposed, and perhaps most vulnerable.

The central thematic and structural interrogative of the novel comes when the prison "charlie" (chaplain) laments: "Does

God want goodness or the choice of goodness? Is a man who chooses the bad perhaps in some way better than a man who has the good imposed upon him?"[1] Such a question, while it affords the concision necessary to a reviewer, is totally insufficient to the critic. For there is something at once delightful and horrible, dogged and elusive in *A Clockwork Orange* that even so profound a rhetorical question cannot contain. There is something about the novel so frightening that it demanded a new language, and something so immanent in the message of the novel that it refused to be separated from the language. Linguistics and metaphysics — the how and what of *A Clockwork Orange* — are the disparate, yet connected threads leading to the Minotaur.

A Clockwork Orange is in part a clockwork, not merely titularly, but essentially. Its cadence and regularity are a masterpiece of grotesque precision. The reader is as much a flailing victim of the author as he is a victim of time's finite presence. He is hurtled into a futuristic book of twenty-one chapters and comes to acknowledge that he, as well as the protagonist-narrator, Alex, is coming of age; that he, too, is charged with advancement and growth. This "initiation" aspect of the novel is not gratuitous — of course. For the novel is further divided into three parts, reminiscent of the three ages of man; and each of these three parts begins with the question scanning the infinite and the indefinite: "What's it going to be then, eh?" Added to both of these devices is the haunting and vaguely familiar setting of the novel that teases the reader into an absurdly disquieting sense of regularity — as numbers have a way of doing — all the more unnerving because such regularity conveys a sense of rhythm about to be destroyed.

The novel's tempo, and its overwhelming linguistic accomplishment is to a great degree based upon the language Nadsat, coined for the book: the language of the droogs and of the night. It is the jargon of rape, plunder, and murder veiled

---

1. *A Clockwork Orange* (New York, 1962), p. 96. Subsequent references are taken from this paperback edition.

in unfamiliarity, and as such it works highly successfully. Anthony De Vitis asserts that Nadsat may be an anagram for Satan'd,[2] but Burgess insists on the literal Russian translation of the word for "teen." The novel makes a fleeting reference to the origins of the language. "Odd bits of old rhyming slang . . . a bit of gipsy talk, too. But most of the roots are Slav. Propaganda. Subliminal penetration" (p. 115).

Close examination of the language reveals a variety of neologisms applied in countless ways. First, there is the overwhelming impact of a Russianate vocabulary that is concurrently soothing and unnerving to the reader. It most certainly softens the atrocities of the book. It is far simpler, for example, to read about a "krovvy-covered plot" or "tolchocking an old veck" than it is to settle into two hundred pages of "blood-covered bodies" or "beatings of old men."[3] The author keeps his audience absorbed in the prolonged violence through the screen of another language. But the Russian has a cruelty of its own; and there are disquieting political undercurrents in Burgess's imposition of Slavic upon English, at least for the tutored ear.

Nadsat, like all of Burgess's conventional writing, harbors a number of skillful puns. People are referred to as "lewdies"; the "charlie/charles" is a chaplain; "cancers" are cigarettes, and the "sinny" is the cinema. There is, to be sure, little room for laughter in a novel as sobering as this, and Burgess's usual authorial grin is only suggested in this very bitter glimpse of tomorrow. Still, there is no absence of satire. In many ways Alex is still a youth, and the reader is repeatedly shocked by a profusion of infantilisms starkly juxtaposed with violence. Burgess flecks his dialogue of evil with endearing traces of childhood in words like "appy polly loggies," "skolliwoll," "purplewurple," "baddiwad," or "eggiwegg" for "apologies," "school," "purple," "bad," and "egg." It is necessary for

---

2. Anthony De Vitis, *Anthony Burgess* (New York, 1972), p. 56.
3. Translations are taken from Stanley Edgar Hyman's glossary of Nadsat appended to more recent editions of *A Clockwork Orange*.

Burgess to achieve an empathic response to Alex, and these infantilisms within Nadsat are reminiscent of Dickensian innocence—serving well as buffer zones (or are they iron curtains?) between the "good" reader and the "evil" protagonist.

Other clues to this grim future world are Burgess's truncated and mechanized synechdoches: The "sarky guff" is a "sarcastic guffaw." "Pee and em" are Alex's parents; the "old in-out-in-out" is sexual intercourse (generally rape!); a "twenty-to-one" (the number is scarcely fortuitous) is a gang beating; "6655321" is Alex's prison name, and "StaJa 84" (State Jail 84) is his prison address.

Closely linked with the mechanical hybrids used in Nadsat are certain words conspicuous by their absence. There are no words, for example, that give positive feelings of warmth or caring or love. When Alex wants to refer to goodness he has to do so by opting out of Nadsat and for English, or by calling evil "the other shop."

Yet the total effect of Nadsat is greater than the sum of its various parts. Alex, in the capacity of "Your Humble Narrator," uses the language to extrapolate a future both vague and too familiar. He sings of a time when all adults work, when very few read, and when society is middle class, middle-aged, and middle-bound. We are told only that 1960 is already history and that men are on the moon. The reader is offered no other assurances. And as the linguistic impact of Nadsat becomes more comprehensible, one is left to wonder if the world of clockwork oranges is so safely distant after all.

When one has truly and carefully followed the linguistic threads of Burgess's novel, the Minotaur guide can be heard arguing a matter deeply tragic in implications. By definition language, like its human author, man, has an essential right to reflect the fits and starts of a time-honed, familiar friend. There ought to be an ordered sense of choice, a spirit of chorus and harmony and solo. Jabberwocky is for fun; Nadsat is a very different construct and far more fearful. Though at times it can be beautiful, there is the lonely wail of tomorrow wrenched from the desperate sighs of today. In Nadsat one finds the

Platonic form of mechanism: the cadence of a metronome and the ticking-tocking ramifications of humanity without its essence.

The deep and hard questions of *A Clockwork Orange*, however, are not veiled by the mechanical language. And standing richer when reviewed in light of the balance of Burgess's cosmogony, they stand even more specifically poignant when played against the panorama of all Burgess's writing. Through a reflective stage-setting, the reader is far more able to cope with the labyrinthine mind behind the dystopian clockwork.

Burgess is fond of envisioning himself as an exile. He has voluntarily absented himself from many situations with the voice of a vociferous (not a whimsical) outcast. He has politically removed his allegiances from Britain. He has removed himself from the aegis of the Catholic Church, voicing preference for a variety of heretical or mystical theologies. Burgess is truly a man of isolation, alone with his own thoughts and his fiction to espouse his maverick philosophy. The exclusive position that Burgess assumes lends his writing a metaphysically unique, if not philosophically original dimension.

Locked within that mind—that mental labyrinth—is a most clever approach to serious metaphysical questions. Burgess has fashioned and shaped a dualist system of eclectic, authentic origin and pitted it against the world of the past, the present, and the future. Burgess's theological contentions are amazingly astute from the point of authenticity, universality, and relevance.

Much of his metaphysics is genuine philosophy given a fresh approach. He has drawn upon Eastern and Western philosophies, concocting a novel brew of Eastern dualism, heretical Manichaeanism, Pelagian/Augustinianism, the cultural mythologies of ancient civilizations, the philosophy of Heraclitus, the implicit teachings of the Taoists, the Hegelian dialectic. The impact of Burgess's metaphysics, however, is not so much the clever jigsaw effect of a master eclectic; rather, it is that out of this syncretism Burgess has presented a serious allegory of the contemporary malaise, which has been diagnosed by all recent Existential and nihilistic thinking. He is answering through his writing the central paradoxes of life posed in Sartre's "nausea," Heidegger's "dread," and Kierkegaard's *Angst* and "fear and trembling."

Basically, twentieth-century man has come to live under the onerous speculations of recent philosophers. He has, in a sense, become a captive of his own (or what he used to feel was his own) universe. Ancient philosophers and artists were dedicated to the simple contention that the universe was a friendly home, divinely designed for mortal existence, and not incidentally mortal happiness. In varying degrees, yesterday's thinkers attempted to explain, rationalize, even challenge man's primacy upon earth; they seldom, however, questioned his right to be here or his natural relationship with the world in which he lived.

The last one hundred years saw the growing disaffiliation from the traditional acceptance of the world as benign. After thousands of years of philosophy dedicated to man's concentric sphere within the universe, nihilists and existentialists were now challenging not only man's place in the system but the entirety of the system itself. No longer was logic, or spirit, or mind, or even God the central force of the universe—these became only alternatives. The center of the universe was now existence; man's solitary life was enough just *in being*. Shockingly, this new paramount position of man left him not the conqueror of the universe but its victim. He was swamped by the very paradox that made his existence supreme. For in accepting and even reveling in the uniqueness of his own individuality, man was forced to accept that he was totally unnecessary. Adrift from the former Divine, or logical, or even scientific plan, adrift from Hegelian systems, humanity was presented with a position of supreme importance and, simultaneously, with the concept of its own total annihilation.

As the world more fully accepted that it was enough just to be, it became aware, too, that an individual existence, while central to that individual, was as nothing in the universe. With World War II and the prospect of total annihilation (not thousands, but millions of deaths and the promise of even greater debacle), the "nausea," "dread," and "fear" that had haunted the ivory towers of philosophers became a part of every living being.

Into this anxiety-ridden arena came the literature that chronicled, prescribed, and diagnosed a series of ways in which man could come to live with relative peace within himself. Yet always the paradox remained: each individual was a unique and single existence that had never been before and would never be again. Yet that same individual existence was nothing. It would die, never return, and the world would go on as before.

Burgess, for good or ill, has generally refused to enter the arena. Indeed, he has steered clear of the mainstream of the philosophical split alluded to above. He has removed himself as thoroughly and totally from this particular dialogue as he has from church and country. He is to be sure a chronicler of paradox. He, too, speaks and writes of polarity, ambiguity, juxtaposition. He does not, however, revile them; on the contrary—and this is perhaps what makes him unique among writers today—he seems to glory in them. Burgess's writing is dedicated to exposing the totality of the paradox and offering humanity an alternative to "fear and trembling." In a single shibboleth, Burgess demands that man first become aware of the paradoxes of life *and then accept them.* The injunction is neither so simplistic nor so naive as it may at first appear.

Burgess offers his readers a cosmogony spinning in exact parallel to their own world. Yet, rather than trembling in the face of paradox, Burgess's cosmogony is energized by it. One is not at all surprised to find living side by side in *The Wanting Seed* "Mr. Live Dog" and "Evil God." "God" and "Not God" thrive in *Tremor of Intent,* and the following references from *A Clockwork Orange* show how energetic such dualisms can become:

> Hell and blast you all, if all you bastards are on the side of the Good, then I'm glad I belong to the other shop. (p. 71)

> But, brothers, this biting of their toe-nails over what is the

cause of badness is what turns me into a fine laughing mal-
chick. They don't go into what is the cause of *goodness*, so
why of the other shop? If lewdies are good that's because
they like it, and I wouldn't ever interfere with their pleasures, and so of the other shop. (p. 43)

Burgess advocates a pure dualism, reflected variously on earth
as "X and Y," "left and right," "black and white," or "lewdies
good and lewdies not good." The names and terms change
with each novel, but the concepts are serious, unswerving, and
consistent—head-to-head combat between equal but opposite
deities who are the forces behind creation.

Although Burgess does not shout innuendos from the novel's
lectern, he does posit dualism as a means for explaining the
unexplainable. Garnered from the fiction itself—for Burgess
has never formally outlined his philosophy—the dualistic system works something like this:

Each of the two divinities created a sphere. The "Good
God" created an ascendant, ethereal sphere. It became a world
of light, and summer, and warmth. Contrarily, the "Evil
God" set his stage. His was a descendant sphere of darkness
and winter and cold. Thus the spinning universe contained the
dual divinity and a massive panoramic background. One, the
"Bog of the Good," all "gorgeousness and gorgeosity made
flesh," gave to man a spirit, while the "God of the other shop"
gave man his flesh—again, juxtaposition, ambiguity, paradox,
and the need to choose.

The first and primary symbols of the Burgess cosmogony are
the sun and moon. They are the mystical, mythical avatars that
preside over the choosing upon the earth. Their qualities, both
natural and allegorical, are the parameters of Burgess's fiction.
Certain secondary symbols are, however, equally important for
directing the protagonists' literal, as well as spiritual movement. From the partial list below, one can discern the two
opposing spheres that directly relate to Burgess's dualistic universe, and the limbo sphere between them.

White ("Good God")	*Gray* ("Man")	*Black* ("Evil God")
sun	earth	moon
day	dawn/dusk	night
birth	life	death
creation	existence	destruction
grace	ambivalence	sin
past	present	future
soul	mind	body
summer	spring/fall	winter

Burgess uses this highly Manichaean and dualistic world for most of his principal settings. His protagonists are allowed to live out their lives until the moment they are embodied in the novels. That moment becomes the moment of choice, and Burgess forces them to exercise the dualistic option. This aspect of choosing and "the choice" mark every plot and direct protagonists from *A Vision of Battlements* to *The Napoleon Symphony*. A novel like *MF* is (if one might forgive Burgess's own pun) riddled with choices. *A Clockwork Orange,* however, is unique of aspect in that Burgess is not working on a multiplicity of levels but concentrating on the *nature* of choice which, by definition, must be *free.* To underscore his message, Burgess is far more translucent about his symbolism in *A Clockwork Orange* than in most of his other novels.

The moon and the night and the winter are Alex's arena. Burgess has always attached allegorical significance to the night and never more heavily than here:

> The day was very different from the night. The night belonged to me and my droogs and all the rest of the nadsats, and the starry bourgeois lurked indoors drinking in the gloopy worldcasts; but the day was for the starry ones and there always seemed to be more rozzes or millicents about during the day. (p. 45)

Scattered throughout the first section of the novel are innumerable references to the night as the time of evil. ("The

Luna was up" and "it was winter trees and dark.") On Alex's final night raid that ends in death, treachery, and incarceration, Burgess is continually outlining in black and white:

> So we came nice and quiet to this domy called the Manse, and there were globe lights outside on iron stalks . . . and there was a light like dim on in one of the rooms on the ground level, and we went to a nice patch of street dark. . . . They [the droogs] nodded in the dark. . . . Then we waited again in darkness. (pp. 60-61)

Burgess continues the imagery—the black of the evening, the light from the windows, the white old woman, the pouring of white milk, the theft of a white statue of Beethoven. Nearly blinded by the most stupid of his droogs (significantly named Dim), Alex is captured by the police, brought through the black night to the white of the police station: "They dragged me into this very bright-lit whitewashed cantora. . . ."

Throughout the remainder of the novel Burgess employs a seemingly confused pattern of white and black. The white-jacketed doctors are evil, and as extreme versions of B. F. Skinner's behaviorists and advocates of "the Ludovico technique," understandably so. In their hands (or rather in their mechanical toils), Alex will become a clockwork orange: a piece of pulpless, juiceless flesh that acts upon command and not out of will. Conversely, the chaplain is a drunk garbed in black, yet he is the only character within the novel who honestly questions the morality of this application of behavioral science.

The white of the doctors, the black of the prison cell, the white of the technicians, the black of the chaplain, the white of the interrogation room, the black of Alex's reentry into society—all are carefully balanced inversions. The reader has often to unravel such inversions—to work, that is, in and out of the maze—particularly within scenes with institutional settings. The same sorts of inversion occur in *The Doctor Is Sick* and in the hospital scenes from *Honey for the Bears*. Burgess generally inverts his black-white imagery in situations where the morality and ethics are prescribed and not chosen. Schools, prisons, military installations, and hospitals—all places calling for Burgess's use of color imagery—underscore, through studied inversion, his perception of a morally inverted, indeed perverted world.

In *A Clockwork Orange* Burgess has crafted a childmachine, placed him in the pit of tomorrow, and "voiced" him with the lament of a world so mesmerized by technocracy that it has lost its essence. Alex chooses to sin and the world cannot live with his choice. Dystopia takes away neither his sin nor his existence, but does take away his right to choose, and thereby his soul:

> Badness is of the self, the one, the you or me on our oddy knockies, and that self is made by old Bog or God and is his great pride and radosty. But the not-self cannot have the bad, meaning they of the government and the judges and the schools cannot allow the bad because they cannot allow the self. And is not our modern history, my brothers, the story of brave malenky selves fighting these big machines? (p. 43)

Alex does what he wants to do, so the world takes away his freedom to choose. He becomes a programmed good machine and no longer a person. Yet there has to be room for freedom, for by design this is a world of man. We are all "malenky selves on our oddy knockies" and the price of freedom runs high. We are a medial element, both desperate and sublime, with our *only* distinction being our right to choose. The paradox is one of enormity, for the stakes are enormous; the only alternative is a mechanized hell.

Oddly enough, Burgess, as man and as writer, is caught in the same paradox he espouses. The mind does not journey far from the body; the medial element, the victimized chooser of Burgess's fictions, is really Burgess himself. The spirit as well as the body yearns for a place, a time to belong. The Far East, England, Malta, are all bridges he has burned behind him. Burgess has, through his fiction, his journalism, his determined stand, cut himself off in principle and in fact from much that he intellectually abhors yet emotionally loves. His church and his

country go on, despite his verbal assaults. Like Gulliver, he
might indeed be genuinely amazed that his satire of the human
condition has not brought about immediate improvement of it.
But then, like Swift—who, too, looks *down* to observe human
nature, rather than *around*—he has been forced to pay for his
olympian vision.

And, unfortunately, for his prophetic vision as well. Burgess's
fiction is more alive today than even in the times it was written.
One reads with amazement, if not indeed horror, that Burgess's
prophecy has become fact. Zoroaster and Manes are dust now.
Dualism is little more than an Eastern etiquette, permeating
the life-style of Asia. Kierkegaard, Nietzsche, and Sartre are
classics, venerable promulgators of the *Angst* and *nausée* that
all of us have subliminally absorbed. But the dualistic paradox
still continues to unwind itself, and we still throb in our gray
cocoons, daring ourselves to opt for emergence into the day
or into the night. Burgess would draw us out of ourselves and
make us choose, would make us commit ourself to choice for
choice's sake. Like Alex, we may become mere mechanism,
or all will, incarnated in flesh and blood: a clockwork, or an
orange. The responsibility is of course ours, and Burgess
brilliantly instructs us how to shoulder the responsibility.

4

Transatlantic Communications: Malcolm Bradbury's *Stepping Westward* (1966)

MARTIN GREEN

Stepping Westward is a great advance over Malcolm Bradbury's first novel, *Eating People Is Wrong*; in fact, it shows a really significant comic talent. Let us take as an example this passage describing the hero's arrival in New York. He takes a cab from the dock to his hotel with the all-too-English girl he has become involved with on board.

> "Okay, let's move," said the cabbie, lighting a cigar with a book-match, and between them Miss Marrow and Walker strove manfully with the heavy luggage, finally getting it all into the passenger area and retaining a tiny intimate spot for themselves. "You just made it, don't you?" said the cabbie, turning round at last. "Where to?" Walker gave the name of Miss Marrow's hotel off Times Square, and his own in Brooklyn Heights. "You two not staying the same place?" said the cabbie. "Come on, why not shack up together, make things easier for all of us. I don't got to drive so far, you got fun. How's that for a suggestion?" He pushed in his gear-lever and they swept under the expressway, over the

cobbles and rail-tracks. "Whadya say, lady?" They turned up one of the crosstown streets, past the unmistakable odour of the abattoir, towards the centre of the island. Dust and paper blew out of lidless garbage cans on the kerbside and iron fire-escapes staggered down the sides of ancient buildings, falling into decay. People sat on stoops, white, coloured. Sun glinted on windows, the city looked dark and hostile, and Walker felt defeated and confused, an animal without a soul, a dead thing. "No," said Miss Marrow, winking coyly at Walker.

A great deal, about the three people involved and about the two environments they represent, is said there with the crispness of expert comedy.

But I don't want primarily to appraise the novel here. I want to reflect on some of its themes, both as Bradbury handles them, and as they exist (in the reader's mind) outside his handling of them. Just what makes him a significant comic talent, of course, is that he puts his finger on material in the reader's mind that stimulates one to this sort of thinking. These themes may be described as some American psychological types and their environment, or the differences between all that and the English equivalent. But in fact, as Bradbury fictionally defines those types, they are something much more sharply challenging and richly suggestive than "types"; they are a discovery of his own, and a discovery for us of our own experience.

The story tells how James Walker, a literary, married Englishman, comes to America on a creative writing fellowship to a Western university, and there encounters a different idea of being a writer and being married. This idea, which is essentially the same mode of being in two different contexts, is in fact his "America." He finds it very exciting and very inviting, and much larger than the English equivalents. But he himself does not measure up to it, and at the end of the book he goes back to England, which means his "large domestic wife" and his writing of querulous comic novels.

The American idea or mode of being is embodied first in Julie Snowflake, a student at somewhere like Wellesley, who

meets Walker on the ship from England, visits him during the
Christmas vacation, takes him off with her to California, and
finally rejects him. This is the sexual, would-be-marital, mode
of the idea. In its literary-intellectual version, the American
idea is embodied in Bernard Froelich, a member of the English
faculty at Benedict Arnold University, who gets Walker the
fellowship, who persuades him to refuse the loyalty oath the
university imposes, and who exploits the resultant scandal to
advance his own interests.

Bradbury has drawn both these figures very well, it seems to
me. It is the things they say that are best—very accurate, very
funny, very interesting and impressive bits of behavior, but he
also knows the house they live in, the books they read, the food
they eat, and so on. The writing about them is on a different
level from the straight satirical description of institutions and
streets and Americana. Bradbury is always sharp in his observation, but when he deals with Julie Snowflake and Bernard
Froelich he is doing more than observe. He is responding to an
idea, and the surface reality interests him also as the expression
of something within, about which he has many powerful and
conflicting feelings.

There is an important difference between the two major
manifestations of the American idea. Froelich condemns himself finally as a bully, a careerist, and a manipulator, while Julie
is none of these things, and remains essentially beyond criticism. She seems to Walker more "beautiful and human" than
anyone he has ever met, and she is presented to us for much
the same response. She deserves to be compared with Margot
Beste-Chetwynde in *Decline and Fall,* and though Bradbury
does not yet have Waugh's dazzling incisiveness and economy
in designing a novel as a whole, his idea of his heroine is really
the more interesting of the two. Julie and Margot both represent "calmness, coolness, freshness" (Bradbury's phrase) to the
young men at the center of the two novels. They are both
quicker, cleverer, gayer, bolder, *freer*—their physical beauty is
supererogatory—than the young men themselves or than anyone else. Above all, they have style; in everything they say and

do they achieve themselves; their behavior is a creation, a work of art. Their moments of self-doubt, the tremors that mar their style momentarily, only make that style more humanly authentic and valuable, more really triumphant.

The fact that Julie is an American undergraduate while Margot is a Mayfair hostess—and white-slave trader—vividly shows us the way the British literary imagination has changed in thirty-five years. It has changed not merely in its attitudes to America and to the British upper classes, but in its modern preference for "life"-values. But what makes Julie a more interesting heroine, and is Bradbury's achievement, is that he has taken his idea more seriously than Waugh or than most comic novelists. We know more about Julie; she is real as much as ideal. When Waugh tried to take Margot seriously, we got something like Julia in *Brideshead Revisited,* something faintly caricatural. Waugh's mind is too powerfully sardonic to leave a heroine free to be herself. Bradbury's mind is looser, more fragmentary, more compelled by things outside itself.

So Julie Snowflake is a much finer manifestation of "America" than Froelich; in fact, it is she who finally judges and condemns Froelich for Walker. But they are still versions of the same idea, only of differing moral quality. For the point about Froelich too is the forcefulness and authenticity of his style; he too achieves himself in everything he says and does. He is aggressive all the time, throwing any onus of embarrassment, anxiety, uncertainty, guilt, onto the other person; but wittily and even winsomely—with style. When we first meet him he quite stupidly damages the car he is driving—which belongs to the chairman of his department—by reversing into a fence.

> "Oh dear," said Walker, coming round the other side of the car.
> "Well, that's how it is," said Froelich; "no matter how careful you are, there's always the other fellow."
> "Bit of a mess, isn't it?"
> "Isn't it?" said Froelich.
> "You must have been in reverse," said Walker, his longish, roundish English face peering seriously into the damage, as

if a word or two from him might rectify the situation.
"Well," said Froelich, "don't just do something, stand
there. . . ."

This, especially with the contrast of Walker's anxious, guilt-
ridden negativeness, is more than mere aggression. But it is still
aggression, and in Froelich's relations with his wife, in his
career, in his literary and political opinions, he is always similarly asserting himself; provoking quarrels, taking over other
people's affairs, ministering to their troubles, challenging any
cool remoteness or mere politeness, any retirement or reliance
on conventions.

But this assertiveness, even this aggressiveness, is true of
Julie, too. It is perhaps clearest in the scene in which she
dismisses Walker, but all the way through it is really unimagin-
able that she should ever be at a disadvantage. She must always
be "cool"; the moment she ceased to be "cool" she would
cease to be Julie Snowflake. She must always assert herself;
behavior that involved no risk, that merely followed convention, would not be a mode of achieving herself, a self-creation.
On the whole this quality in her is shown always in its attractive
aspects, but I think most readers will feel surprised, at one
moment or another in the action, that the novel is finding her
(or Froelich) quite so impressive as it is. The explanation lies,
of course, in the character of Walker, who is so remarkably
negative and passive, scrupulous and uneasy, physically and
psychologically uncoordinated, *unstylish*. He has never achieved
himself in a piece of behavior in his life. He is necessarily
fascinated by even the worst sides of this American type, hypnotized by even Froelich's aggressiveness.

Walker represents England, and English liberalism, we are
told. Bradbury offers us some quite elaborate analyses of those
concepts. I am unconvinced. Politically, Walker is a lower-
middle-class conservative, it seems to me; ideologically, he is a
romantic pessimist with a horror of the technological future;
and I don't see anything valuably English about those
categories. (I mean, of course, that *his* England does not im-

pose itself on me as even comically authentic.) But Walker does represent his kind of negativeness quite vividly, and thereby gives full value to the American positiveness. He "brings out" the other characters. And since this American quality is so powerful even when not brought out, is so much a feature of the cultural scene, Walker's experience does represent that of Englishmen (among others) when in America.

That quality we can perhaps analyze a bit further by starting from a remark about Froelich by his wife, Patrice—that he is a hundred percent ego. It is the first part of the phrase that is the more important, that he—like Julie—gives the sense of being *fully* expressed in every gesture and every silence, every action and reaction. The word *ego* should not be taken to mean selfishness, in the old-fashioned moralizing sense. In that sense, Walker could be condemned as being just as egotistic, and in a meaner style. What *ego* means here can best be explained by reference to Norman O. Brown's book *Life Against Death*. He there sets the human body, including the instinctual drives and premental responses, in opposition to the cultural abstractions that derive ultimately from instinctual repression. What Froelich has, what "America" has, and what Walker has not, is an egotism of the body. This American type, though involved so much in intellectual activities, is dedicated to self-expression and self-enforcement in immediate relationships, tests of strength, and direct sensual-emotional contacts. The English equivalent expresses himself and enforces himself much more through his identification with cultural abstractions—in Walker's case, through his writing.

One of the puzzling things about Walker, as a person, is the completeness (the 100% quality) of his self-negation. He has *no* convictions, *no* opinions, no power to assert himself, no power to cope with the world or with other people; the reader wonders how he holds together. And yet we are told that Froelich "envies and admires" him; and Julie seeks him out and gives herself to him. Why? Because of what he has written, in both cases. And that is obviously not a matter of mere talent, if we separate that off from the personality it expresses. We need only turn to the book flap to remind ourselves, with a glance at Bradbury's own career history, how much seriousness, industry, energy, ambition, and sheer force of will go into becoming what James Walker is. This too is self-creation, and of a kind that impresses the other two.

Julie and Froelich, though so much more impressive in their social performances, even as people of intelligence, are probably not going to achieve anything in the world of literature, or of any other kind of "abstract" activity. They put a lot of their energy into such activities, but not of the best *kind* of energy. Froelich is going to be chairman of his department. He is writing a book on the plight of the twentieth-century writer, and we are given to understand that it will be just another such book. All that inventiveness in immediate contacts becomes sterile academicism in the world of thought. And I think the reader knows instinctively that Julie too will always be able to express herself in the world of immediate contacts too completely to need, or be capable of, any large-scale venture into abstractions. People like her have great psychological trouble with their Ph.D. theses just because they can't achieve themselves in those terms, and can't bear to do anything that is not a self-achievement.

It seems to me worth bringing in *Life Against Death* here because the fullness of the ego is linked with "the body" in so many ways in *Stepping Westward*. There is much stress on Walker's paleness, flabbiness, paunchiness, physical uninterestingness, and on these being English qualities in him. The attractiveness of Julie, and of American girls in general, is located in their physical firmness, litheness, springiness. Much is made also of his clumsiness, his gracelessness, his lack of physical coordination — his ineptitude in the swimming pool and at changing a tire. Julie's first attempt to reform him is an attempt to teach him to "relax physically." And after his few months in America, Walker does become browner, leaner, fitter, more interesting physically — and the mere approach to the boat home sets him sneezing again. America is the land of bodies, as Dr. Jochum, a European wiseman, tells Walker.

It is also, and relatedly, the land of intense emotional relationships. Walker finds America very confusing because he
cannot tell whether people are being friendly or hostile. "Most
of the time they seem to be both simultaneously." Froelich
embodies this trait. As Patrice says, being liked by Bernie is a
full-time job—he is so hostile to the people he likes. She also
says that when you see two Americans quarreling, you know
they are preparing to go to bed together. "It's a relationship.
Hostility is so much more friendly than total indifference." And
she complains of Walker's English comic novels that they
hadn't enough affection in them; the characters were too rational, not intuitive enough. The lines of contrast between the
two countries are therefore clearly drawn.

America is finally the land of freedom, of anarchy, in every
cultural, moral, and sexual way. The campus buildings are a
riot of architectural styles, the students are extravagantly
sophisticated and extravagantly naive, the married couples on
the faculty swap partners for the night. A part of Walker's
fascination with America is his sense that anything goes; right
and wrong are irrelevant there. And this too is an important
element in Brown's complex of ideas in *Life Against Death;* this
full, free, sensual and emotional life of the body demands a
breaking down of moral and intellectual categories.

Not that Julie Snowflake and Froelich represent moral and
intellectual breakdown; quite the reverse, and it is the novel's
generosity and justice toward them in this way that is one of its
best features. Both are keenly interested in ideas and in making sense of life; both are full of that self-respect which derives
from embodying the principles one believes in. But there are
one or two qualifications to make to that. Both are in a sense
childish, compared with Walker. They reach out for everything
they want, rather poutingly; they expect an amused, admiring
indulgence from everyone else—from the universe. And it is
notable that Froelich, by the end, has used the loyalty-oath
issue to make himself chairman, and is using his new power to
abolish the writing fellowship and establish a magazine that will
publish his own articles. This is notable because it *isn't* a

dramatic betrayal of his old standards. It is more like a translation of them into action. For his old standards were that one should get the power into the right hands. His hands are the right ones because they are alive, able to touch, full of love and anger; and they are alive because he believes in himself. This does involve a certain betrayal of abstract principle. When Froelich is getting Walker to refuse the loyalty oath, Patrice says, "You didn't stand. Why should he?" "I did stand. I crossed my fingers when I signed it," said Froelich. "No, look, this is the point, friends." He is quite in earnest when he says that, and perhaps for him "standing" means being able to say that—being able to take the moral tone fully even when one's actions have not entitled one to it; his moral *personality* triumphs.

If we may call the cultural abstraction of the personality the mind, then what we have in Julie and Froelich is a marriage of body and mind that allows the body a decisively larger role than it has in that marriage in Walker's type. Their interest in ideas, without being insincere in the ordinary sense, is at the service of their "bodily" selves. Walker has a very uncertain sense of that self in him. The ideas he deals with loom much larger in his life—which is not to say that he takes them more seriously in the old-fashioned moralizing sense. This is a contrast in personality structure. Froelich establishes himself in terms of immediate power—confrontations, tests of strength, embraces, alliances, defeats, triumphs; while Walker establishes himself in terms of impersonal cultural performances—lists of publications, and invitations to speak, impartial surveys of other people's books, comic novels. After his loyalty oath stand, Walker finds that in his creative writing class, he is "freely spoken of as a 'genius.' It struck him as odd, yet not inconsistent, that this praise came, not because he wrote like a writer, but because he had spoken like one." This is the American idea as contrasted with the British.

The Americans that Julie and Froelich can be said to represent must be primarily the intellectuals. But in a longer perspective, surely a great deal of the country can be said to be, as it were, focused through them. They are experimenters, morally, socially, and intellectually. Their personality style promises to be able to handle difficult and conventional situations — to be able in ten minutes to establish them as what they are, with total strangers, unprotected and unsponsored — to be able to sell themselves. And this is what nonacademic America seems to Walker, a series of alarmingly difficult and unconventional situations. His two great failures with women are over car breakdowns — the classic American situation. Froelich would not have so failed. Not because he has any mechanical aptitude, nor because he has any considerateness for the women, but because the personal-social problem of getting the car fixed is just the kind of thing he is organized to do.

And surely Bradbury has the right to identify America with this kind of personality structure, in which the ego is located much more in the area of direct emotional-sensual relations, direct and "childish" affections and hostilities, and every kind of cultural abstraction is distrusted, from formal manners to state socialism. It presumably has something to do with the much more permissive system of child-rearing in America. This is the America that erupted in the Berkeley students' movement, and this is the America one can place in opposition to the official personality of Communist Russia.

One of the reasons Froelich seems so interesting and representative to me is that through his voice I hear that of Henderson the Rain-King and other of Saul Bellow's heroes. Henderson, Herzog, and Tommy Wilhelm all have the same interest in their own bodies, the same emotional fullness, the same organizational anarchy, the same intellectual looseness. Even the writing of these novels gives the same impression, of a man very much interested in thinking, in working out the truth, but a good deal more interested in himself in the act of thinking — never quite able to forget himself, and hence always comic and childish; a man pointing fervently at some saving truth about the human condition, but with his eye on himself in the mirror, so that the finger is not pointing at anything in particular, after all. And Bellow is, as we know, a great representative figure for intellectual Americans. Moreover, if Froelich's book were better than it is promised to be, it would perhaps be *Love and Death in the American Novel*. For of course people like Froelich do sometimes write books, and they are sometimes very good books; full of a sense of the author as a big personality, mischievous, unpredictable, and brilliant. (Froelich and Julie are almost certainly Jewish, incidentally, but that fact has only representative significance. The point is that they are American.)

Walker represents an opposite type at least half against his own will. He believes in American-style "freedom" before he comes to America, despises his own domesticity, and is only halfhearted about the English virtues of politeness, detachment, not hurting people, and so on. He sees England much as his American friends see it, as a damp dugout for the damp of soul, a national funk hole. And at the end he completely accepts Julie's indictment and dismissal of him. And it is in the completeness of his failure that the punch of Bradbury's story lies.

Julie and Froelich were attracted to Walker partly by his negativeness; in their world he is a curiosity of almost pornographic interest; he is a nudist among knights in armor. They took him into their favor, offered to play the games of life with him, promoting him over the heads of a hundred other people nearer their own size and weight. The moment they forgot to give him extra advantages, the moment they began to use both hands, he was hopelessly outclassed. He was knocked to the floor and trampled under foot. Bradbury is saying that this is likely to happen every time between an Englishman and an American—at least, as long as the Englishman accepts the American standards, the superiority of the psychological structure that is described as "American." And that Englishmen should do that seems to be part of American cultural dominance today.

I wrote the preceding remarks in 1965, immediately after

reading *Stepping Westward*. Now, in 1972, it seems worth adding a few more, which derive from the events of the seven years that have passed since then. It is now *not* true that Englishmen "must" accept American cultural standards or psychological structures.

In America, a great deal has happened that can be summed up by saying that we have entered upon an age of revolution. A considerable number of bright young people have made up their minds that a revolution must happen, and everyone who thinks has been forced to declare himself for or against the idea, and to say why. The American personality type that Bradbury presents as material for comedy has begun to deal in death. Its love of freedom has ceased to mean mostly sexual license. It has taken on political functions.

If Julie Snowflake were created today, she would perhaps be called Firebrand. She would certainly be a much more extremist personality than the one Bradbury describes, both in political ideology and in life-style. She might either have gone underground, into some Weatherwoman group, or to live in a commune. Froelich would not be involved in loyalty oaths and wife swappings, but in trashings and bombings, draft office raids and prison terms. Moreover, though the two personalities might be in some sense the same despite the change in their activities—the same as far as their contrast with Walker goes—their whole environment, and so their meaning, has changed. America is no longer the land of comedy. It is a land of tragedy now, and Julie and Froelich, even seen from this book's angle, would not be comic characters. Of course, they *could* be seen as comic again, but that would need a new angle of vision, which has yet to be fixed.

For perhaps the most interesting thing that the seven year lapse measures is the way "reality" has changed while the literary conventions have not. (By "reality" I mean that consensus view of America which is powerful and general enough to force itself on a writer as much in touch as Bradbury.) I have read several other British comic novels since 1965 that took the same angle on America as *Stepping Westward* did. Some of them were published slightly before, but essentially they were contemporary with it, and David Lodge's *Out of the Shelter* was considerably later. Two of them, Julian Mitchell's *As Far As You Can Go* and Kingsley Amis's *One Fat Englishman* were of comparable literary interest with *Stepping Westward,* and Andrew Sinclair's *The Hallelujah Bum* was at least lively. In all of them (they form a distinct genre of modern British fiction) the view of America and the way its idea contrasts with the English idea is the same. In them all the central character, who represents the novelist, comes to the U.S.A., responds reluctantly to its various challenges and invitations, gradually makes up his mind for it as opposed to England, but (usually) returns home nevertheless, feeling unable to meet those challenges adequately. And though they do not deny the tragic elements in the American situation, they respond more to the comic elements. They see even the tragic as comic, in the sense that it is another manifestation of the whole country's size and vitality, its oppositeness to the smallness and claustrophobia of Britain.

Of course the heroes do not all represent the same England as Bradbury's Walker does. Amis's hero is more like Evelyn Waugh's early figure, Basil Seal, and his novel might be given the title that Waugh gave to a late story, "Basil Seal Rides Again," since Amis also is confronting Tory amoralism with the challenge of young America. This marks Amis's definitive affiliation to Waugh—his turn away from the "British decency" of *Lucky Jim.* It thus marks his self-affiliation to that earlier mode of British sensibility, which was much more aggressively anti-modern and anti-American than Bradbury's. But even Amis's hero is morally intimidated by America, in the same way as Walker. The differences between the heroes illustrate the range of British types involved in this imaginative encounter with "America" during the sixties.

Moreover, during these years we also saw America produce comic work that corresponds to the British, in the sense that it issues from the identity that Bradbury attributes to Froelich—I mean the comedy of Heller and Pynchon and *M.A.S.H.* and above all John Barth. *Giles Goat-Boy* is surely the supreme manifestation of that aggressive, extrovert ebullience, that harsh, gross body-humor, which Bradbury describes as "America."

But both these styles seem to have been by-passed by events. America is no longer triumphantly comic, for its citizens or for its visitors. It is perhaps a sign of the times that John Wain, one of the first Angry Young Novelists, recently published a novel in which another British anti-hero is humiliated by a golden American girl in the first episode; but this one goes on to retrieve himself by rooting himself in a Welsh village. In *A Winter in the Hills* the hero (who like others of his type has become dangerously dessicated by academic life) does *not* leave England for America to find regeneration. He goes back to the world of *Lucky Jim,* and to the virtues of the working class and the trade union, to comradeship and decency. He learns again to be the kind of Englishman I described in *Mirror for Anglo-Saxons,* to practice the sort of style that Richard Hoggart has represented in British public life.

Moreover, among the Englishmen I have recently met over here, more and more seem to have that sense of themselves, and of their style as Englishmen, in America. They move through the thundering ruins of this great, gaudy, wicked Hollywood set, this *Day of the Locust* scenario, openly keeping a tight hold on their integrity—publishing a sense that they belong to a tight little tradition, unambitious and untriumphant, but simple, solid, cautious, durable. It is a vastly more attractive posture than that of James Walker. Morally they have every advantage. Imaginatively, however, I suspect that the disintegrated looseness and openness of the comic heroes of the sixties promised more in the way of new life for British comedy.

5

Looking for the Simple Life: Kingsley Amis's
The Anti-Death League (1966)

BERNARD McCABE

"What do you think about death?"
"Death, sir?"
"Yes, death. What do you think about it?"
"I never think about it, sir."
"Never?"
"No, sir."
"Right. Next. What do you think about death?"
"It's nothing to do with me, sir."

The grotesque interrogation continues, and apart from being what it's about, goes on sounding like any ordinary army confrontation. It is typical of this strange Amis novel. *The Anti-Death League* keeps shifting us disturbingly from the matter of fact to the mysterious and back again. These soldiers are doing what a lot of people in *The Anti-Death League* do, they are not "coming clean about death," and that is what the novel implicitly claims to be doing; its subject is the problem of evil.

Amis comes at the problem from many angles. "The steering

67

failed to respond" is the last sentence of the book, and in a small accident a lonely man's old dog is run down. But by then we have already seen a young soldier killed in a similarly pointless way, another young man dies suddenly of meningitis, we contemplate a third who is living a vegetable life of "total withdrawal." And there is the young and beautiful Catharine, who in a difficult life seems at last to have moved on to a new plane of love and happiness, to have found "a signal, a guarantee that the real joyful life existed somewhere." Then she discovers that she has cancer of the breast. "Out of a clear sky. Act of God you might say."

Act of God. In Amis novels friends and enemies are usually very quickly identified and established as such. And in *The Anti-Death League* Amis as usual provides a choice group of human malevolents, "pro-death" people. But then in a sudden shift of focus we are pushed beyond the here and now to find that the ultimate enemy is God. In *The Anti-Death League* God gets the sort of treatment that Professor Welch gets in *Lucky Jim*, or that the newspaper editor, Harold Meers, gets in *Girl, 20*, a sustained offensive. In a poem "To a Baby Born Without Limbs," written by Max Hunter, the novel's central character (the latest variation of Jim Dixon, now alcoholic and homosexual), God as source of human misery, is made to say:

> But just a word in your ear, if you've got one.
> Mind you DO take this in the right spirit,
> And keep a civil tongue in your head about ME.
> Because if you DONT,
> I've got plenty of other stuff up MY sleeve,
> Such as Leukemia and polio,
> (Which incidentally your welcome to any time,
> Whatever spirit you take this in.)
> I've given you one love-pat, right?
> You don't want another.
> So watch it, Jack.[1]

---

1. The illiteracies are deliberate, for complicated plot reasons. The whole poem is near-Amis in style, could almost have come out of his latest collection, *A Look Around the Estate*. Compare the sardonic poem "New Approach Needed," addressed to

God, apparently benevolent ("100% loving"), is the root of evil, and he is relentlessly attacked. Or more precisely, he is attacked as he exists in the minds and mouths of his admirers ("to believe in any sort of benevolent deity is a disgrace to human decency and intelligence . . . ," this is the army chaplain speaking). Hunter's attack on death and God is an attack on the ways people find to evade the problems of evil and of death. Amis, again as usual, is pursuing the dishonesties of thought, word, and deed that surround these topics. He gives them the shock treatment, in *Lucky Jim*'s iconoclastic "filthy Mozart" style. "God giveth and by Christ God taketh away," or, as the disasters pile up, "God's having a whale of a time."

The truculence is familiar, as is the exasperation and the impatience, an impatience that keeps well clear of righteous indignation—one of Amis's regular targets. His protagonists, from *Lucky Jim* onwards, have been characteristically violent and compulsive. Caught in worlds of frustration, they have something of the feverish urgency for instant gratification that we associate with the "deprived child." Amis is fascinated with the possibilities of simple action. Lucky Jim swallowing down great pints of bitter at high speed, or bolting whole at breakfast-time a finger-held fried egg, sets the pattern. If you are hungry, grab the food. If you want a girl, get her drunk, as does the hero of *Take A Girl Like You,* or assault her, as does his *One Fat Englishman,* or, more nastily, exploit her fears, in the aptly titled *I Want It Now.* If a man is a fool, laugh at him and hurt him. Bash your way through the niggling or the sentimental or the socially constricting barriers to the truths of the will. Do what you want and don't do what you don't want (a fresh message for pawky postwar England). Amis, needless to say, is not *prescribing* such conduct, but his novels contemplate the possibilities of anger and violence as a quick and effective way out of the cramping conventions, gentilities, and cultural orthodoxies of contemporary life.

Christ on the cross: "Come off it/And get some service in/Jack, long before you start/Laying down the old law. . . ."

Bullied by the world, the Amis protagonist quickly bullies back. Find the enemy and get him. In *Lucky Jim*, Dixon knocks down Bertram, his nice girl's awful, intruding, arty fiancé, and in his famous drunken lecture on medieval history he sends up (as the English say) the groves of academe by knocking them about a bit. In *The Anti-Death League*, Max Hunter behaves in the same way when he literally "sends up" St. Jerome's Priory, using a small atomic weapon. He is making a frontal attack on the home of "God the Father Almighty."

A specialist in a sort of controlled but peppery irritation, Amis invites the reader in his plain commonsense speech to recognize the enemy. The enemy, largely, is mean-spiritedness in its many manifestations—in cultural, social, sexual situations, for instance. In human terms the smallest touches are enough. Anger at the man who keeps his change carefully in a small leather purse, or who wears a bow tie, or a furry gray-blue waistcoat, or wears dark sunglasses on a dull day, or who talks in a certain way about art or music or wine, or who works at "trendiness" in speech or point of view, or who—the versions multiply. In these apparently arbitrary notations Amis asks us quite seriously to assent (often, but not always with amusement) to his recognitions of moral stinginess, of the evil forces that work against—well, against what? Mostly against good people loving one another.

Amis seems recently to have become interested in rendering evil as some form of positive presence. It is one of the ways in which he works to get new dimensions into his comedy, which by its very nature risks limiting itself to satiric social comment.[2] These deeper excursions have almost the air of respite from the pressures of his satirical intelligence. It is hard to move anywhere from the jocular and sardonic; Amis finds the grotesque a possible route. In a later novel, *The Green Man*, equally strange and experimental, he goes further, exploring the supernatural survival of past evils in the natural present.[3] In *The Anti-Death*

---

2. David Lodge makes this point in the interesting section on Amis in his *The Language of Fiction* (New York: Columbia University Press, 1966), pp. 243–67.

3. Perhaps he is beginning to believe in the Devil. G. K. Chesterton says some-

League the apprehension of evil is reinforced by a curious metaphor that runs in the mind of a young officer, James Churchill (Catharine's lover). As the novel opens, in some strikingly foreboding pages, Churchill begins to feel that he is moving into a concentration of evil, a feeling that grows when the young army dispatch-rider is suddenly killed under a truck. Speaking of this impression, he says to a brother officer:

> "You probably have heard of these things they call lethal nodes. You don't have battles any more, you have small lethal areas it's death to enter. Well, we're in a lethal node now, only it's one that works in time instead of space. A bit of life it's death to enter."

The military, or pseudo-military, metaphor is apposite, because the principal setting of the novel is a military camp. In this setting we become involved in a spy-mystery story, in which the interactions between the evil camp and an evil mental hospital next door are articulated in terms of assumed identities, disguise, incriminating documents, a pursuit, even a big shoot-up in the end. Rather tiresome terms, on the whole, silly with something of the silliness, or childishness, of *The Egyptologists*, the spoof-novel Amis wrote in collaboration with Robert Conquest. Yet Amis does achieve an extraordinary intensity in his evocation of evil as an all-embracing presence.

The camp is at the heart of the novel. In it a group of mostly young officers live semi-isolated in sybaritic luxury. All the compulsive appetites that are typically frustrated in earlier Amis novels are quickly gratified. The food is princely, whiskey and wine flow like water. And down the road in a sort of "Rapunzel's castle" the charming Lady Hazell practices "promiscuous polyandry" with no questions asked. Lucky Jim's early dreams come true—except that the military establishment has a dark secret: the soldiers are there for training in the use of a particularly terrible total-war weapon, a form of

---

where that that is a good route toward beginning to believe in God. So who knows where Amis may end up?

plague that is to be used against the communist Chinese. There are spies and counterspies, doubts and fears, nervous collisions of personalities and temperaments; it is a world of "boredom, depression and weariness," peopled by men like the biological-war expert, Venables, a self-sufficient, indifferent scientist and impatient rejecter of the irrelevancies of social discourse and friendship—"I depend on nobody"—and the expert intelligence officer, Ross-Donaldson, coldly professional —"Not my field, what people suffer from"—and clearly identified—"It's our job to be pro-death." The prison-like mental home is dominated by wicked Dr. Best, manipulator and exploiter of troubled psyches, discoverer of hostilities and aggressions in all apparently natural impulses:

> "as I've warned you several times before, whenever we go down at all deep we're virtually certain to find something rather unpleasant waiting for us. Do you follow? Something that must be pretty shocking or it wouldn't be hid away from us like that." . . . Dr. Best chuckled.

Ranged against this accumulated evil are the forces of "human intelligence and decency," equally recognizable: James Churchill, who rescues Catharine from the hands of Dr. Best, Catharine herself, the bountiful Lady Hazell, and Max Hunter, kindly orgiast, who mounts his secret campaign against death and against God, his one-man Anti-Death League, as "a way of voicing some sort of objection." The simplicities of human affection—"I love you." "I know."—and the simplicities of protest—"I've got it in for God"—are the only armor against the arbitrary attacks of accidental death, disease, and general malevolence, human or divine. Goodness wins out, as usually happens in Kingsley Amis's moral fables. The lovers, James Churchill and Catharine, stay together, Max Hunter finds it possible at one blow to settle accounts with both God and Dr. Best, and the Army's plan to use its death-dealing biological weapon is abandoned. But, as in *That Uncertain Feeling*, the victory is tenuous. Catharine and James's love idyll lies under the cloud of her sickness, Max Hunter's "campaign" has an edge of desperation.

A simple moral fable:

> Churchill went back into the bedroom and started dressing. Lady Hazell had apparently fallen asleep. He wished that those men had not been in the house when he arrived, and that he had come on his own. At this stage it was clear to him that he would not be making another visit here. If he did, he would probably like it less. Or he might like it more, in which case he would mind about the other men more. Or, possibly, he might find himself eventually minding about them less. That was an unpleasant idea.

Young James Churchill, emerging from a session with Lady Hazell, is working out his moral position, and he does it in a way that the Amis reader will immediately recognize. At various points in the novel other sympathetic people — Max Hunter, the Indian officer Naidu, Lady Hazell herself — will think or speak with the same tone and diction, as sympathetic people do in all Amis's novels, and as the narrator does. The deliberate simplicity, almost ingenuousness, almost naiveté, almost innocence of this language intends to suggest and succeeds in suggesting clarity of mind, an honest and decent moral perception, untrammeled by false sophistications, self-deceptions, pretentious abstractions, the philosophical or ethical or cultural jargon that gets in the way of seeing things as they really are. Like Wordsworth in his *Preface,* the sympathetic figure in an Amis novel endeavors to look steadily at the subject and convey his deepest feelings and judgments on morals and manners in "simple and unelaborated expressions." The subject is often himself, as in this case, for it is an essential part of the Amis strategy that the protagonist be on the alert for and seize on evidences of mean-spiritedness in himself as much as in others. The fairly loud applause that we are invited to accord the protagonist of *Lucky Jim* is occasionally muted even there, and it requires frequent modulation in succeeding novels, where the centers of virtue and vision engage in more complex self-confrontations. For this simple painstaking language, which is Amis's distinctive invention (and the effect of which is enhanced by our awareness of the sophisticated intelligence behind it), becomes a weapon of great skill and subtlety. This skill, together with his sharp ear for the pompous cliché, the quick seizing on verbal slips that reveal self-importance, self-deception, or mental laziness, and his trick of catching and turning and twisting the ordinary words of the enemy, gives Amis his great strengths as a satirist. And of course he is brilliantly and delightfully funny. Amis, like Evelyn Waugh and like his contemporary, Anthony Burgess, has that special gift; he can always surprise us into laughter.

Fools are put down smartly: the professor in *Lucky Jim*, the novelist-critic in *I Like It Here*, the psychoanalyst Dr. Best in *The Anti-Death League*. Yet satire can be a dangerous weapon that backfires. Dr. Best is effectively realized as a representative of evil, a monster who exploits his patients and abuses their psyches for his own delectation. He is also a delightfully monstrous figure of fun: "I've always thought there was a certain amount to be said for Bach, though his hysterical emotionalism is a grave limitation," or: "A deeply anxious mind, that of Mozart" —(someone answers, "Yes. Good in other ways, too.") But the principal joke about Dr. Best is that he goes about labeling lovers as aggressors, "Pulling them apart . . . asking them whether they thought they were going the right way about bringing their repressed hatred of each other out into the open," and that he finds repressed homosexuality everywhere, even among practicing homosexuals. This seems rather elementary satire on psychiatry, undergraduate humor at best. More unsatisfactory still, Dr. Best, as often happens to Amis villains, is the victim of a huge practical joke, engineered in this case by Max Hunter, who has him arrested as a spy. Schoolboyish. But the result for Dr. Best is a sudden and complete breakdown, and the articulate, excessively coherent psychiatrist jabbers away about his delusions of power (" 'Best,' said the chief, 'the world is in danger of destruction by death-rays.' Best knew he was the only one who could save them") and about his homosexual fantasies. The bully is discomfited, as in Billy Bunter stories, but it is not a very funny joke. We have stopped laughing at lunatics. In situations like this Amis's poise sometimes leaves him, we get a "tough" act, and the anger emerges as the raspy edge of vulgarity.

These excesses stem from Amis's seriousness. For the amusing Amis has always been a serious novelist. It is worthwhile making the solemn affirmation because he has been too easily accepted or dismissed as a mere railer, a twentieth-century Thersites. Q. D. Leavis, drawing in her serious skirts in the recent excellent Leavis book on Dickens, treats him simply as an irresponsible: "Our only bastions against barbarism . . . are the consistent objects of Amis's animus: in turn his fictions have taken as targets for denigration the university lecturer, the librarian, the grammar school master, the learned societies, the social worker . . . ," and she warns that he will be attacking the parson next, as indeed he does to some degree in *The Green Man*. Apart from the most un-Leavis-like implicit attack on satire as such (where does such a catalogue of protected professions leave Pope, for example?) Q. D. Leavis's comment ignores or denies the evidently serious moral concerns in these novels.[4] Although there are tensions and sometimes ambiguities in the shift between knockabout manner and fundamental intention, Amis *is* seeking honesty and clarity about life as it is lived. All the fury about "culture-talk" in his novels, and especially about religious, ethical, and psychiatrical talk in *The Anti-Death League*, is not simply nihilistic, any more than is Stephen Dedalus's attempt to shake off the "nightmare of history" in *Ulysses*. And one can say this while recognizing that consummate skill carries its own dangers with it, and that seeking for the simple formulation *can* lead to simple-mindedness.

---

4. The spectacle of a Leavis springing to the defense of the "clerisy" in this indiscriminate way has its own sad ironies, and seems doubly unfair to Amis who, rightly or wrongly, has got himself a notably reactionary reputation as defender of "traditional" educational values. His Philistine pose has always been a game with the public, asking to be recognized as such. Even the anti-academic *Lucky Jim* was a very "literary" book, full of disguised quotations, in fact.

Amis at times has insisted on his own seriousness. Probably his most self-revealing novel is *I Like It Here,* which has a hero, Bowen, who is a novelist himself, and who may be taken, cautiously, as an Amis self-portrait. Bowen makes the following comment on Henry Fielding, a novelist whom Amis has gone out of his way to praise on several occasions:

> Bowen thought about Fielding. Perhaps it was worth dying in your forties if two hundred years later you were the only non-contemporary novelist who could be read with unaffected and whole-hearted interest, the only one who never had to be apologized for or excused on grounds of changing taste. And how enviable to live in the world of his novels, where duty was plain, evil arose out of malevolence and a starving wayfarer could be invited indoors without hesitation and without fear. Did that make for a simplified world? Perhaps, but that hardly mattered beside the existence of a moral seriousness that could be made apparent without evangelical puffing and blowing.

No doubt a vulnerable piece of lit-crit; a romantic travesty of the eighteenth century, for example, surely *not* one of the best centuries to be a starving wayfarer in (if there has been one, yet), and other things sound wrong too—the question-begging behind that "unaffected and whole-hearted interest," for example. But it is most interesting as a view of the world Amis harks back to, or can imagine harking back to—"How enviable to live in the world . . . where duty was plain"—a world where simplicity and moral seriousness go hand in hand (as do the romping and buffoonery and practical joking). The fact that Hunter's attack on the problem of evil is very simply stated does not mean that the problem is not real, or not acutely realized in sufficiently disturbing ways, in this serious novel.

Fielding has been mentioned, and we are on the brink of fitting Amis into a Tradition—an inescapable fate for important English novelists when the critic gets at them. He is surely the immediate heir of twentieth-century England's major comic-satirical novelist, Evelyn Waugh. When Amis reviewed

Waugh's army-life book, *Officers and Gentlemen*, in *The Spectator*, he spoke of the latter's "disconcerting blend of the funny and the horrific," a blend that *The Anti-Death League* has quite exactly remixed and reused. Remember the initial interrogation about death, and its context, for instance. Amis's writing, his technique, often recalls Evelyn Waugh. In its economy, for instance; the self-damning phrase simply left to stand there without comment (Dr. Best on Bach can be compared with Waugh's treatment of Hooper in *Officers and Gentlemen*, or of Fr. Rothschild in *Vile Bodies*) or the quick, loaded exchanges where one voice appropriates the other's phrase and underlines its folly. They are temperamentally akin, too; it is not irrelevant that Amis has assumed the same testy, letters-to-the-editor role that Waugh played so hard in the last years of his life—brief, caustic, expertly phrased communications to *The Times* and *The New Statesman*, complaints from the Right about sloppy punctuation and sloppy politics.

Both authors are interested in and like to write about "good living." *The Anti-Death League* has almost as much about "wine-and-foodery" (though it is more ironically presented) as *Brideshead Revisited*. Both enjoy schoolboy larks almost as much as sophisticated wit: skylarking in the Officers' Mess is an approved feature of *The Anti-Death League* as well as of *Officers and Gentlemen*. Waugh's Basil Seal, whether he is painting a ginger moustache on the masterpiece of Poppet Green, avant garde (and superbly silly) artist in *Put Out More Flags*, or eating his mistress in a stew in *Black Mischief*, must have been an Amis Ur-hero. The conservative Waugh obviously delighted in Basil Seal's flouting of the acceptable moral and social order, his liberating anarchy. Amis shares a contrasting attachment to conservative, "traditional" values and an immediate imaginative and creative sympathy with the anarchic.

But this is always an escape-hatched, witty anarchy. Martin Green, a critic who has paid frequent attention to Kingsley Amis, recently placed him beside Norman Mailer, the U.S.A.'s self-styled "Left Conservative," as a writer who has moved beyond the liberal, humane, traditional culture—"antiliberal,

antigenteel, antimoralist"—into a Faustian search for the forbidden.[5] The parallel is suggestive, and could lead in many
directions, but I would like to pursue it with some reservations.
It is true that Amis, like Mailer, sees anger and violence as an
underlying psychic truth of contemporary life and, like Mailer,
uses anger and violence as an important way out of its frustra-
tions. But the essence of Amis's wit and intelligence and the
nature of the appeal he makes keep him well within a traditional, an accepted and sufficiently indicated set of social
norms. His appeal is to an anticipated assent, whereas Mailer is
a truly radical novelist who seeks, as deeply original writers
sometimes do, to reforge his audience and make it anew: "I
will settle [says Mailer in *Advertisements for Myself*] for nothing
less than making a revolution in the consciousness of our time."
Amis, with his "Watch it, Jack," knows he has an audience
ready-made who will quickly pick up his allusive wit, who are
ready to be delighted, diverted, even instructed, but not to be
saved.

   Mailer, as well as Amis, knows about the deprived child (see
his essay on *The White Negro* for example), and one might, for
the purposes of comparison, place Marion Faye, from his *The
Deer Park*, beside Max Hunter of *The Anti-Death League*. Marion
Faye, pimp, diabolist, murderer, homosexual, saint,
"philosophical psychopath," the *White Negro* fictionalized: Max
Hunter, whiskey-swiller, self-deprecator, yearner for love,
homosexual, would-be seducer of nice young men, practical-
joke-player—next to Mailer's apocalyptic heights and depths
we can easily measure the precisely understood domestic liberal limits of Amis's range. Mailer describes his political novel,
Barbary Shore, quite accurately, like this:

   It had in its high fevers a kind of insane insight into the
   psychic mysteries of Stalinists, secret policemen, narcissists,
   children, Lesbians, hysterics, revolutionaries,—it has an air

---

   5. Cf. Martin Green, *Cities of Light and Sons of the Morning*, (Boston: Little, Brown,
1972), pp. 78–81.

which for me is the air of our time, authority and nihilism stalking one another in the orgiastic hollow of this century.

Amis simply does not want to write like this. The anarchic Max Hunter is no Stephen Rojack (though he might have found some sharp things to say about the hero of *An American Dream* on the lines of the Amis poem "Outpatient"—"Right, then, mine's a lobotomy"). Amis in the end prefers the world of Tennyson's Telemachus, "Decent not to fail/In offices of tenderness . . . " to that of his Ulysses, "Life piled on life/ Were all too little. . . ." Mailer's romanticism is no doubt tradition-based also; his radical urgency finds energies in the hallowed impulse to come to terms with the American Savage as much as with the American City. But Amis, despite his forays into the irrational and supernatural in *The Anti-Death League* and *The Green Man*, is not interested in exploring Mailer's radical worlds of alienation, contradiction, and disorder. He does not see much point in straying far from the quick wisdom that the City of London provides. When we switch from Mailer's apocalyptic New York to the England that Amis wants, the contrast can be striking. Here is Max Hunter in *The Anti-Death League* urging the pressing need for positive action when faced with the problem of evil:

> "Sometimes you've got to be impractical and illogical and a little bit useless, because the only alternative is to do nothing at all, and that would simply be offensive. You can't just let things like this go sliding past without any kind of remark, as if nobody noticed or cared."

How sane and sensible this seems; it is what we all should want to hear. Yet there *is* a touch of schoolmasterly, pipe-in-hand uplift about this kind of thing—apparently a risk that Amis runs in the service of a final simplicity.

He is in a very English comic tradition after all. Once the satiric mask falls away, we can see romantic smiles, even a little sentimentality. Sharp comedy alternating with indulgent sentiment moves us back to the grand master Dickens (who grew up on Fielding). One recalls Dickens's marvelous ear for the revealing turn of phrase, his irrepressible buoyancy and inventiveness, his eye for the mean and hypocritical, his world of good folks and bad, his streak of vindictiveness (he liked to deal out smart punishments for crimes), his ready sentimentality, the basic conservatism, and above all, the confident simplicity that emerges in a wonderful complexity of observation and incident. It helps when reading Amis to keep Dickens in mind, nothing more nor less than that. Amis is one of those novelists whose presence is quite palpable behind every page that he writes. Of course, Dickens is another; Orwell once remarked that when reading him he was always aware of a particular face behind the page, "laughing, with a touch of anger behind the laughing . . . the face of a man generously angry." That description fits Amis at his best, too.

6

The Fool's Journey: John Fowles's
The Magus (1966)

MARVIN MAGALANER

For all its trappings of myth, symbol, and necromantic hocus-pocus, John Fowles's *The Magus* is essentially and patently the story of a human being and his quest for the true path to fulfillment. "Charting the voyage" (p. 552)[1] in ways conscious and unconscious eventually becomes the obsession for Nicholas Urfe as he relates the history of his existence from birth to adulthood. The details of that journey are vividly clear. What is deliberately murky for a long time in the narrative is the direction that the travel will take and, metaphorically, the destination at which the protagonist will, at the end, arrive. In the elucidation of these significant mysteries, Fowles obviously intends the Tarot pack of cards to be helpful.

The author prefaces the novel with a quotation from Arthur Edward Waite's *The Key to the Tarot*, describing one of the Trumps Major of the deck:

> The Magus, Magician, or Juggler, the caster of the dice

---

1. John Fowles, *The Magus* (New York, 1970); page references to this book will be given in parentheses throughout this chapter.

81

and mountebank in the world of vulgar trickery. This is the
colportage interpretation, and it has the same correspondence
with the real symbolical meaning that the use of The Tarot
in fortunetelling has with its mystic construction according to
the secret science of symbolism. . . .[2]

On the table in front of the Magus are the symbols of the
four Tarot suits, signifying the elements of natural life,
which lie like counters before the adept, and he adapts them
as he wills.[3]

As Waite provides a voluminous gloss on the *seventy-eight* cards
of the Tarot, the *seventy-eight* chapters of *The Magus* will offer a
gloss on Nicholas Urfe's quest, based in part at least on stan-
dard interpretations of specific cards of the Tarot, particularly
the Zero card—the card assigned to The Fool. But before
these views of The Fool card can be meaningful here, something must be said of Fowles's story.

The author carefully establishes the character of Nicholas in
the first few pages of the novel. In the second sentence, Urfe
discovers that he is "not the person I wanted to be" (p. 11).
The revelation is bolstered by psychological details: oppression
by an overbearing military father, contempt on the part of both
parents for his artistic leanings, and the trauma of his stint in
the army. The necessity to lead two lives—"aesthete and
cynic" (p. 12), poetry lover and army man, sexual adept and
unloved, unloving adolescent—obscures, however, the discovery of his "real self" (p. 13), "I had got away from what I
hated, but I hadn't found where I loved, and so I pretended
there was nowhere to love" (p. 13). On leaving Oxford, Urfe
concludes, "Handsomely equipped to fail, I went out into the
world" (p. 13) and proves himself prophetic in short order by
resigning from his first job as schoolteacher. The last paragraph
of the first chapter sums it up:

It poured with rain the day I left. But I was filled with

---

2. Arthur Edward Waite, *The Pictorial Key to the Tarot: Being Fragments of a Secret
Tradition Under the Veil of Divination* (Blauvelt, New York, 1971), p. 12.
3. *Ibid.*, p. 75.

excitement, a strange exuberant sense of taking wing. I
didn't know where I was going, but I knew what I needed. I
needed a new land, a new race, a new language; and although I couldn't have put it into words then, I needed a
new mystery. (p. 15)

At this point, consideration of the Tarot, particularly of the
Zero card called The Fool, is instructive. Waite's description
(accompanying a reproduction of this trump card) of the young
men depicted in most Tarot decks reads in part this way:

> With light step, as if earth and its trammels had little
> power to restrain him, a young man . . . pauses at the brink
> of a precipice . . . he surveys the blue distance before
> him—its expanse of sky rather than the prospect below. . . .
> The edge which opens on the depth has no terror. . . . His
> countenance is full of intelligence and expectant dream. . . .
> He is a prince of the other world on his travels through this
> one. . . . The sun, which shines behind him, knows whence
> he came, whither he is going, and how he will return by
> another path after many days. He is the spirit in search of
> experience. . . .
>   . . . . The conventional explanations say that the Fool
> signifies the flesh, the sensitive life, and by a peculiar satire
> its subsidiary name was at one time the alchemist, as depict-
> ing folly at the most insensate stage.[4]

The degree to which Nicholas Urfe fits the description or
fails to fit it should be meaningful in Fowles's construction
since the end of the journey will depend on the qualifications of
the neophyte who undertakes it. The expectation of taking
wing is there in both, the intelligence and the anticipation.
Urfe and The Fool share an innocent lack of terror at the trials
that may lie ahead. Where the figure of the Tarot ostensibly
parts company with Fowles's protagonist is in Waite's reference
to the depicted person as "a prince of the other world on his
travels through this one." Yet Fowles has figuratively prepared

---

4. *Ibid.*, pp. 152–55.

the reader to consider even this possibility. Nicholas has led "two lives" (p. 12), and he has in the army gone on "leading a double life" (p. 12), no matter how unprincely, until he is unsure of his identity or, as he puts it, of his "real self" (p. 13). In the sense that Waite records his own view of The Fool as a "prince of the other world on his travels through this one," and at the same time records the conventional view of The Fool as "the flesh, the sensitive life," of *this* world exclusively, Nicholas Urfe's uncertainty as to his real self might appropriately apply to the Tarot figure as well.

Like Joyce, Fowles is a most self-conscious artist. His protagonist's name itself is as heavily weighted with associative undertones as Stephen Dedalus's was. Nicholas may be a saint (the recent reservations of the Catholic Church notwithstanding), but he is also a Devil in this other world of which Waite writes. And Urfe may be a name "remotely allied to Honoré d'Urfé, author of the seventeenth-century bestseller L'Astrée" (p. 11), but etymologically the dictionary reveals "urf" to mean "a stunted person, esp. a child."

Mouni Sadhu's reading of The Fool card in the Tarot pack comes closer to the view that the man pictured on the card is indeed stunted, ridiculous, and tragic at the same time.

> On a rock leading to a precipice a Man is hastily walking. On his head we see a ridiculous cap, something like that of a circus clown. The fool's cap is of three colours, white, red and black. . . . His clothes are good for many things except to be worn, and still less for traveling. . . .
>
> He does not look at what is awaiting him at the bottom of the precipice, a crocodile, with wide open jaws [not in the Waite version]. . . . The Man turns his head away and looks somewhere in the sky. The left leg of his ridiculous and indecent attire has been torn by a vicious dog. . . .
>
> Who is this traveller? . . . Incarnate Man is evidently created to live on the *physical plane*, according to the laws of that world; but the fool is heading towards the abyss.[5]

---

5. Mouni Sadhu, *The Tarot: A Contemporary Course of the Quintessence of Hermetic Occultism* (North Hollywood, Calif. 1972), pp. 453–54.

The traveler here is a far cry indeed from the prince of the
other world. The "gorgeous vestments" of Waite's Fool have
become the "indecent attire" of Sadhu's, and the journey to
which the former looks forward expectantly is doomed to end
for the latter in the crocodile's jaws.

Between the one version and the other stands Nicholas Urfe,
the human character in *The Magus*, who leads two lives and
seeks his real self. It must be obvious by now that the novel
will strive, if not to reconcile these two views, at least to deal
with them meaningfully. Eden Gray tries to do just that with
conflicting views of The Fool in the literature of the Tarot.[6] In
doing so, she apparently rejects the "court jester" view, prefer-
ring Waite's interpretation. "The Fool's Journey" is important
enough to Gray to merit a separate chapter. In it, she sees The
Fool as representing "the soul of everyman, which, after it is
clothed in a body, appears on earth and goes through the life
experiences depicted in the 21 cards of the Major Arcana,
sometimes thought of as archetypes of the subconscious."[7]
Gray exhorts her reading to find in the journey of the Fool "his
own map of the soul's quest, for these are symbols that are
deep within each one of us."[8] She then draws this map ver-
bally, outlining in broad terms the directions taken by the Fool
as he encounters the similarly archetypical figures on the other
trump cards. Without seeking to construct a one-to-one analog-
ical relationship between the Fool's journey and Nicholas's
quest, the reader can profitably note the principal analogies.

"In the Magician and the High Priestess, the Fool learns the
uses of the conscious and subconscious aspects of the mind in
order to create the bounty of Nature, as pictured in the Empress."[9] One of the givens of the book is the identification of
Maurice as the Magus. Not content with calling him "Conchis," Fowles is careful to have the character point out that he
prefers the "*ch* soft" (p. 76), so that the association with

6. Eden Gray, *A Complete Guide to the Tarot* (New York, 1972).
7. *Ibid.*, p. 228.
8. *Ibid.*
9. *Ibid.*

conscious becomes inescapable. To the Magus, Waite assigns a godlike role, which attempts to fix the "unity of individual being on all planes"[10]—precisely the kind of help The Fool (Nicholas) requires in order to stop living two lives and attain wholeness. Until he is successful with his subject, Nicholas must inhabit the "waiting room" of Bourani, a kind of limbo from which only his own awareness can rescue him. The unity that Nicholas must acquire will eventuate in an equilibrium of idea and feeling, desire and emotion, conscious and subconscious. If Gray is correct, therefore, Maurice Conchis "represents Man's will in union with the Divine achieving the knowledge and power to bring desired things into manifestation through *conscious* [italics added] self-awareness."[11]

If Nicholas learns the uses of the conscious from Maurice, his subconscious is aroused by Lily Montgomery who, in *The Magus,* bears a resemblance to the High Priestess of the Tarot trumps. Waite's interpretation of that card associates the High Priestess with the moon, pomegranates, the Garden of Eden, gauzy vestments, and with Isis.[12] Fowles arranges for Nicholas to be present at a nocturnal masque that strains the limits of reality and consciousness. In it, Lily is "metamorphosed" into Apollo's sister. In a "long saffron chiton," she carries arrows and bow and walks a "huntress walk. . . . Artemis-Diana" (pp. 178–79). Conchis had also first seen Lily in a garden, the spell her appearance had woven for him being summed up in the image "The broken pomegranate is full of stars" (p. 110). And later in the novel, Lily is described as "ISIS, ASTARTE, KALI . . . AND AS THE CAPTIVATING LILY MONTGOMERY" (p. 470). Gray sees this Priestess as "the eternal feminine, sometimes called Isis or Artemis" and likens her "even to Eve before her union with Adam." Her task is "spiritual enlightenment, inner illumination," for she is "the link between the seen and the unseen."[13]

---

10. Waite, p. 75.
11. Gray, p. 20.
12. Waite, pp. 76–79.
13. Gray, p. 22.

The unsentimental education of Nicholas by Lily and Conchis culminates in the elaborate ceremony of judgment,
psychic and psychological, in the huge underground hall. Here
the phantasms that have tormented the protagonist are given
animate form behind the outlandish masks and costumes they
assume. And here the author makes the most obvious use of
the colors and forms and symbols of the Tarot.

Black, white, and red dominate the room. Urfe is decked out
by his captors in a black mouth mask, white ribbons, and
"bloodred" rosettes. The room itself is black and white, re-
lieved only by a painted red rose. A white-haired woman in a
witch costume wears a black hat and red apron. The goat-
headed figure is dressed in a white smock that has two black
bands round the sleeves. He carries a "black staff in red-gloved
hands." The oft-repeated color scheme is clearly deliberate and
most probably selected by Fowles to reinforce the position of
Nicholas as the center of the action: the reason for the ritual
(pp. 444–54). For these are the colors of The Fool. In Sadhu's
version, on The Fool's head "we see a ridiculous cap, something like that of a circus clown. The fool's cap is of three
colours, white, red and black."[14]

The jury of macabre creatures files in: the goat-headed man,
the man with a head like a crocodile (see Sadhu's description of
the dangers that beset The Fool), the skeletonlike man, the
vampire, the witch, and the rest. Finally, the curtained, black
sedan chair is carried in, its occupant hidden. "On the front
panel was painted in white the same emblem as the one above
my throne—an eight-spoked wheel" (p. 450). The reader
never finds out who, if anyone, sits behind the curtains. Conchis says that the chair is vacant, but it is plausible to imagine
the drapery concealing the goddess Ashtaroth (p. 454). Interpretation of the Tarot has it otherwise. To Waite, the chariot
contains "an erect and princely figure" representing "triumph
in the mind."[15] And Gray expands on that formula to declare

---

14. Sadhu, p. 453.
15. Waite, p. 96.

that the chariot "stands for the human personality, which can be a vehicle for the expression of the Self." She then identifies the royal figure in the chariot as The Fool, who "has reached an outer triumph and is ready to learn further lessons. . . ."[16] To the extent that he can be "master of his passions," Gray tells us, The Fool can ride the "Chariot of success."[17] Urfe himself thus metaphorically seems to occupy the chair.

But why should the sedan chair (The Chariot) be decorated with the Wheel of Fortune? This venerable symbol, principally Egyptian, constitutes the tenth trump card of the Tarot and, indeed, has the letters "T-A-R-O" around its circumference. The Wheel, with the Sphinx above it, represents "stability amidst movement, suggesting that we are not always governed by chance and fatality but that we have the power to change our lives."[18] Thus, "when the Fool reaches the Wheel of Fortune, his apprenticeship is over. From now on he is on his own, to rise or fall, while the sphinx of his soul looks on."[19] It is quite conceivable, in this view, that Nicholas, the prisoner in body, should look on at his other self in the chair-chariot, the part of the self that is now triumphant, free, and ascendant.

Once Nicholas the man is actually unfettered, Fowles makes much of the fact that he is free to make choices. These must be presented to him by those who have enticed him into the "godgame" for his own ultimate good. Conchis and Lily de Seitas take over the task of instructing their initiate in the ways of consciousness and unconsciousness in order that he may "create the bounty of Nature, as pictured in the Empress."[20] This Tarot figure sits on a throne, a field of ripening corn behind her, a water fall beyond, and she represents "universal fecundity." Holding the key to life in this world, she guards the secret of the path from this life to the life beyond. To Gray, she is the Goddess of Love: "As the High Priestess is Isis veiled,

16. Gray, p. 32.
17. *Ibid.*, p. 228.
18. *Ibid.*, p. 38.
19. *Ibid.*, p. 228.
20. *Ibid.*

the Empress is Isis unveiled."[21] She typifies to her the "productive, generative activities in the subconscious after it has
been impregnated by seed ideas from the self-conscious. The
subconscious has control over all the steps of development in
the material world. . . ."[22]

Fowles gives over the entire final section of the novel to this
Empress figure, whom he calls Lily de Seitas. Seeking to track
down the *personae* of Bourani, Nicholas is led to St. John's
Wood in London and eventually to the country house where
this mature woman plays her imperious role. "She sat in an old
wingchair covered in pale gold brocade; very erectly" (p. 544),
like the woman on the Tarot card. She is revealed to be the
mother, not of thousands perhaps as in Tarot lore, but of Rose
and Lily and Benjie. "I knew she was sitting there, in her
corn-gold chair, and that she was like Demeter, Ceres, a goddess on her throne" (p. 547). Like Venus too, she is old and
wise in the meaning of love, a wisdom that she tries to impart to
Urfe, the stunted child of the early chapters who has suffered
and endured to the point at which the lesson may be meaningful. Her name, de Seitas, perhaps associated with the medieval
Latin *seitas* (oneself), may underline the importance of selfhood, the recognition of the reality of Self.

Her "sermons" to Nicholas, whose voyage of self-discovery
is almost at its termination, stress truth and trust in human
relationships. She admits even that she and Conchis and the
younger Lily have been "charting the voyage" for The Fool,
and that such duties require the employment of a morality
quite unfamiliar to one reared in the vestiges of Victorian *mores*.
Unlike a conventional Venus, who might have restored the
beloved to the swain through miraculous intervention, Mrs. de
Seitas invokes the waiting room again, insisting that any miracle be wrought by the Self of Nicholas.

Urfe must grow from within. He must find his way out of the
magic mists of Bourani, out of the craziness of the rituals he has

---

21. *Ibid.*, p. 24.
22. *Ibid.*

undergone, in order to reach and regain Alison. Even with his new-found strength of character, he will not attain his goal without first proving in the real world the reality of his new being. Only then may he hope for union with Alison, whose name, as Fowles points out, means "without madness" (p. 514). Consequently, Nicholas must experience the interlude with Kemp—a meaningful friendship with a woman of no physical attraction—plain, vulgar. He must also come to the realization that Lily de Seitas is not an adversary but, if anything, the Wisdom within himself:

> There was something discreetly maternal in it [Lily's tone], a reminder to me that if I rebelled against her judgment, I rebelled against my own immaturity; if against her urbanity, against my own lack of it. (p. 574)

Her parting remark demonstrates to Nicholas that he must carry the ball in any further plays. "Alison," she tells him, "is not a present. She has to be paid for. And convinced that you have the money to pay" (p. 579). Part payment is Urfe's treatment of Jojo, the nubile adolescent who offers him her love and her body, but who is given "great affection, and not the least desire" (p. 585). Or, as Gray puts it, "the Fool can ride the Chariot of success as long as he can be master of his passions."[23] With his confession to Jojo comes Nicholas's epiphany that salvation is bound up with "choosing Alison, and having to go on choosing her every day" (p. 589). Now he understands that "adulthood was like a mountain, and I stood at the foot of this cliff of ice, this impossible and unclimbable" (pp. 589–90), as The Fool does in the Tarot pack. But the realization of what and where he is brings Alison back, for all the world like "a priestess from the temple of Demeter" (p. 599), back to face the same choice as Nicholas has had painfully to make. The "godgame" is over.

Most commentators on the Tarot see the cards as a "symbolic record of human experience,"[24] in which The Fool plays

---

23. *Ibid.*, p. 228.
24. *Ibid.*, p. 7.

the role of Everyman. Those who lean toward modern psychoanalytical explanations of the power of Tarot see this figure as a disturbing Jungian archetype with roots in the Collective Unconscious of mankind. Those oriented toward religion accent the affiliation of the same figure with Gabriel, for instance, showing forth the ultimate victory of Spirit. Devotees of *The Golden Bough* study the Tarot in terms of the mythical world. All of these would probably find the analogy made by Eden Gray congenial:

> It may be helpful to think of the Tarot as representing the spokes of a huge wheel upon which each of us travels during his life on earth, experiencing materials (*sic*) and spiritual ups and downs. These are reflected in the cards when they are laid out by a Reader—their positions, juxtapositions, and combinations are all significant. The Fool, representing the Life-force before it comes into manifestation on the earth plane, is in the center of the wheel, moves to its outer edge through 21 phases of experience, and then returns to the center whence it came.[25]

In like fashion, the author of *The Magus* becomes the "Reader" of the cards, laying out his seventy-eight chapters in such a manner that he can present his Fool in a wide variety of stances vis-à-vis the reality of this world. It will be recalled that Nicholas Urfe first encounters Alison on page nineteen of the novel and thus briefly and unwittingly has reality within his grasp. His fate, however, is to lose her and what she represents, moving through numerous "phases of experience" until he finds Alison again on page 596. From the loss to the recovery, this Fool is thoroughly tested in the manifold relationships he assumes with the other metaphorical characters of the Tarot pack.

Even though the author is assigned the task of laying out the cards, the ultimate Reader in the situation is the reader of the novel. For the meaning of Nicholas's encounters with Maurice or Lily or Mrs. de Seitas is at bottom a matter of judgment and

---

25. *Ibid.*, p. 14.

interpretation. Fowles, as Joyce's artist-god of creation, plays the "godgame" within his seventy-eight chapters. But the significance of what God has wrought depends upon where along the journey of life the reader of the story finds himself. This very accessibility to multiple interpretation that *The Magus* affords is one of the marks of the serious novel.

7
Rosamund's Complaint: Margaret Drabble's *The Millstone* (1966)

PETER E. FIRCHOW

Virtually unknown in this country only a few years ago, even though she had been publishing novels with industrious regularity since the early sixties, Margaret Drabble has now "arrived." The American Academy of Arts and Sciences has welcomed her into its membership; *Critique* has feted her in a special issue (in 1973); and *Contemporary Literature* has interviewed her. Those novels of hers that had been allowed to fall out of print—that is, all but one—have now fallen back into it again. The conventional repositories of knowledge, such as *Contemporary Novelists,* have begun to notice her; and the day is not far off when the annual bibliography of the Modern Language Association will be officially aware of her existence.

Why this favor after such neglect? Difficult to know, though probably and a little ironically it stems from the splash her last novel, *The Needle's Eye* (1972), made on this side of the Atlantic, the only one of her novels to attract considerable attention here; and partly because it looks as if she has finally caught the crest of the neofeminist wave, as a writer who speaks pointedly about the condition of the modern woman. Though here again there is a kind of paradox, for as she herself has pointed out (in the entry in *Contemporary Novelists*), none of her novels is "about" feminism. Feminism for her, she maintains, is not so much a subject as a *sine qua non*, an atmosphere that her characters breathe without having to think about consciously.

In Britain, however, Margaret Drabble's reputation has been less given to flux and fashion. In an unobtrusive way, she has been emerging as one of the most successful and least publicized novelists of the past decade. There all her novels are readily available in Penguin paperback. The degree of her popular success can be gauged by the fact that *The Millstone* was recently republished, along with a specially written preface by the author, in a vaguely casebook format suitable for use in secondary schools.[1] Perhaps even more to the point, *The Author*, the official publication of the Society of Authors, not long ago expressed horror at the spate of pseudo-Drabblerians beginning to haunt the literary landscape.

Moreover, Margaret Drabble herself has, through a little discreet puffing of her own—articles in *The Listener*, *The Guardian*, and *Encounter*, as well as occasional TV appearances—assisted in increasing her sales, if not always her reputation. Indeed, the excessively domestic character of her journalism has probably done her more harm than good, and may have contributed to the frequently patronizing air of even well-intentioned reviewers. It is difficult to take someone seriously whose most intense personal preoccupations, to judge by what she is impelled to make public, concern the care and feeding of babies. An important subject, to be sure, but not one that seems likely to attract the attention of intellectual literary circles. Nor was her first critical book, *Wordsworth* (1966), sufficiently impressive to allay doubts whether Drabble really was worthy of serious attention. Perhaps the more ambitious study of Arnold Bennett that has just been published will alter the situation and encourage critics to take a closer look at her. I certainly hope so, for, as this essay tries to show, she is a serious and, in some respects, a quite remarkable novelist. Deliberate unpretentiousness and appar-

---

1. Margaret Drabble, *The Millstone* (London: Longmans, 1970).

ent anti-intellectualism are part of the wide Puritan streak in her[2]—and in many of her characters—which leads her to concentrate on "ordinary" vices and virtues, and to hide her lights in rough homespun.

Nevertheless, her writing is unmistakably distinctive. Once one has read a Drabble novel, one never confuses it with someone else's. On the most simple verbal level, her books bear eloquent witness to the pains she has taken to fashion the "lucid" medium on which reviewers have repeatedly remarked. There is a sense always of a slow, methodical, yet paradoxically playful investigation, a very gradual passing from familiar to less familiar, an exploration, usually, of a physical or mental interior. In the compass of novels that rarely exceed two hundred pages, Drabble manages to convey an agoraphobia reminiscent of Proust. People do not move or act much in her world, and when they do, they are punished for it. The ratio of plot to story (in the Forsterian sense), or of monologue to dialogue, is unusually high, though in contrast to Proust, the ruling passion of the major figure—Drabble's novels are often built around a single main character, as befits her solipsistic theme—is moral rather than psychological.

An "uncomplicated Murdoch," one reviewer called her, and others have compared her to Woolf, to James, and to Austen. Of the last named, Drabble herself has little good to say; Woolf she had, by her own confession,[3] begun reading only after she had already published several novels; and James is too much interested in technique to be truly pertinent. Jane Austen, despite Drabble's displeasure, is still the novelist who most readily springs to mind, for Drabble too is fond of female heroines with identity crises, and has a penchant for middle-class subjects in very narrowly circumscribed settings. And like Austen's, Drabble's controlling intelligence is ironic without being caustic, and her plots are clearly focused on a discoverty

---

2. In *Arnold Bennett* (New York: Knopf, 1974), p. 24, Drabble touches on the subject of her family's roots in the frugal Methodist Midlands.
3. "Margaret Drabble," in *The Writer's Place*, ed. Peter Firchow (Minneapolis: University of Minnesota Press, 1974), p. 115.

of the self's proper social and moral place. She is very much in the English tradition of novelists—like Waugh and especially Forster—who are much more than they seem.

Hence it is no doubt appropriate that Drabble should have suffered, as Austen did, from a habit of mind that confounds smallness of scope with smallness of mind. To be sure, as yet no latter-day Walter Scott has appeared to congratulate her on painting on a square of ivory. The work of the miniaturist, it seems, is at present in even greater disrepute than it was a century and a half ago. In order to succeed, the modern major work of art must advertise itself as much, either by bulk or choice of theme. "It is the vice of a vulgar mind," E. M. Forster writes in *Howards End,* and his remark could well serve as an epigraph for both Austen and Drabble, "to be thrilled by bigness, to think that a thousand square miles are a thousand times more wonderful than one square mile, and that a million square miles are almost the same as heaven."[4]

The comparison with Iris Murdoch is less appropriate. Resemblances, of course, there are—solipsism, "this strange disease of modern life," love or its impossibility—but the differences are greater. Whereas Drabble and Austen inhabit a Newtonian physical and moral universe, where effect follows cause, this is by no means the case with Murdoch. The psychology and especially the emotional make-up of the characters of the two novelists are, in consequence, radically different. One need only juxtapose a figure like Honor Klein in *A Severed Head* with Rosamund in *The Millstone* to see how different they are: the former full of certainty, passion, mystery, a paradoxically two-dimensional embodiment of primitive life and will; the latter controlled, introverted, uncompelling, a three-dimensional surface. Honor Klein's actions—sudden, strange, and imperious—if they are to be understood, must be translated back to earth from a mythological and philosophical plane, whereas Rosamund, if she ever leaves earth at all, does so in order to ascend to a rational, moralistic purgatory.

---

4. E. M. Forster, *Howards End* (New York: Vintage, n.d.), p. 29.

The plot of *The Millstone,* Drabble's third novel, is very "clever," turning as it does on a reversal of the traditional plight of the violated maiden. Rosamund at twenty-five is still burdened with her virginity, for reasons that she cannot wholly fathom herself. Since her late teens she has been sleeping with men, but never allowing their caresses to proceed beyond a "certain point." Nevertheless, Rosamund enjoys and even fosters a reputation for sexual promiscuity, going out at the same time with two men, each of whom is convinced she is sleeping with the other.

Thus far, as I say, all is very clever and modern and sophisticated. We are amused: this seems (and is) so obviously ingenious a vehicle for satire on the contemporary liberated woman. So this is what happens to Clarissa without Lovelace, to Hetty without young Squire Donnithorne, to Nora with Torvald. Independence, we gather, is not a wholly unalloyed good: it must be paid for, and the price is loneliness and confusion of social roles and moral values. The old words cannot be used anymore, at least in the capitals that convey a spiritual as well as physical meaning. Love exists only in a world where one makes it, art where one advertises it, and charity where one goes to the National Health scheme or Welfare Agency for it. Yet somewhere below the surface the residue of the old ethic and aesthetic makes itself felt; the desire to escape a world conceived wholly in lower case remains. As Rosamund herself recognizes, she is a Victorian in mod clothing.

Drabble, however, is not content with simply developing and varying the initial satiric theme of the young intellectual female abandoned to her own devices. She deepens and enriches that theme by devoting much the greatest part of the novel to something as unsophisticated and shockingly ordinary as a baby—the "millstone" to which the title, in one sense, refers. Suggestively named after the feminist reformer Octavia Hill, the baby is the fruit of a remarkably reticent and underplayed sexual encounter—Rosamund's first and, so far as we know, last—between herself and a diffident BBC announcer named George. I shall return to this scene of shadowy intercourse later, for it provides essential clues to Rosamund's character, but for the moment I want to stress that it is what happens to her as she tries to cope with her pregnancy and then with her baby that forms the substance of the book. *The Millstone* is less of a satire and more of a study, conducted with unusual subtlety, of moral and emotional growth.

What strikes the reader about Rosamund from the very first paragraph is her determination to be strictly honest. "My career has always been marked," she begins, "by a strange mixture of confidence and cowardice: almost, one might say, made by it. Take for instance, the first time I tried spending a night with a man in a hotel. I was nineteen at the time, an age appropriate for such adventures, and needless to say I was not married. I am still not married, a fact of some significance, but more of that later. The name of the boy, if I remember rightly, was Hamish. I do remember rightly. I really must try not to be so deprecating. Confidence, not cowardice, is the part of myself which I admire, after all."[5] Here Rosamund strikes the note of dualism that is to be richly orchestrated during the rest of the novel, but, less obtrusively, she also makes us see that very same dualism and her refusal to hide it, at work. "I do remember rightly"; how revealing this qualification is! In that brief sentence one catches a glimpse of a world of pretense and pseudo-sophistication where it is sinful to admit to sexual inexperience. But we see too that, although Rosamund is willing to play the game of deceiving others, she will not agree to extend that deception to herself. Her honesty to herself, in fact, is almost pathological. Registering with Hamish at a hotel, after having agreed to act the married couple and elaborately equipping herself with baggage and a curtain ring, she nevertheless signs her own name. Later on she embarrasses one of the nurses by insisting, in spite of her physical condition, that she is Miss, not Mrs. Stacey. Rosamund is continually impaling herself upon the ironies of life, and bleeding.

---

5. Margaret Drabble, *The Millstone* (Harmondsworth: Penguin, 1969), p. 5. All further references are to this edition and are included in the text. The American paperback edition is published by New American Library under the title *Thank You All Very Much* (from the film of the same name based on *The Millstone*).

Ironic, for example, is the circumstance that Rosamund is writing a doctoral dissertation on the Elizabethan love poets and is herself lamentably ill-informed about love. When George, who does not appear to be particularly well-informed himself, makes love to her, she closes her eyes tight, perhaps pursuant to the advice Victorian mothers gave their daughters: "Close your eyes and think of England." When she first becomes aware that she is pregnant, Rosamund makes a rather ludicrous and amateurish attempt at self-abortion, using a recipe of gin and hot baths derived from cheap fiction. Rosamund is all theory and no practice, and even her theory is rather shoddy. Nor, despite their greater sophistication, do her friends seem more adept. Though, unlike her, they clearly do practice the "new morality" they preach, they seem as fundamentally incapable of understanding others, or themselves, as Rosamund. Witness the novel Lydia is furtively writing about Rosamund's condition, in which her reasons for having the baby are reduced to the level of Dear Abby psychology. For that matter, though Rosamund's relations with others are generally disastrous, there is scant evidence of anyone else being appreciably more successful. Significantly, not just Rosamund, but all her friends and acquaintances are either writing themselves or else in some way involved in the communications business. Yet none of them communicates successfully.

Though she does not presume to answer for others, Rosamund is profoundly disturbed by her emotional self-imprisonment. Like the enlightened intellectual she is, she discovers the root of her difficulty in sex. "My crime," she admits quite early in her confession, "was my suspicion, my fear, my apprehensive terror of the very idea of sex" (p. 17). But though she recognizes and censures her "crime," she is nevertheless incapable of coming to grips with what continues to force her to commit it. "I have thought of all kinds of possible causes," she goes on, "for this curious characteristic of mine—the over-healthy, businesslike attitude of my family, my isolation (through superiority of intellect) as a child, my selfish, self-preserving hatred of being pushed around—but none of these imagined causes came anywhere near to explaining the massive obduracy of the effect" (p. 18). One of the reasons why she seems able to make love to George rather than to the sexually aggressive and symbolically named Joe Hurt is because she considers George homosexual, an impression not entirely effaced by her "seduction." In some way the sexual act means for her a violation of a private sanctum, a sacrilegious trespass upon the sense of self. The implications of this, essential for understanding Rosamund, I shall explore later on in this essay.

Though Rosamund initially professes to be unable to account for her behavior, she soon shifts her ground and tries to thrust the blame onto her parents. This, aside from being good Freudian strategy, is in part confirmed by the preliminaries to the seduction scene. Just before George and Rosamund make love, she remembers "what was at the back of my mind" and proceeds to inform him how her mother was "a great feminist" who raised her to be "equal" (pp. 28–29), and used to tell her stories about Queen Elizabeth (the virgin queen, one recalls). Only a few moments earlier, she had recounted, in mocking terms, an anecdote about her parents' ridiculous attitude toward life. Both quixotic socialists of a vaguely Bloomsbury stamp, her parents had done absurd things like "making the charlady sit down and dine with us, introducing her to visitors, all that kind of nonsense" (p. 27). Their reward for doing so had been for the charlady to run off with the silver, despising them and knowing that they would do nothing about it. "My God, they made themselves suffer," Rosamund exclaims, implying strongly, however, that they did not exclude their children from that suffering. Worst of all, perhaps, their "disastrous experiment in education" (p. 28), instead of removing class prejudice in their children, only served, by reaction, to increase it.

Sometimes Rosamund is even moved to wonder "whether it is not my parents who are to blame, totally to blame, for my inability to see anything in human terms of like and dislike, love and hate: but only in terms of justice, guilt and innocence" (p. 84). This is the expense of spirit in a waste of sociological pity, where spontaneity is stifled by duty, and the love of men replaced by love of man. Woman, Rosamund affirms, cannot live by reason alone, and the attempt to do so leads to the drastic dysfunction of emotional response. Not that Rosamund holds her parents exclusively and personally responsible for her emotional frigidity. She is perceptive and intelligent enough to see the general in the particular, and to recognize in her parents only the most powerful (for her) human embodiment of modern society. The repression of natural impulse and the insistence on a social conscience are, she knows, principles that have conditioned not only her own life, but the lives of an entire generation. "Authority, the war, Truby King,"[6] she reflects in her hospital bed. "I was reared to believe that the endurance of privation is a virtue, and the result is that I believe it to this day" (p. 111).

The conflict working itself out in the breast and womb of Rosamund is, in one respect, a reprise of the great nineteenth-century argument between the values of Bentham and of Burke, of Thomas Gradgrind and of Sissy Jupe, of the machine and the heart, with Octavia in the latter role and socialism and Truby King in the former. The very first episode of the novel—the fiasco of trying to spend the night with Hamish in a London hotel—illustrates this theme. Here Rosamund's inadvertent lapse into honesty—signing her own last name, instead of Hamish's—brings the machinery of social convention momentarily to a halt. The clerk, significantly, does not react with anger or the indignation of offended virtue; she merely evinces a "weary crossness" brought on by having to perform an extra task. "I was stopping the machinery." Rosamund realizes, "because I had accidentally told the truth." What Rosamund understands only imperfectly at this point, how-

---

6. The reference is to Sir F. Truby King's *Feeding and Care of BABY*, which has gone through many editions since it was first published in 1908. The following observation, taken from the section entitled "Foundation of Character," is fairly typical: "The establishment of perfect regularity of habits, initiated by 'Feeding and Sleeping by the Clock' . . . is the ultimate foundation of all-round obedience. Granted good organic foundations, truth and honour can be built into the edifice as it grows." (Auckland, 1937), p. 222.

ever, is that it was probably the "machinery" of their affair that prevented her and Hamish from reaching a satisfactory sexual rapport in the first place. Significantly, when Rosamund does reach such an understanding, faulty though it is, with George, the reason is partially because it is so spontaneous and unexpected. It is no coincidence that just before it happens, Rosamund is about to get up to turn off the radio. Indeed, it is her intention to do so that precipitates their lovemaking, so that for once life triumphs over the machine.

When one bothers to notice them, one finds "machines" lurking at various important places in the novel. Apparently trivial, but certainly symptomatic, is the water heater whose finickiness helps to frustrate Rosamund's attempted abortion. Of roughly the same order is Lydia's whimsical account of her dealings with the post office, and its refusal to register a package containing the manuscript of her novel. This, to be sure, "had turned out to be a question of sealing wax and string, but she had taken it for some more prophetic assessment of her packet's worth, and had indeed been so shaken by its unexpected rejection that she had taken it back home with her and put it in a drawer for another three months" (p. 11). Then there is Lydia's experience of grappling with the legal machinery designed to permit abortion, an experience that, ironically, concludes with an accidental abortion caused by her nearly being run over by a less sophisticated machine, a bus.

More important is the social machinery Rosamund encounters when she seeks medical care under the National Health scheme. It is an experience that radically alters her outlook on life, for it forces her to realize that her independence was illusory, as all independence must be. An assured income, an apartment in the right section of London, and a naive faith in the effectiveness of the social apparatus can insulate one from too direct a confrontation with reality, but the protective illusion cannot survive giving birth to an illegitimate baby. This is not to say, by any means, that the machinery is all social or even external. Rosamund recognizes very clearly that a part of the machine is herself. "When Hamish and I loved each other for a whole year without making love," she remarks sadly, "I did not realize that I had set the mould of my whole life. One could find endless reasons for our abstinence—fear, virtue, ignorance, perversion—but the fact remains that the Hamish pattern was to be endlessly repeated" (p. 7). Where one thinks one can freely choose to commit or abstain from an action, one really chooses a habit, for conditioning works quickly and imperceptibly; and instead of being master of one's fate, one ends by becoming its victim.

The question that this leads to is whether or not independent or freely willed action is possible at all. Nor is this, in the context of the novel, by any means an academic matter, for on it hinges, as Rosamund knows, her having the baby. The question is broached by Rosamund in response to Lydia's account of her accidental abortion, when she suggests that Lydia put the incident in a novel:

"Oh, I couldn't possibly," said Lydia. "It's so unconvincing. Far too unrealistic for my kind of novel. It sounds like something out of Hardy's *Life's Little Ironies*."

"I've always thought *Life's Little Ironies* had rather a profound attitude toward life," I said truthfully.

"Have you really?" said Lydia. "I don't find it profound at all. It's so mechanical. Not real." (p. 65)

Rosamund goes from this to ponder how reports of accidents of even absurd kinds had moved her deeply, accidents like "Killed While Adjusting Safety Belt, or Collapsed Night Before Wedding."[7] The question here goes far beyond the conflict of social machinery and the human soul. It goes to the human soul itself. That is, are we free agents or the executors of fate, of some "different, non-rational order of things" (p. 66)? Do we partake of a universal machinery? Rosamund, perhaps surprisingly, answers this question in the affirmative. For her the pregnancy is no accident, because ultimately there are no acci-

---

7. This theme is developed more fully in Drabble's next novel, *The Waterfall* (1969).

dents, because "had it belonged to the realm of mere accident I would have surely got rid of it" (p. 66). The inexorable machinery of her body, proceeding independently of her will, has, Rosamund decides, connected her with the machinery of Nature, not to say of God. "Really, it was a question," she concludes, "of free will; up to this point in my life I had always had the illusion at least of choice, and now for the first time I seemed to become aware of the operation of forces not totally explicable, and not therefore necessarily blinder, smaller, less kind or more ignorant than myself" (p. 67). Beyond the machinery of man, there stands the superior machinery of the universe. It is Wordsworth and Hardy pitted against Bentham and Marx.

It is as if, being impregnated with Octavia, Rosamund had been filled with meaning. Unlike the Rosamond of Samuel Daniel's *Complaint* (1592), whose sexual transgression was punished with death, Drabble's Rosamund gains new life thereby.[8] Giving birth, she is herself reborn. It is not merely that she gains additional knowledge, but that she knows what she knows differently—with the heart and the body, not merely with the head. This is symbolically rendered, in an almost Wordsworthian fashion, by means of a middle-aged woman who one day at the clinic thrusts her damp baby into Rosamund's arms while she goes to be examined. Later, leaving the hospital, Rosamund sees the woman agin, as she stolidly makes her way down the street in the company of her two children. "There was a solemnity about her imperceptible progress," she observes, "that impressed me deeply: she stood

---

8. Daniel is, one should remember, one of the poets whom Rosamund is working on. His poetical spirit of a maiden wronged suggests, interestingly enough, a similar preoccupation with fate:

Then write, quoth she, the ruin of my youth,
Report the downfall of my slipp'ry state;
Of all my life reveal the simple truth,
To teach to others what I learnt too late.
Exemplify my frailty, tell how fate
    Keeps in eternal dark her fortunes hidden,
    And ere they come, to know them 'tis forbidden.

there, patiently waiting, like a warning, like a portent, like a figure from another world." Trying to formulate her experience shortly thereafter for a group of old college friends, Rosamund discovers that she cannot do so. Even she herself cannot entirely make it out, so it would be folly to expect others—especially friends like these—to grasp its significance. But a fragment she understands already: I saw that from now on I, like that woman, was going to have to ask for help, and from strangers too: I who could not even ask for love and friendship" (pp. 71–72). Another fragment that at least the reader is asked to understand involves the will-less, mechanical behavior of this woman. Dependence seems to imply becoming part of a larger mechanism, one that overrides the individual ego. But for Drabble, unlike Bergson, the appearance of the machine in man is far from comic.

Paradoxically, as the realization that she is not and cannot be independent begins to seep into her, Rosamund's sense of self takes shape as never before. The fact that another being is now utterly dependent on her impels her to overcome her ingrained diffidence and self-effacing ways. This process culminates in a magnificent confrontation between Rosamund and a head nurse who, with all the might of the hospital machinery at her back, refuses to allow her to visit Octavia, just then recovering from a serious operation. At first yielding to what seems overwhelmingly superior force, Rosamund eventually returns ready to risk a scene, no matter what the embarrassment or the consequences. As she is about to be pushed out of the lobby, she closes her eyes and begins to scream at the top of her voice. " 'I don't care,' I yelled, finding words for my inarticulate passion, 'I don't care, I don't care, I don't care about anyone, I don't care, I don't care, I don't care' " (p. 134). This scream echoes not only the earlier official "I don't care" of the nurse, but also the despairing cry of Sandra, the little lower-class girl who, because she was considered a bad influence, had been excluded from playing with her sister's children.[9] Like Sand-

---

9. One of the alternative names Rosamund had considered for her child was Sandra.

ra's, Rosamund's scream is the voice of nature in revolt against the artifice of man. It is also, as the repeated "I don't care" indicates, the assertion of the self against the other, the assertion of the primacy of the living individual over the abstract social interest. Like Helen in Forster's *Howards End*, Rosamund has learned to say "I" because, by virtue of her experience, she has gained an "I" to say it with.

Once again Drabble renders Rosamund's new insight symbolically, this time by means of a woman whose children have inherited the same congenital defect (examples, no doubt, of the natural machines gone wrong) and who, like Rosamund, spends much of her time visiting her children in the "forbidden" ward. There, surrounded by the whimperings and unattended sufferings of multitudes of other babies, cared for only by the machinery of the state, Rosamund wonders what to make of "them": don't their mothers care, and how can they be helped? The answer she gets seems, on the face of it, crass and selfish: nothing can be done, one must look out for oneself and for one's own. These children used to bother her conscience, Rosamund's interlocutor confesses, but no longer: " 'My concerns are my concerns, and that's where it ends. I haven't the energy to go worrying about other people's children. They're nothing to do with me. I only have time to worry about myself. If I don't put myself and mine first, they wouldn't survive. So I put them first and the others can look after themselves' " (p. 140). These are clichés and, as Rosamund the "good socialist" recognizes, they are Tory clichés. She has heard them all before. But she does not react to them on the level of politics or cliché. Instead she is touched nearly to tears. It is as if she possessed some new organ of perception that equipped her to understand as she has never understood before; and the new organ, of course, is Octavia. What she could not accept on the plane of the intellect or of art, she accepts in the body. The machinery of man is again subordinated to the machinery of biology or fate. "Thus gently put forward as the result of sad necessity," Rosamund feels, the clichés reveal the truth.

This is not simply mindless egotism. Her shouts of "I don't

care" are preceded and must be preceded by caring on the deepest level. In fact, Rosamund does *not* care for the first time, because she *does* care for the first time. It is the intensity of her love for Octavia which makes her push herself forward. Rosamund quite consciously translates in her mind this growing selfishness into "maturity," which might be roughly defined as the knowledge that love is never found in nature separate from selfishness. From the perspective of this presumptive maturity, Rosamund even allows herself to look down on the quixotic idealism of her parents. Their problem is really that they have never grown up. "My parents are still children, maybe," she reflects; "they think they can remain innocent" (p. 145).

The direction in which Rosamund's "moral fable" finally moves, I think, is of questioning the Christian/Rousseauian/Marxian ethic underlying the modern welfare state. Man is not master of his fate and the notion of universal brotherhood is a lie. "Whoso shall offend one of these little ones which believe in me," the passage in Matthew reads from which the title of the novel is taken, "it were better that a millstone were hanged about his neck, and that he were drowned in the depths of the sea." And who is it that offends him? The hosts of babes crying in the wards make their accusatory reply. And whom do they believe in? Octavia's radiantly smiling face as she greets her mother, who had "deserted" her for a day, provides an equally certain answer. The state as God cannot escape responsibility and hence hanging with a millstone of guilt. For a child the true God is the parent, and only through the parent's love can the millstone be avoided. For the millstone is part of man's satanic machine; the mother, part of divine Nature's.

As if to make certain that this point shall not be lost on the reader, the novel concludes on Christmas Eve, with another "accidental" meeting of George and Rosamund. Rosamund, the suggestion seems to be, is Mary, a "virgin" who has given birth to a child; George is Joseph, a father who is nevertheless not a father. The message of this modern Christmas, however, is not one of universal love and brotherhood. Sitting across from

George, Rosamund feels sorely tempted to break out into screams once more, this time of "I love you." But she restrains herself. The spark of love requires enormous voltage and the space it can leap is very small; it extends to Octavia but not to George. The Christmas message here is "love theyself," or love extensions of thyself, for that is all you can ever love. Even George, it appears, could once have entered into this narrow circle of possible love because he so very much resembles Rosamund. At the time of their brief physical encounter Rosamund had already sensed this, wondering if her reticence were not matched by his. Now the identification is explicit. "I neither envied nor pitied his indifference," she reflects, as they both gaze upon the sleeping child, "for he was myself, the self that but for accident, but for fate, but for chance, but for womanhood, I would still have been" (p. 172). The love for George has been displaced by love for Octavia, because finally Octavia, even more than he, is herself.

8

The Artist and the Introvert: Nigel Dennis's *A House in Order* (1966)

ROBERT PHILLIPS

In *Cards of Identity* (1955) Nigel Dennis displays his ability to create a novel that continues to reward on each reading. A long satire, an inventive fable, a philosophical inquiry into modern man's problem of identity, it prompted W. H. Auden to declare, "I have read no novel published during the last fifteen years with greater pleasure and admiration."

Auden, and the rest of us, had to wait another twelve years before Dennis produced a third novel. (*Boys and Girls Come Out to Play*, the first of his novels that Dennis was "prepared to take responsibility for," appeared in 1949.) And while Walter Allen called Dennis, on the strength of *Cards of Identity*, "the most considerable satirist to have appeared in English fiction since Wyndham Lewis," *A House in Order* (1966) seems to me no satire at all. Wickedness and folly *are* depicted, but not censured; there is little mockery, raillery, or ridicule, and no invective. It seems rather to resemble more closely the dark allegories of Kafka or the philosophical novels of William Golding.

I say "seems" because *A House in Order*—like Shirley Jackson's *The Sundial* and a few other modern novels—defies description just as it defies yielding an absolute meaning. It is a multidimensional work that reveals to us the variety of levels on which we live—dream and act, past and present, personal and collective. When the American edition appeared in 1967, the reviewer in *New York Review of Books* proclaimed, ". . . no mere reviewer can hope to penetrate all—or even most—of its deeper implications." I should like to touch upon six such implications, with a full discussion of two.

The first level, the level of action on which the novel must be read, is as a suspense story. No reader needs critical aid here. Dennis's story of an ordinary soldier who is captured and temporarily held by the enemy in a greenhouse while opposing forces decide his fate—greenhouse or prison camp, life or death?—moves swiftly and unpredictably. It is a joy to read.

A second level of action, suggested by Dennis's English publisher in the dust-jacket blurb, is that of the struggle between personal obsession and social duty. The individual who chooses to defend the lives of some struggling house-leeks and cranesbills—rather than conform to expectations in the service of the defense of his country in a time of total war—can be seen as a unique study of the problems of identity in our mechanistic society. Yet Dennis himself, on the same dust jacket, asserts that a study of the problems of identity is "exactly what it is not."

An exploration of the difference between fortitude and courage is another "meaning" that has been suggested, which could lead to a comparison between *A House in Order* and Stephen Crane's *The Red Badge of Courage.* The theme is given point by the inquisitor's speech, late in Dennis's novel: "My friend! Are you prepared to pretend to this Court that you endured silently and without complaint a captivity that would kill an ordinary person, and did so not because it suited your bold plans but only because you were born with the heart of a chicken?"[1] Yet such an interpretation seems much too narrow, and focuses on but a portion of the book's larger concerns.

---

1. All quotations are from the British edition (London: Weidenfeld and Nicolson, 1966). The American edition (New York: The Vanguard Press, 1967) is still in print.

A much broader reading is to see, as I suggest one must, the novel as an allegory of the human condition, with the abandoned greenhouse of the protagonist's civilian life a symbol of Paradise lost, his exile from Eden. His symbolic act of saving plants from destruction can be read as his desire to preserve his Edenic past or Dantean Paradise. The hero is Adam outside the Garden, and his retreat into a second greenhouse is his Paradise regained. In this sense man, tempted by the wiles of war, loses his paradise, as did Adam in Milton's first epic. But Dennis's hero resists the temptations of that war (as Jesus resists temptation in *Paradise Regained.*) Like Jesus, Dennis's hero regains Paradise through resistance.

One does not, however, have to inflict a Christian framework upon the allegory for it to represent man's lot. Caught by unnamed captors who do not understand a word he says, sitting all day in a glass house but "simply not being seen by anybody at all," the protagonist's alienation is representative of the problem of communication in the world. And he himself is no paragon in a world gone wrong: He keeps losing his glasses—his own ability to see. He also is blind to the beauty of autumn outside his greenhouse until he works at cleaning the glass. He does not even recognize the miracle of the resurrected houseleek: "The evidence was there, plain to see, but it was no more seen by me than I, open and upright on my chair, had been seen by the scores who passed me on my first day" (p. 26).

This problem of man's alienation and personal dissociation is implicit in the hero's situation: He is neither an official prisoner (like those in the camp) or a free man (like those at home). He is wanted neither by the Department of Horticulture nor by the Prison Commission. He is merely an accident in a political tug-of-war. Unwanted by anyone, he becomes a solipsist in his dissociated condition, and comes to the knowledge late that, while he thought he alone was watching the prison, 800 prisoners had been observing him. We are not alone; war is not forever; we live by growing things.

While the prisoner is segregated from his fellow man, he becomes trained to a symbolic vocabulary of subtle human relations and odd strivings in the world of plants, a vocabulary he can, if he will, apply to equivalent patterns of human experience. For what is a greenhouse if not a place where life is intensified, a place where spring comes sooner? Early in the novel the prisoner realizes that his choice of the greenhouse is a hanging of his survival upon a thread of self-will: "Clearly it was up to me to decide whether I wanted to live or die" (p. 39). And die he almost did, spiritually as well as physically, at one dark moment seeing his choice of the greenhouse as a mistake engaged upon through pride. Yet, when spring comes, both he and the plants are survivors. The man who knew just how much plants could endure had to have his own spirit tested. Spring gives him new life "such as a baby might make on starting to recognize things" (p. 48). When a prisoner escapes from camp, the church bells ring "as if it were a day of feasting or resurrection" (p. 107). His own spiritual rebirth is symbolized by the resurrection of the house-leek, no ordinary leek at all, but rather the reappearance of an extremely rare species, the *Sempervivum melitense*, not seen for over a century—a symbolic message that out of suffering and dirt can come glory.

Dennis's novel, then, asks some basic questions about man's existence and survival. Can life (green things) survive in the modern mechanized technological world? The book is an allegory of survival of the spirit, of spiritual man (green being the color of hope) in the modern world of war. The journey to the underworld of the mind (or soul) is communicated, as in the poetry of the late Theodore Roethke, by a symbology of shoots and roots and muck, with the mystery of death and resurrection embodied in the annual cycle. Further, just as a greenhouse catches and multiplies the power of the sun, Dennis's greenhouse is a many-faceted and potent symbol. The greenhouse here becomes a Ship of Life, symbol of the voyage of the physical and spiritual body through time and space. To live in a glass house is to travel through space to other worlds, to inhabit an Ark with a necessary cargo for survival of plants instead of beasts.

Implicit in all of this, Jungians would tell us, is the inevitable drift toward death of the Ship of Life sailing toward the end of worldly existence, carrying with it the captive and his deep-rooted memories. It is also the desire for transcendence. In emblematic terms the greenhouse, with its verticality and height, with its supports forming a mast in the center of the vessel as well as a cross or Cosmic Tree, can be at once the Ship of Life and symbol of the inexhaustible life processes of growth and development.

This particular greenhouse also functions as a microcosm of all that the protagonist has sought to escape, the trash heap of common lives, with its old pipe, old hat, and well-chipped Madonna littering the shed, "the very shambles I most detested and despised in the human race" (p. 9). Instead of adding to the destructiveness and folly of the race, he chose to spend the war growing plants, a positive act in the face of so much negativism and destruction. He even dreams of appeasing the enemy with flowers! Yet the fragility of his four glass walls underscores the frailty of his (and our) illusions. He was not really "safe" there at all. One of the book's central paradoxes, in fact, is that to be in prison is to be free, to be outside the confining walls is to be unsafe. Other paradoxes are that the actions of a truly decadent family made possible the restoration of a rare species of flower only an exceptional few can appreciate, and that, for a garden, absolute neglect is better than half-witted care by blunderers. Such paradox and irony lend to Dennis's novel an aura of life through the looking glass, and the author seems to echo Lewis Carroll when he declares, "All behaviour is both quite natural and quite absurd" (p. 8). The book also resembles Kafka's *The Trial*. Both examine a spirit under *arrest* by the official world. And like the trial scene in Carroll's *Alice in Wonderland*, Dennis's book reveals the absurdity of appearances.

At novel's end we find that the captive would rather remain a prisoner than go free. But the agronomist forces him to escape. Once free, he seems to approximate the circumstances of his captivity: He returns to his own greenhouse, and he chats evenings with a uniformed authority (albeit the village policeman). His main regret is not that he was imprisoned, but that he may have failed to recognize other rare plants that he might have saved. But man, like the policeman with his own unheated greenhouse, must "always be limited in what he is best at" (p. 115). The moral is, "It's what you allow to happen that counts" (p. 117).

Yet, I maintain that one must recognize another meaning within Dennis's brief allegory—that of a portrait of the artist in society today. The gardener *is* an artist. He is the artist/priest/poet/celebrant whose celebration of nature is a celebration of the spirit of man. While he earns his living drawing maps (the surfaces), his real joy comes from planting and feeding roots (the depths). In his art for the sake of art, his is a brave figure in the materialistic world, a world that leads many to live half-lives. As the inquisitor puts it, "And you insist that most of your countrymen are like you—that they give their best to their hobbies and try to forget what they do for a living?" (p. 98). Exactly. The Deputy's questions reflect popular culture, indicating that if the prisoner's plants were edible, at least his work could be seen as useful. The deputy cannot acknowledge so much labor for the sake of "mere" beauty.

Thus *A House in Order* proclaims that, for the house of our lives to be in order, it must exist not only on the external level, but on the internal as well. In a highly poetic novel, Dennis has discarded realism to find true reality, drawing upon the ideas and the images of the mind to construct the world of his protagonist, an artistic man whose unconscious thoughts and dreams are parents to his conscious acts. The symbols of the greenhouse and the plants unite and synthesize the various levels of the prisoner's reality. It is because the unconscious functions exist in an archaic and animal state that Dennis's protagonist must so exist as well. Not merely a little mapmaker (whose job clearly was suppressed by the unconscious), the unnamed prisoner of the novel must be said to be all poets. The gardener is to the earth what the conscious (rational) is to the unconscious (irrational). The rare plant is that work of art which miraculously survives the wars of men.

This leads directly into the final level of meaning in *A House in Order*—the psychoanalytic. By this I do not mean that I intend to psychoanalyze Dennis, though it may be instructive to learn that, early in life, he has retired if not retreated from his native London and later habitat of Manhattan to the Isle of Malta, an act that some might liken to living within a greenhouse. Rather, it is the mind of Dennis's protagonist that must be analyzed, to show that the author has truly written of the human condition as it is embodied in the predicament of a particular human type.

The true artist (as opposed to the dreamer on the one hand and the crank on the other) represents the normal introverted type as set forth by Jordan and Jung. The introvert tends to confine himself to the perceptive character of intuition, and to the shaping of his perception. He has, usually, an inferiority "complex with contracted consciousness," as set forth by Otto Gross in 1902 and later adopted by Jung. He is one for whom ideas have a lasting influence and for whom impressions go deep. His associations are restricted, frequently narrowed down to a single theme or obsessions (around which other associations build, of course) to consolidate one particular complex of ideas from which all else is excluded—a phenomenon Gross (borrowing from Wernicke) calls "sejunction." In extreme cases such sejunction can become an "over-valued idea," or "spleen," or—in pathological cases—an unshakable paranoid idea.

Could a better description of Dennis's protagonist be found? Indeed, he appears to have just such a rigid inner cohesion of a complex (though hardly paranoid, not at all pathological). He resists influence from the outside world to the extent that he is rigidly secluded from it (with a corresponding accumulation of libido within). This accounts for his extraordinary concentration on inner processes (his own as well as the plants') and on the physical sensations of heat and cold, light and dark, dry and moist. As a subject for analysis, he would belong to the "sensation" type: inhibited, absorbed, even distracted, he can (and does) sit for an entire day in one chair. His is the distinct tendency toward solitude, as opposed to participation in external life. Such solitude is compensated for by his special love of plants.

In Adlerian psychology the plants are "auxiliary devices" (compensations), which the prisoner establishes as "guiding fictions" to help balance his sense of inferiority. (The "guiding fiction" is a psychological system that endeavors to turn an inferiority into a superiority.)[2] On the other hand, Jung would view the plants as a functional adjustment in general (not just of feelings), an inherent self-regulation of the psychic apparatus, a balancing of the one-sidedness of the prisoner's general attitude produced by the function of the consciousness.[3]

The theme of alienation, then, can be seen not only as the result of an indifferent world, but more correctly as the introvert's inability to communicate with that world. Such introverts are, on occasion, subject to sudden explosions, alternating defensiveness with taciturnity. The prisoner's wild waving and dancing behind his glass cage, as well as his outburst in the first sentence of the novel ("Take me, take me! I am a prisoner too"), are indicative of such behavior.

Another essential feature of the introvert is his solitary pleasure in elaborating personal thoughts and acts for their own sake, regardless of external reality. This is the same as the artist's dedication to art for art's sake. The introvert, like the artist, achieves sufficient distance from life to perceive acts and objects in their symbolic rather than their "realistic" aspects. He is, according to Jung, the "cultural genius"—one concerned with abstract invention (as opposed to the extroverted type, the "civilizing genius" concerned with practical achievement).[4]

---

2. See Adler's *The Neurotic Constitution*, trans. Bernard Glueck and John E. Lind (New York, 1916).

3. "On the Importance of the Unconscious in Psychopathology," in vol. 3 of the Collected Works of C. G. Jung, *The Psychogenesis of Mental Disease* (Princeton, N. J., 1960).

4. "The Type Pattern in Psychopathology," vol. 6 of the Collected Works of C.

The Jungian introvert does not orient himself to the object, or by objective data, but through subjective factors. He places a subjective view between himself and the object of perception. Such a predominance of the subjective factor in the introvert's consciousness naturally involves a devaluation of objects. Dennis carries this devaluation to symbolic extremes through his protagonist's living in a house totally void of *things* — no rugs, no lamps, no pictures. (The junk left by the degenerate family rests in the adjoining shed.)

Accepting Dennis's protagonist as prototypical introvert/ artist, what then are the psychological implications of his novel? Under such an assumption, the book becomes an allegory of the introvert's constant fear of falling under hostile influences. As Jung says of the type, "His ideal is a lonely island where nothing moves except what he permits to move." This of course is the situation of the greenhouse, where the gardener plays God in the selection of which plants shall live and which die, and in exterminating grubs and vermin.[5] Dennis's introvert's acts are the basis of subjective factors determining his judgment.

The greenhouse/prison camp split represents more than mere dissociation. The men in the camp on "the other side" represent that other side of his personality to which passage across is blocked by conscious resistance to any subjection of the ego to the realities of the unconscious. The glass house is the feeling function, the prison camp is "the other side," the thinking function. Jung would call the protagonist's state of dissociation "a neurosis characterized by inner debility and increasing cerebral exhaustion," symptoms of psychasthenia. In his selection of plants as love objects, the introvert's aim is, like the aim of Dennis's slender but not slight novel, intensity rather than extensity in thought.

G. Jung, *Psychological Types* (Princeton, N.J., 1971, p. 289.) I have made extensive use of Jung's theories of the type problem in human character in this essay, and unless otherwise identified, the terminology is Jung's.

5. For similar fictionalized insights into this aspect of the introverted personality, see Frederick Theodor von Vischer's novel *Auch Einer* (Leipzig, 1902).

When the gardener gladly endures without complaint a captivity that would kill an ordinary person, he fills the bill of Jung's introvert's suggestibility to personal influences:

> He lets himself be brutalized and exploited in the most ignominious way if only he can be left in peace to pursue his ideas. He simply does not see when he is being plundered behind his back and wronged in practice, for to him the relation to people and things is secondary and the objective evaluation of his product is something he remains unconscious of. . . . His work goes slowly and with difficulty.[6]

When he pursues his would-be captors, who do not understand his language, the protagonist is like the classic introvert who, according to Jung, is by turns taciturn or else hurls himself on those who do not understand him, which he takes as one more proof of the abysmal stupidity of man.

Thus life in a glass house becomes a symbolic equation for the introvert's painful anxiety to escape notice, and the condition of being a prisoner dramatizes the introvert's exclusion of outside influences. The basic struggle for warmth and for life within the greenhouse underscores the supreme importance the introvert places on what secretly concerns his own person, owing to the subjectivization of consciousness that results from his lack of relationship to objects. The glass house moreover is a symbolic, frail, defense mechanism behind which the introverted thinker hides from troublesome outside influences. It is his "protective shield" against all objective (outside) forces.

In a more pathological case, such a man would be said to operate in an archaic reality (though his lack of comparative judgment would keep him unconscious of the fact) in which insects and plants appear as malevolent demons and benevolent deities. The outisde, objective world would appear make-believe or comic. But for Dennis's protagonist, the outside world is all too real. As a rule he "resigns himself to

---

6. Jung, *Psychological Types*, p. 385.

his isolation and the banality of the world, which he has unconsciously made archaic" (description in Jung's words.)[7]

Such a psychoanalytic interpretation actually supports my claim that the novel is an allegory for the role of the artist in society. In the general Western view, the artist is a minority figure, and any "subjective opinion" is held to be an unacceptable or inferior one in the world of hard facts. The introvert/artist, on the other hand, breaks with the things that are, in order to unite with the things that may be. Yet he finds himself in a world that would force him to join it in an extroverted overvaluation of things. The introvert/artist is made to feel inferior because he does not depend on his subjectiveness the way his opponents depend on the object. When Jung says, "Introverted sensation apprehends the background of the physical world rather than its surface," we recall Dennis's gardener and not the cartographer. The mapmaker is merely a face that the protagonist prepares to meet the faces that he meets.

The protagonist's ability to see not the reality of an object, but the reality of the subjective factor (or of the primordial images that constitute the psychic mirror world) is symbolized when he discovers the century-old flower, surely a totem for the *sub specie aeternitatis*. In this act, Dennis's hero sees not only time present, but past and future as well, the truly introverted (poetic) sensation. The plant here is one which, as symbol, is covered by a patina of age-old subjective experience and a shimmer of events yet to come. Ultimately, Dennis is saying, the difference between artist and nonartist, extrovert and introvert, is the difference between prose and poetry. One is literal, the other dimensional. And in his fight for survival in the literal world, Dennis's hero sows seeds—a psychic functioning of the whole ancestral line and, in general, an accumulated experience of the organic life.

---

7. *Ibid.*, p. 402.

9

Myths of Identity: Alan Sillitoe's *The Death of William Posters; A Tree on Fire* (1965, 1967)

JAMES W. LEE

Saturday Night and Sunday Morning was not only the finest novel of 1958; it was to be *the* classic novel of the angry decade. *The Loneliness of the Long-Distance Runner,* published the following year, achieved almost the same stature in the field of shorter fiction. The eight books of fiction published since 1958–59— six novels and two collections of short stories—have satisfied very few reviewers and critics. But there was no way for Sillitoe to have won anyway. When he kept strictly to the Nottingham- shire working classes, he was decried for not spreading his wings over new fields. When he tried to go outside the indus- trial Midlands, he was accused of betraying the forces that shaped him. He wrote a futuristic allegory, *The General,* in 1960 and John Dennis Hurrell wondered if he wrote it out of a "desire not to be thought ignorant."[1] Hurrell liked *Saturday Night and Sunday Morning* as much as everyone else did, and he

---

1. John Dennis Hurrell, "Alan Sillitoe and the Serious Novel," *Critique* 4(1960–61):6.

hated the thought that Sillitoe was "abandoning the sources of his inspiration" in order to treat "overtly serious themes." Hurrell even found some creeping seriousness in *Loneliness*. In order to be unfairly fair to Hurrell, I should quote two of his passages:

> The volume of short stories is not yet pretentious—in fact, taken by itself it is a most satisfying piece of writing—but it is approaching the pretentious. . . . In *Saturday Night and Sunday Morning* Sillitoe has written a good serious novel because he has not attempted to be . . . serious . . . in *The Loneliness of the Long-Distance Runner*, however, the desire to be "serious" is apparent on the surface. (p. 5)

> Perhaps Anthony West was right [Reviewing *SNSM* in *The New Yorker*, West said "Even if he never writes anything more, he has assured himself a place in the history of the English novel."]; if Sillitoe has a place in the history of the English novel it will be for *Saturday Night and Sunday Morning;* his literary identity in the other two books has been submerged under a desire to be "significant"; in an important sense Alan Sillitoe has *not* written another novel, even though two more books have appeared under his name. Neither is this an isolated case; one could cite other examples of the intentional abandonment by an author of the sources of his inspiration, in the search of an overtly important theme. (p. 6)

Hurrell is accusing Sillitoe of a crime against his *literary* identity because he has chosen to explore his *personal* identity in a different way. After Sillitoe, in his first two works, had attempted to make some sense out of the Midlands working-class life that he had lived, he sought new characters and new situations to use in probing the questions of being *versus* nonbeing, of valid human living *versus* the automatic reactions of social automata. The search for identity is surely the main theme of modern art, and it is a theme, moreover, that has in some degree held the attention of man always. Serious writers all write, I think, in an attempt to make sense out of their world; modern writers, who frequently see themselves as strangers in a strange universe, often attempt to approach the question of identity from a variety of angles. Sillitoe's first two works were fairly simple and fairly predictable: Who am I in the context of my birth and my time? As Alan Sillitoe matured as a writer, he began more sophisticated searching, and often the novels failed to satisfy those critics who expected him to continue writing about men as simple as Arthur Seaton. *The General* is a novel on the same theme as *Saturday Night and Sunday Morning,* for the protagonist is being faced, on a more complex level, with the question of his identity: is he a construct of the state he serves, always obliged to obey blindly, or is he a human being responsible to himself for his activities? Arthur Seaton and Smith, the runner, lack the General's insights, but the problems are the same. The General's choice may lead to his physical death; Arthur's will lead to his existential death—in front of the telly, smoking Woodbines.

The question of Frank Dawley's identity in *The Death of William Posters* and *A Tree on Fire* is one of Sillitoe's most interesting explorations of the question of authentic being as opposed to the dead, automatic life. Frank Dawley is Arthur Seaton after a half decade of marriage to Doreen. He is more mature than Arthur and slightly better educated, but he is equally angry at having let himself get turned into an automaton by marriage, by the factory, by the "kid-noise," and by the social structure.

The two novels, *Posters* (1965) and *Tree* (1968),[2] have been much misunderstood, for critics and reviewers have seen them as handbooks for revolution and treatises on class conflict and social upheaval.[3] Certainly the characters talk incessantly about the coming revolution, and Frank Dawley does go and fight in

---

2. *The Death of William Posters* (New York: Knopf, 1965) and *A Tree on Fire* (New York: Doubleday, 1968). Further references will be to these editions and will appear in the text in parentheses.

3. See Allen Richard Penner, "The Political Prologue and Two Parts of a Trilogy," *University Review* 35(1968): 11-20; and Stanley S. Atherton, "Alan Sillitoe's Battleground," *Dalhousie Review* 48(1968): 324–31.

the Algerian revolt. But I think Sillitoe is much less concerned with establishing a blueprint for conflict than with seeing how certain people create a revolution within themselves. Men like Frank Dawley, men poorly educated and long stifled by automatic life, often lash out fiercely when they begin seriously to face the questions of why they live and what they live for. The militancy, it should be remembered, of Billy Budd only came about because he was unable to speak in the presence of Claggart and Captain Vere. Sillitoe's Frank Dawley goes to war because he cannot think and speak until he has purged himself, until his brain becomes like the gray ash of burned desert trees and then, like them, flowers anew. Once he has had his revolution of heart and mind, he may be able to answer his questions of moral integrity and identity in less violent ways. Other Sillitoe characters have.

It is just barely possible that the third volume of the trilogy may show the futility of revolution and the inefficacy of attempts to achieve world brotherhood through violent action. If Sillitoe is as good a novelist as he sometimes seems to be, it is not without the realm of possibility that the first two volumes are ironic, and the salvation found by Frank Dawley and the Handley menage at the end of *A Tree on Fire* is as false as most other "isms" have been found to be. If, on the other hand, we see in Volume 3 the creation of a Utopia based on the destruction of all the "dark Satanic mills" of England, I can see why the book is taking so long.

Before the harpies Speculation and Prediction conquer all in their path, it might be a good idea to look carefully at *The Death of William Posters* and *A Tree on Fire.* The two novels brought the wrath of the reviewers down on Sillitoe. John Davenport thought the first book one of the "most atrociously boring novels" he had ever read,[4] and Martin Seymour-Smith found the second volume "atrociously silly, immature and humorless. . . ."[5] Not everyone was equally harsh, but there were no

4. "Zentimental Journey," *Spectator* 214(1965): 640.
5. "Thinking Pink," *Spectator* 220(1968): 43.

raves. Detractors saw Sillitoe as a "simple-minded Red" and attacked the books for their Communist propaganda and their attempt to "set the little streets upon the great."

In the trilogy, Frank Dawley abandons his family and sets out "on the road." He is seeking the meaning of life, if indeed life has any. He goes from Nottinghamshire to Lincolnshire, where he moves in with Pat Shipley, the district nurse. The fact that the district nurse serves frequently as a midwife should not be overlooked, for Pat serves as a *mid*wife to Frank in that she is the "wife" between Nancy, whom he left, and Myra Blassingfield, with whom he ends up. He stays with Pat Shipley until her estranged advertising copywriter husband appears and causes trouble.

During his stay with Pat, Frank meets Albert Handley, a primitive painter and part-time con man, and establishes a relationship that endures throughout the books. Handley lives in a ramshackle house with most of his seven children, his wife, and his eccentric brother. The brother, who plays an ironic John the Baptist to Frank Dawley's ironic Christ[6] and Albert Handley's ironic Creator, stays all alone in his elaborate radio room waiting for a definitive message from God. While waiting, he also intercepts all sorts of other shortwave messages from revolutionary groups around the world. The rest of the family is made up of some equally strange folk: there is nubile Mandy, whose sexuality is exceeded only by her desire for a "new red Mini"; Ralph, a twelve-year-old who plays with a double-barreled shotgun; and several others who grind out revolutionary tracts on a printing press and plan for the armed conflict to come.

Frank moves from Pat Shipley—his first encounter with the Handleys is very brief—to London, where he meets a now-successful Albert Handley, who has been discovered by Pat's husband, Keith. At a showing of Handley's work, Frank meets Myra Blassingfield and begins a relationship that continues throughout *A Tree on Fire*. Myra's husband tries to run over

---

6. I am indebted to my student Larry Williams for calling the John the Baptist and Christ parallels to my attention.

Frank in his car but misses, and is killed. Myra and Frank now go to Majorca, then to Spain, and finally to Tangiers, where Frank signs on to smuggle arms to the FLN. *The Death of William Posters* ends as Frank begins his long trip into the desert, on the run to find out why he is on the run, as he says earlier. Myra, pregnant with Frank's child, is left on her own to find her way back to England if Frank does not return from the desert within a few days.

The first novel ends abruptly, and it is no wonder the reviewers were dismayed at this strange ending—no one had been informed that this was the beginning of a trilogy, apparently. From the rather unsatisfactory summary above, it is not hard to see that *The Death of William Posters* is a strange book. But it is no more "atrociously boring" than *A Tree on Fire* is "atrociously silly." The plot of *Posters* is episodic, and the plot of *Tree* is not always satisfactory because of all its shifting back and forth between Frank's desert odyssey and the stories of the Handleys and Myra back in England. The title of the first book comes from the announcements on walls all over England that "bill posters will be prosecuted." Bill Posters, or more formally William, is the character Frank imagines to be always on the run, as he himself is. The whole world is after William Posters, and only by supreme cunning does he keep a step ahead. William is Frank's alter ego, and Frank learns that it will be necessary to kill that frightened, hiding part of himself if he is ever going to be free. The death of William Posters is necessary to insure the existence of Frank Dawley.

A Tree on Fire takes Dawley deep into the desert, where he actually joins the FLN, kills French soldiers, attacks a couple of air bases, sees his friend Shelley Jones[7] die of gangrene, almost dies himself, and finally returns to England to join Myra and his hitherto unseen son and the Handleys in a sort of revolutionary commune. Much more happens in the novel.

---

7. It hardly needs to be pointed out that the name Shelley Jones is a combination of Percy Shelley and the ordinary and practical American. Sillitoe's character is much like Shelley in his rather fanciful idealism, but he is quite practical in his logistical arrangements.

John Handley more or less regains his sanity and goes out to Algeria to bring Frank back. Incidentally, John Handley does not just slip quietly away to Algeria; first, he burns down Albert's house. He puts Frank on a plane at Gibraltar and takes a train—he is afraid the plane will crash—and just before he gets home, he commits suicide. Also, we see a great deal of Albert Handley in the novel and get a look at the struggle between his creativity and his destructive tendencies. There are some fine scenes centering around Mandy, who gets her "new red Mini" and spends three weeks on the M1 between London and Lincolnshire racing anyone who will race and sending home postcards of the rest stations. At the end, Frank, back with most of his loved ones, hopes to persuade his wife, Nancy, and his children to come share his new life.

Again, the summary is unsatisfactory; it is a better novel than my précis reveals. There is not *a* tree on fire, but several. Frank Dawley comes to the desert "burning, burning, burning" with rage, lust, and class consciousness; it is necessary for him to go through the purging flames of battle, heat, and thirst to have his "foul crimes burnt and purg'd away." Albert burns with self destructiveness, and he must burn with Pater's "hard gem-like flame" of artistic creativity in order to complete himself. John burns, too. The verb is transitive and intransitive: he burns with a desire to hear God's voice, to hear God tell him that, as a precursor of Christ, his work is finished and he can give up the head that has so long burned with the fever of insanity. And he burns out the Handleys, hoping "that he had succeeded in consuming the destructive pride of the family" (*Tree*, p. 394). A whole forest is on fire in the novel, and when the fires burn away the pride, rage, and hatred, the trees will flourish. The burned trees in Algeria serve metaphorically: "such wilderness trees always grew again . . . leaves would grow greener than before, trunks less beautiful, but branches stronger" (*Tree*, p. 220).

It may be that these two novels are, as Allen Richard Penner says, paeans to violence.[8] And it may be that John Handley

---

8. "The Political Prologue and Two Parts of a Trilogy," p. 19.

speaks for Sillitoe when he says, in a passage that Penner quotes, "The police, the armed forces, civil defense personnel are an army of occupation. Those who join their ranks are traitors. Those who sit on jury service are traitors. Those who hold state secrets and do not try to divulge them to the enemy or to make them public knowledge are also traitors" (*Tree,* pp. 269–70). Penner then says, "One might hope that Sillitoe does not intend such ravings to be taken seriously, but the case seems to be otherwise" (p. 19). It can certainly be argued that an uncomfortably large number of Sillitoe's characters talk very much as John Handley does. Arthur and Brian Seaton and Smith, the long-distance runner, all sound exactly like Frank Dawley and the Handleys. But there is a rather large number of Sillitoe's characters who have no interest at all in revolution and who lead distinctly quieter, but no less desperate, lives. If my argument seems excessively weak, consider these comments of Sillitoe's:

> I don't believe in working class; any class. I just give my characters the finest sensibilities I can according to my art. . . . To think of an individual in terms of class is irrelevant. I've never thought of anything like that when I'm writing; it's anathema to me. What other people say about my writing is their business, but my stories are not class conflicts: they're just individual psychotic, psychological or whatever conflicts. If a man tries to hang himself because he's miserable it's not because he's working class; he's just miserable.[9]

It may be argued that artists are among the last persons to be listened to in such matters, and I generally agree. But not this time. I happen to believe Sillitoe because there is too much in his writing that seems to bear him out. It seems to me that he takes a character of a certain sort and lets him move freely toward some personal determination. That his characters are almost always working class says more about his "source of inspiration" than about his political stance. In two of his novels—*The General* and *Travels to Nihilon*—he finds consider-

---

9. John Hall, "In a Class By Himself," *Guardian Weekly*, April 4, 1970, p. 21.

able dissatisfaction with states that probably grew out of revolutionary societies. Most states do, ultimately. So, he is an anarchist. Probably no more so than most of us in moments of social frustration—at tax time and when the red and blue lights flash on the police car behind. Sillitoe may be very much in the New Left, but I still insist that the themes he explores are much more personal than political.

In the two novels under consideration, the main characters do seem to find, for a time, their salvation in political terms. But revolution may be the only game in town that Frank Dawley can really play in. He was "bleeding to death" in marriage at the start of *Posters,* and his relationships with Pat and Myra offered little more opportunity for finding himself than his marriage to Nancy had. It is not as if he set out to find a war to fight; it is that the rebellion offered him a place for trial by fire. Once caught up in militance, he has not yet found, at the end of Volume 2, a way of life more satisfactory.

It is probably unfair and unscholarly to point to a solution that one of his characters finds in a later novel. In *A Start in Life* Michael Cullen, after having been "on the road" as a real *picaro,* retires to the unused railway station he has bought and is seen at the end happy among the radishes and nasturtiums. I suspect—and timorously predict—that the Dawley-Handley group may find a similar way to build a new Jerusalem in "England's green and pleasant land."

There is much to suggest, I feel, that Sillitoe's picture of the revolutionary—the thinking Handleys and the warring Frank Dawley—is ironic. Albert Handley's sons conduct, on paper, a battle of Britain. They rush into the room from time to time and announce that their guerilla forces are fleeing toward Wales and that the forces of reaction are in pursuit. They ask Albert's advice about battle plans, and he suggests countermovements and guerrilla fade-outs with the air of a man humoring small children. They need fifty pounds for a printing press to print revolutionary handbills on, and he gives the money in almost the same way that he buys silly Mandy a "new red Mini." Their paper war is not much different from her assault on the freeway in her car.

And their war, I think Sillitoe is showing us, is not much different from Frank's in the desert. (Of course, it is easier to get killed in Frank's.) Shelley Jones, Frank's revolutionary mentor in the desert, is a childlike intellectual who is not far removed from one of the young Handleys. Shelley Jones—like his namesake, "a beautiful but ineffectual angel"—is pictured by Sillitoe in this way:

> His tall, thin figure walked ahead, caught by a set of ideas that replaced a burned-out childhood; ideas that seemed to suit him far better than if he had retained the golden aura of some far off blissful infancy. In one sense, his ideals made up for a manhood he could never have attained, and gave him a far bigger personality than if he had. (*Tree*, p. 162)

And it needs to be remembered that Shelley Jones is forced into the desert almost at gunpoint by Frank, when gun-running is not enough to satisfy Frank's desire for a cleansing experience. Frank feels that he must experience more than the moderately dangerous smuggling, and he forces Shelley into real revolution and causes his death. Frank knows that he has sacrificed Shelley Jones's life to his experience, and I think Sillitoe makes that point to show us—and Frank, one hopes—that revolutions of the soul are preferable to those which require real bullets. The scenes in the desert, which parallel the revolution being carried on in England by the Handleys, are, I think, more than anything anti-revolutionary. There are dozens of scenes pictured—children blown to pieces, women murdered, old men tortured—which make the point that ideals can better be achieved in more peaceful ways. As Frank observes once, "Slogans, ideals and beliefs weakened when you pulled the warm bodies toward the holes you had lain in while you waited to kill them . . ." (*Tree*, p. 216).

The revolution back in England takes place on two fronts—the mock fight of the Handley young and the very real fight in Albert Handley's soul. Handley the artist is constantly tormented by Handley the radical, who is on the raw edge of violence all the time. But Albert Handley, who does not really understand his art—"a theory is only a way of explaining how your art died" (*Tree*, p. 40)—knows that it is both fed and consumed by his violent nature. He must keep his rage alive but under some control if he is going to continue painting. Like Yeats, who said that all he had in old age were rage and lust "to spur [him] into song," Handley knows something of the relationship between inspiration and fury. Frank's desert journey may be to learn how to suffer, but Albert has already learned. Through his suffering he creates. When Frank learns to create rather than destroy, he will be as complete a man as Albert Handley is.

In the two volumes of the trilogy, Alan Sillitoe has been exploring a theme centered around a search—or several of them—for identity. He has not been proclaiming an answer; he has been working toward one. The best authors always do that, and Sillitoe's willingness to search for moral solutions is what marks him as a serious writer. The critics who call his trilogy a handbook for revolution fail, I think, to see what he is aiming at, how he is using revolution to consider much more serious matters than politics and class. Like Albert Handley, he is seeking to reconcile rather than to destroy.

10

Substance into Shadow: V. S. Naipaul's *The Mimic Men* (1967)

ROBERT K. MORRIS

The Mimic Men (1967) is one of the most arresting and original books to emerge from England's postwar literary renaissance, and the acme to date of a career that has proved both distinguished and unique. Such was not always the case. Up until 1967 there seemed little to separate V. S. Naipaul from a clutch of articulate authors who wrote for the prominent periodicals, who imposed civilized sensibilities on a range of personal themes, and who so sprawled their talents over the fields of belles lettres, history, biography, and travel that it was hard to know whether their cultural criticism was meant to be a by-product of novel writing or vice versa.

More prolific than most, Naipaul seemed for almost a full decade willing to let his imagination and style find their base level in familiar subjects, but in no way go beyond them. He was regional; he was perhaps even parochial; he tacked too close to the narrowest reaches of Shaw's epigram that "the man who writes about himself and his own time is the only man who writes about all people and all time"; for even his art of capturing the public and private, the real and fantasy lives of characters inhabiting a world he knew well never carried experience much past the immediate, or enlarged essential truths about them into questions of existence that went outside the confines of the particular novel itself.

His first novel, *The Mystic Masseur* (1957), published when he was twenty-five, became prototypical of the kind of fiction he wrote in the next five years: tragi-comedies of aspiring little men who, trapped by habit and culture, seek to resurrect change from the debris of a stagnant society. Trinidad was the society in question, soon turned into the microcosm of early novels like *The Mystic Masseur, The Suffrage of Elvira* (1958), and *A House for Mr Biswas* (1961)—certainly fit inspiration, this world, for a writer who had been born and educated in it, and made to suffer there a sense of alienation even before self-exile to England, but equally a failing inspiration, undermined at its heart by an obsession that Naipaul wrote about shortly after revisiting the Caribbean in 1961:

> I had never examined [my] fear of Trinidad. I had never wished to. In my novels I had only expressed this fear; and it is only now, at the moment of writing, that I am able to attempt to examine it. I knew Trinidad to be unimportant, uncreative, cynical. . . . Power was recognized, but dignity was allowed to no one. Every person of eminence was held to be crooked and contemptible. We lived in a society which denied itself heroes. . . .
>
> It was a place where the stories were never stories of success but of failure. . . . It was also a place where a recurring word of abuse was "conceited," an expression of the resentment felt of anyone who possessed unusual skills. Such skills were not required by a society which produced nothing, never had to prove its worth, and was never called upon to be efficient.[1]

One needn't read the Caribbean books too closely to see how this expressed fear provided the thrust for Naipaul's fiction, even as it screened his field of vision. An expatriate novelist

---

1. V. S. Naipaul, *The Middle Passage* (Baltimore: Penguin Books, 1959), pp. 43–45.

who writes about his native country at a distance and with disaffection labors, even more than the writer who has never left home, under the twin shadows of the past: memory and history. Clearly for Naipaul, the privileged and damned expatriate who straddled two periods and two cultures, the temporal-cultural gulf separating Trinidad and England was at first something lonely and frightening, something to sheer away from. For sounding the depths might set up resonances that an inexperienced novelist was not yet ready to control.

A look at a theme central to these early novels may partially explain my meaning. *The Mystic Masseur* and *The Suffrage of Elvira* are both broadly concerned with the success of the little man. In the one, the effete, naive autodidact, Ganesh Ramsumair, mounts, through a combination of chance, island superstition, and corruption, to become first a popular masseur, then a mystic, writer, politico, and finally a representative in the assembly. Ganesh eventually exchanges his constituency and title of M.L.C. (Member of the Legislative Council) for an M.B.E., loses his status as cult figure and hero of the people, and even changes his name to G. Ramsay Muir. In *The Suffrage of Elvira*, Surujpat Harban's shaky course to the Legislative Council careers through the comic intrigues, boondoggling and logrolling attending democracy's rise in Trinidad and its first general election. He sells out totally to win the seat, and winning, disowns all those factions that helped him—Hindu, Moslem, Black—surrendering honesty, innocence, and wonder to the fascination for the power that transports him from Trinidad's backward counties to Port of Spain.

If Ganesh and Surujpat free themselves from their imprisoning environment, they do so by breaking the links with their culture; and if they win new identities, they do so by losing whatever value their old selves had. No one, "the little man" least of all, can resist that first taste of power and prosperity that nourishes the starved ego. But as Naipaul's cumulative ironies make clear, success bought at the expense of spirit, and through an evasion that means moral eviction from the rest of humanity, must count as the greatest failure. The snobbism of the turncoats who succeed generates a cultural isolation far more damning and damaging than the insulation of those who fail.

The pose of those Trinidadians who "make it" is relatively simple to understand; the position, however, is a bit more complex. Perhaps it is really analyzable only by one who has personally experienced the shifts accruing from separation, reorientation, and change. By tunneling outward from the core, Naipaul may well be the first contemporary writer to penetrate the confusion surrounding the plight of the British colonial minority cultures. Compare Naipaul on Trinidad with Forster on India, Orwell on Burma, Burgess on Malaya to see how the Englishman's exploration of interior regions, however compassionate, sensitive, or intelligent retains the anxiety and guilt of the white man's failure to "only connect" the British and colonial cultures. At least in *The Suffrage of Elvira* and *The Mystic Masseur*, Naipaul is far more objective in writing about the disparity, far more willing to relieve the white man of the white man's burden; and to recognize that in his desire to dispense with the *substance* of his older culture, the minority colonial who would succeed had little choice but to ape the mere *forms* of his adopted culture. In perfect outline, but with many of the details yet to be fleshed out, the unresolved themes and paradoxes of these Caribbean novels anticipate those in *The Mimic Men*. Ganesh and Surujpat are in fact Naipaul's first "mimic men," still lacking the force of art or history behind them to thrust them into tragic significance.

The Mimic Men was not, however, the direct consequence of Naipaul's expatriation from the West Indies and his return there; nor was it inspired solely by what I would call his Caribbean period. He seemed to have played out the main theme of the colonial's success and failure with his best work on Trinidad, *A House for Mr Biswas*, and indeed appeared to have freed himself from that world in his following novel, *Mr Stone and the Knights Companion*, which deals strictly with English characters in an English setting. Save that Mr. Stone is another little man—insulated, eccentric, static, visited only months before he is to be superannuated by an inspiration that changes his life—the connection between this novel and the Caribbean novels may seem tenuous and somewhat perplexing. One could note merely that Naipaul in this well-knit, low-keyed, subtle work of perception and revelation works in the tradition of the novel of sensibility, and in the vein of James, Elizabeth Bowen, and the Angus Wilson of *The Middle Age of Mrs Eliot*. In retrospect, though, the very writing of the book can, almost independently of what it has to say, be seen as an advance in Naipaul's more complex response to an England, and more particularly to a London, that later reassert themselves as the actual framework for *The Mimic Men*.

The fact is that the novel manages to say a good deal as well: not only about individual growth and insight in relation to collective and cultural influences, but about man's relationship to forces higher still. Much of this is crystallized in Mr. Stone's long-awaited epiphany in the final pages of the novel:

> And as he walked through the long, dull streets [of London], as with each step he felt his hips and thighs and calves and toes working, his mood changed, and he had a vision of the city. . . . He stripped the city of all that was enduring and saw that all that was not flesh was of no importance to man. All that mattered was man's own frailty and corruptibility. The order of the universe, to which he had sought to ally himself, was not his order. So much he had seen before. But now he saw, too, that it was not by creation that man demonstrated his power and defied this hostile order, but by destruction. By damming the river, by destroying the mountain, by so scarring the face of the earth that Nature's attempt to reassert herself became a mockery.[2]

Yet, apart from setting it down, what was Naipaul to make of this belated vision of human power lodged in human weakness, of this recognition of a solipsism so perfect that the confined

---

2. V. S. Naipaul, *Mr Stone and the Knights Companion* (London: Andre Deutsch, 1963), p. 158.

ego could define itself at the expense of either creation or destruction? In the present work not very much. *Mr Stone and the Knights Companion* was no more able than the Caribbean novels to accommodate Naipaul's disparate experiences, his developing epistemology, or his shifting attitudes toward the culture he had absorbed or that had absorbed him. Was he, that is, to continue writing about England as an outsider turned insider? about Trinidad as an insider now become outsider? What seemed absent from all his books, what prevented any one of them from becoming his "big" book, was that fusion of theme and character capable of creating the artistic illusion beyond the lifelike reality.

The synthesis that finally came with *The Mimic Men* was foreshadowed, I believe, in *An Area of Darkness*, the penetrating account of Naipaul's *Wanderjahre* in India. The experience was both illuminating and shattering. India stirred atavistic memories; lured Naipaul into almost believing that he belonged there. But, in the end, his quest for those roots which his grandfather had transplanted in Trinidad, and which had fed Naipaul's own conflicting attitudes and allegiances as an inheritor of three cultures, confirmed more deeply still his sense of permanent deracination. Modern India appeared to Naipaul even more a cultural-colonial paradox than the modern West Indies:

> The outer and inner worlds do not have the physical separateness which they had for us in Trinidad. They coexist; the society only pretends to be colonial; and for this reason its absurdities are at once apparent. Its mimicry is both less and more than a colonial mimicry. It is the special mimicry of an old country which has been without a native aristocracy for a thousand years and has learned to make room for outsiders, but only at the top. The mimicry changes, the inner world remains constant: this is the secret of survival. . . . Yesterday the mimicry was Mogul; tomorrow it might be Russian or American; today it is English.[3]

3. V. S. Naipaul, *An Area of Darkness* (Baltimore: Penguin Books, 1968), pp. 56–57.

Thus much for the outward show, the facade, the "casual confidence trick" the English had played on the entire society. The more indelible impression on Naipaul's psyche was realized after his return to London: when, "facing [his] own emptiness, [his] feeling of being physically lost," he recollected how such a world of mimicry and shadows was too easily absorbed into a Hindu world of illusion, and how *that* world might absorb anyone who at last grew tired of the game:

> It was only now, as my experience of India defined itself more properly against my own homelessness, that I saw how close in the past year I had been to the total Indian negation, how much it had become the basis of thought and feeling. And already, with this awareness, in a world where illusion could only be a concept and not something felt in the bones, it was slipping away from me. I felt it as something true which I could never adequately express and never seize again.[4]

This is, however, precisely what Naipaul did seize upon and express three years later. Nor is it very difficult to understand why. The corollary to his having confronted a complex of attitudes, been tempted to succumb to them, mastered the impulse to do so, and written a book about the experience, was to write another book showing how different the design might have been had he yielded to the initial temptation. The necessary changes already made, *The Mimic Men* seems to me this book. Autobiography becomes fiction; the "area of darkness" that is India becomes, through a shift in the spirit of time and place, a composite of Trinidad and England; the mimicry of the Anglo-Indian becomes that of the British-educated Hindu colonial; and "negation" becomes the analogue for the game of illusion that has been the life of the refugee-immigrant narrator-hero, R. R. K. Kripalsingh (Ralph Singh) who, at forty, having exhausted his role as friend, countryman, lover, son, husband, student, businessman, politician, and diplomat, now

---

4. *Ibid.*, pp. 266–67.

writes his life from an "unchanging room" in a middle-class London hotel, and strives to secure in the "inaction" imposed upon him "the final emptiness."

Singh's room provides the literal framework for *The Mimic Men*, but, as the end of the novel clarifies, it has all the while been somewhere near the symbolic center as well. I say room; more exactly it is two rooms, though each is congruent with the other—the two sides of the same worn and spent coin that is Singh's life. The first is the attic room in the boardinghouse in Kensington where he takes up temporary residence after the war, and from the occupation of which he dates his "preparation for life": his initial taste of unlimited freedom outside the dusty village on "Isabella" (Trinidad); his entanglements with the great and chaotic city of London; his strange, questing career as student and voluptuary; and his marriage to the white girl Sandra. The second room, that in the hotel, he inhabits fifteen years later. Now in exile and obscurity, ravaged and drained by the flux of history, defeated by personal, social, political, and cultural forces, fragmented, he seeks to understand and ratify through the writing of his life the final "withdrawal" from it.

Rooms are the alpha and omega of Singh's life, but not its antipodes. Naipaul extends the range of his symbol by fusing, rather than opposing certain major ambiguities inhering in it. In a novel dealing with displacement and loneliness, with desolation, dissolution, with failed ambitions, the final room becomes a mausoleum of claustrophobia and deadness. It images the no-exit of Sartrean confinement, the paralysis of Beckettian silence and inaction. At the same time it is a Proustian room in which Singh tries to reconstruct from memory—memory being but another mimic action of reality—the "parenthesis" of a life enclosed by the only two fixed points he has ever known, the "twin ports" between which he has experienced the "shipwreck" that is his life. Logically, the two rooms would seem to mark this beginning and end, the "preparation" and "withdrawal"; metaphysically, though, they are continuous, the last an inevitable consequence of the first.

For while an inhabitant of the first, Singh, the imperfectly Westernized Hindu, becomes dominated by the driving illusion of Western man, lodged (as Lévi-Strauss tells us in *The Savage Mind*) in the psychological materialism of Marx: the idea of a goal.

> The living material of Freud aspires to the nirvana of inert matter; it wants to come to rest at unity but it is doomed to move and divide, to desire and hate the form it engenders. The historical man of Hegel and Marx wants to suppress his otherness, to be one again with others and with nature, but he is doomed to change himself constantly and to change the world.[5]

It is this belief in a goal—most immediately embodied in the libidinous, protean, "whitey-pokey" Sandra—that Singh takes back with him to Isabella; this belief that initiates his drive toward wealth and power; this belief, and in the end this mere illusion, that amplify the discord between what he is and what he thinks he is.

Thus the last room offers the devastating reduction of the illusion, the true annihilation of substance for Singh. He sees that what he believed to be the substantive part of his life was mere shadow, mere mimicry. He writes his history hoping in part to abolish it, as though perhaps through disintegration only can he assess its meaning. In part, too, the writing itself becomes a process of life that reconciles Singh to his lost heritage. Like his father, "Gurudeva," who leaves his family to become a mendicant and holy man, a *sunyasi,* Singh, a waiter, need no longer regard change as a manifestation of energy (a Western prejudice), but, Brahmin-like, as the illusory realm of impermanence. To appreciate Naipaul's irony of allowing a Hindu whose philosophy teaches the negation of history to withdraw in order to write history, we must understand that Singh's life shows how the world of varied, chance events leads to an

---

5. Octavio Paz, *Claude Lévi-Strauss: An Introduction* (Ithaca, N. Y.: Cornell University Press, 1970), p. 125.

empty region where being and nothingness are reabsorbed. In his last room, tricked by what he imagined was permanent power and the illusion of freedom, by the chimera of a goal, Singh now contemplates "an apparatus which knows no activity other than repetition, and which lacks a goal."

There is yet a more unifying irony that relates to my conviction that this last room is at the novel's symbolic center and provides an opening for my discussing *The Mimic Men* in terms of its themes and overall structure. The irony is developed at the heart of a brief but significant passage from which I have already quoted phrases here and there.

> It never occurred to me that the writing of this book might have become an end in itself, that the recording of a life might become an extension of that life. It never occurred to me that I would have grown to relish the constriction and order of hotel life, which previously had driven me to despair; and that the contrast between my unchanging room and the slow progression of what was being created there would have given me such satisfaction. Order, sequence, regularity: it is there every time the electric meter clicks, accepting one more of my shillings.[6]

"Order, sequence, regularity!" The pattern for which Singh has quested all along, hoping to understand how seemingly random events and accident have created the fractured self he now is—the quest for the matrix within the parenthesis—is revealed in the emptiness of an exile's room. The irony is that the revealed pattern is only a shadow of the real pattern he has lost. But the revelation comes without éclat. Singh's beast does not spring from this jungle of tangled relationships, fraudulent motives, conditional acts. It continually and elusively circles him. He is drawn, rather than galvanized into knowing why "[his] own journey, scarcely begun, had ended in the ship-

---

6. V. S. Naipaul, *The Mimic Men* (New York: Macmillan, 1967), p. 293. Subsequent page references will be to this edition and found in parentheses following quoted extracts.

wreck which all [his] life [he] had sought to avoid." And in pondering why in his freedom to choose he had at every turn made the wrong choice, and why he continued to enforce the imagined projection of himself and fill the void with the mimicry of coherence, he unveils by degrees how the quest for order dissolved into chaos, how sequence surrendered to contingency, how regularity whirled off into eccentricity.

These are, I think, the principal movements in *The Mimic Men* that articulate many of its themes and structures. And since the second of these movements is wrapped up with the novel's plot, I should like to discuss it first.

Singh's reconstruction of the past is, one may remember, more than autobiographical. His life is interwoven with the political and social changes that take place on Isabella, and consequently aspires to be pseudo- or quasi-history as well. Yet the idea of any sequence common to the writing of history is undermined by the nature of the narrative itself: a scrupulous sifting of facts by memory, rather than an impartial, logical presentation of them. What I mean to suggest here is that the novel's architectonics seems at odds with the idea of historic continuity, with the pattern that Singh would like, but is unable to realize. Less abstractly, the novel covers over a quarter of a century: from about 1930 when Singh is ten, until 1960 when he is forty, opening at a date midway between (1946), and moving backward in time before moving forward. A modern reader has no trouble accepting this device as a conventional mode of memory-narrative, but Naipaul works a curious (and as far as his theme is concerned, pertinent) variation on the technique. Singh's memory seems to blur as the novel comes closer to the present. Facts become opaque; gaps appear between large chunks of unaccounted-for time; events are taken less as certainties than as contingencies as Singh himself withdraws further and further into the shadows, until by the end of the novel he is no more than a face peering out from behind a pillar.

Thus the second and longest section of the novel, dealing with Singh's childhood, adolescence, and initiation into manhood is the most vivid. Isabella, not yet a dream but still a reality, is fixed in time and space, and given historic solidity in that James Anthony Froude had once visited there and written about it. For Singh, son of a poor schoolteacher, though allied on his mother's side to the millionaire owners of the Bella Bella Coca-Cola Bottling Plant, the island is a place of paradox and tensions. He is fascinated by wealth and poverty alike; he is drawn to his rich cousin Cecil and to the less rich but more aristocratic Creole family of the Deschampsneufs; yet he is equally attracted to the struggling, ambitious blacks like Hok and Browne. Like them he loathes the daily "betrayals into ordinariness," cherishes their secret dreams of escape from Isabella, but dreams himself, inflamed by his reading in *The Aryan Peoples and Their Migration*, of fulfilling the prophecy incarnate in his surname ("one of the warrior caste") by perhaps ruling the island.

Up to a certain point in this section, Naipaul appears to be reworking the themes of escape and betrayal found in the earlier Caribbean books, with the exception that something complete seems struggling to be born out of Singh's half-formed ego. But whatever it is fails to materialize. Chance thwarts will. His search for continuity, his desire to participate in life, is deflected by a series of fortuitous events that confirm how much easier and more natural it is for men to destroy than to create. Mr. Stone's revelation is brought home to Singh in a dozen ways, and at each turn he is maimed anew. His uncle's shame and savage desire for revenge after the near truck collision with some workers imbue Singh with intimations of power; his father's desertion and subsequent affiliation with radical insurgents shatter his foundations of family and stability; the drownings at the beach and the gross attitudes of the fisherman desensitize him to pity, make him retrench further into the role of observer in order to avoid further wounding; the devisceration of the Deschampsneufs' prize race horse (by his father's followers and according to the ancient Indian blood rite of *Asvamedha*) renders obscene his long love affair with Aryan myth; and the urging of the now-dissolute Cecil to shoot his

(Singh's) half-brother during a macabre bach ramble almost pushes him to becoming a participant in destruction, rather than a mere observer of it.

These lacerations of the child and young man partially prepare for the insulation and masochism of the adult. Singh's responses to events in England after the war (his womanizing with pick-ups and prostitutes, the disturbing and febrile courtship of Sandra, marriage to her), and those covering a decade on Isabella before his final exile (his shabby dealings and calculated successes in real estate, Sandra's divorce and departure, his period of solitude in the "Roman" house, the founding with Browne of *The Socialist,* his rise to power as head of the country, and his ouster) are all conditioned by the maiming in youth.

Yet, however juxtaposed, these events are unshaped by meaning and stripped of consequence, for they only drive Singh to total negation. The more powerful he becomes publicly, the more isolated he becomes privately; the more he exercises control over others, the less he can avoid the encroaching impotence of mind and body, enter the mainstream of humanity, or control himself. *"Je vens d'lué,"* he says at the end of the novel, using the patois of Isabella. *From* where we know. But *to* where? Singh has so realized his youthful avowal to "eliminate" all superfluous things from life, to "simplify," that he has pushed elimination and simplification to the near vanishing point, and with it all feeling, contact, desire, growth. Annihilated by the forces of contingency that he has permitted to control it, the sequence of his life is now merely a matter of record: as accurate, unvaried, embalmed as the striations on his desk and the patterned wallpaper in his "unchanging room."

Singh's quest for "sequence," the historic order of *The Mimic Men,* is synchronous with the search for "regularity" or personal order. In one way this particular movement very much hangs together through Naipaul's use of motif: here a symbol, there a phrase, but in either case peculiar to the patterns eluding Singh throughout. Motif is not baffling in *The Mimic Men;* on the contrary, it is rather transparent, for much of the novel's irony is lodged in Singh's refining to obscurity what should have been so patently obvious. One sees, for example, that reiterations of the "two landscapes of sea and snow"—Isabella and England—between which Singh is restlessly driven, correspond to his private "shipwreck" and the perfection of his desolation. Or that the periods of his life are linked to the women he has known—his mother, Lieni, Sandra, Wendy, Stella, indeed Isabella itself—and betrayed, or with whom infatuation has fallen into ennui, disgust, impotence. A phrase returns to mirror his *Sehnsucht* (*"Who comes here? A grenadier. What does he want? A pot of beer."*); another to echo the cry of the defeated in the war between master and slave ("The Niger is a tributary of that Seine") and to inspire his first paper on political theorizing; still another (*"Quantum mutatus ab illo"*) to invoke the discontinuity he experiences through personal change and loss.

These motifs are neither difficult to trace nor many. Nor are they intended to involute even further the difficulties of Naipaul's demanding narrative. Like similar motifs in James and Proust, those in *The Mimic Men* force breathing spaces between the closely-woven textures of prose, bridge or merge the past and present, and sustain the exchanges between time and memory. Yet in the last analysis they are pendants to the larger theme, spinning off with variations from the title, and setting in motion the cycle that returns Singh to the "regularity" of his room. The theme is of course mimicry. And the specter of simulation haunts Singh from childhood onward: quite consciously at first, but then so mechanically that those defenses of concealment and protection raised by the ego to keep at bay defeat and anxiety soon become a biological art. Singh perfects his mimesis until the real cannot be distinguished from the counterfeit.

In his initial impersonation—when a boy of about ten—he "suppresses the connection" with his father's family, for "to be descended from generations of idlers and failures, an unbroken line of the unimaginative, unenterprising and oppressed, had always seemed . . . to be a cause for deep, silent shame." He temporarily shuffles off the shame by signing his compositions "Ralph Singh," instead of Ranjit Kripalsingh, but a piece of him gets lost in that shuffle and in subsequent ones. A witness to his Uncle Nana's fiasco with the lorry driver, he learns that "a man was only what he saw of himself in others"; at school he falls easily into the role of "natural impersonator"; and a dangerously unsporting attitude is formulated on the cricket field:

> An audience is never important. An audience is made up of individuals most of whom are likely to be your inferiors. . . . The successful performer in whatever field operates, not perhaps from contempt, but from a profound lack of regard for his audience. The actor is separate from those who applaud him; the leader, and particularly the popular leader, is separate from the led. (p. 136)

Yet, though Singh grows more calculating in developing those powers of mimicry that finally generate the mimicry of power, he cannot escape the atavistic taint—the unaccountable proclivity to be enslaved by his own expertise, cast by it into an existential limbo:

> We, here on our island, handling books printed in this world, and using its goods, had been abandoned and forgotten. We pretended to be real, to be learning, to be preparing ourselves for life, we mimic men of the New World, one unknown corner of it, with all its reminders of the corruption that came so quickly to the new. (p. 175)

This, perhaps the most crystalline perception in the novel, is never surpassed. It becomes both justification and rationalization for Singh's strange *decision*—I italicize the word to make it clear that he has not yet relinquished the illusion of freedom—to purge inward "corruption" by allowing it to taint others. Devious and eccentric acts become the foundation for a barrier in front of which he can mime public gestures, behind which he can retreat into a private fantasy of coherence. Against tradition he marries a "whitey-pokey," thereby cutting himself off from Isabella's society. He plays the arch-capitalist by engineering a condominium development called, in honor of his father, Kripalville, and sees the name ironically changed by popular wits into a symbol of his own maiming: Crippleville. He entombs himself in the opulent, grotesque Roman house, setting the stage for his rise from patrician to politician. And even when he and Browne create the "movement" on Isabella (or, as he conjectures, when the "movement" creates them), there is a fraudulence latent in his idealism; for he capitalizes on the rumored intimacy between himself and Wendy Deschampsneufs, becoming, "at least in so far as appearances went, what others saw in me. It was play for me, play for her."

Except the play, the mimicry eventually becomes life. Every act, gesture, plan, and detail effected by Singh is done with an eye to the drama. Game playing is no longer the means to an end but the end in itself, since it brings with it its own rules, its own sense of personal order. But if gamesmanship and drama account for Singh's success, they also engineer his failure. What he discovers too late—and much of Naipaul's art in *The Mimic Men* is to keep this awareness always lagging a bit behind the tempo of events—is that the master of a role is only one miscue away from becoming its prisoner. Singh falls from power with all moral and material substance dissipated. And having given over at forty the complexities demanded by life, he can only drift away from "responsibility and attachment" toward the "final emptiness," retreat into shadowy simplicity, and become a slave to the total and useless freedom he has so long courted.

In the end, such freedom negates all will, all desire to be anything but free. There is a more terrifying paradox reserved for Singh, a unique tragedy for the "warrior" who is left with the "fear of action," for the virile politico who is reduced to sterility and impotence. As Lawrence wrote over fifty years ago in *Women in Love,* this sort of freedom is "the substitution of the mechanical principle for the organic, the destruction of the organic purpose, the organic unity, and the subordination of every organic unit to the great mechanical purpose. It was pure organic disintegration and pure mechanical organization. This is the first and finest state of chaos." Singh's resolution into a mechanical order of all conflict that makes life go is the sag into chaos. And it is this idea that Naipaul uses as the organizing metaphysics of the novel, beyond which even Singh's quest for historic and personal order pales: his making tangible the chaos from within.

The textures of *The Mimic Men* and its leaps back and forth in time make it difficult to assess the exact moment that the movement from "playacting to disorder" realizes the final pattern. And perhaps this kind of assessment would be of no particular value. Naipaul's metaphysics is not generated through a dialectic but through opposition of forces. Every action of Singh's is greeted by an opposing counteraction. Marriage ends in divorce; activity in inactivity; creation in destruction; riches in poverty; success in failure; power in powerlessness; respect in scorn; popularity in isolation, et cetera, et cetera. In every way Singh's immersion in life and history brings about exile from them. Beginning with "the human instinct for order," he steers voluntarily toward "shipwreck." Certainly this abiding metaphor of *The Mimic Men* has caught exactly the whole dreary, conscious drive toward "controlled chaos."

Still, in a novel emphasizing that drive toward a goal desiring nothing but its own goallessness, Naipaul does make an assessment of sorts. He compresses the ideas sketched in the Caribbean books and *Mr Stone and the Knights Companion* into several major statements on chaos, order, politics, and power, working all four themes together impressively and according to the novel's design. It is not accidental that Singh first collides with this sense of metaphysical order after the near collision on the dusty road in Isabella; it is not accidental either that he dreams, at that moment when the political and dramatic are violently yoked together, of becoming head of the country; and it is not accidental, finally, that when he is top dog on the island, these particular ideas of order just as suddenly vanish. With Naipaul these things are not, I repeat, accidental, though for Singh they could well be. In the one case—that of the boy and his uncle and a lorry driver on a road—Singh resurrects a vision of order from potential chaos; in the other—that of the

vulnerable politician in the Roman house—chaos has devolved
from the height of order. It is hard under these circumstances
not to accept as compelling such paradoxes of existence
whereby chaos and order, almost interchangeably, lead to an
identical nullity:

> My career is by no means unusual [writes Singh retro-
> spectively at the opening of the novel]. It falls into the pat-
> tern. The career of the colonial politician is short and ends
> brutally. We lack order. Above all, we lack power, and we do
> not understand that we lack power. We mistake words and
> the acclamation of words for power; as soon as our bluff is
> called we are lost. Politics for us are do-or-die, once-for-all
> charge. Once we are committed we fight more than political
> battles; we often fight quite literally for our lives. . . . For
> those who lose, and nearly everyone in the end loses, there is
> only one course: flight. Flight to the great disorder, the final
> emptiness. (pp. 10–11)

Though in the way of all "colonial" novels *The Mimic Men* is
political as well, thematically bound up with the nature of
power, Naipaul has tried to extend this almost ungraspable
concept beyond aphorism and "vague and unreliable" generic
definitions. For Singh—the participant in an ambiguous
drama, a man who does not possess the "frenzy, the sense of
mission, the necessary hurt" required for the professional
politician—power goes beyond the impudent, the corrupting,
the mechanical, the dehumanizing. It is something more than a
historic adjunct to the Hobbesian contract emerging from the
chaos of meanness, shortness, brutality, nastiness. It is a logical
phenomenon, but it is also a manifestation of chance and revelation. It is a frightening noumenon of time and place; it is a
destroyer of substance, a creator of shadow men; it is a self-
generating entity feeding upon itself only to devour itself and
all allied with it. "The tragedy of power like mine," writes
Singh, "is that there is no way down; there is only extinction."
    Merely to encounter this rather overwhelming meta-
physic—power as leading to "extinction," nothingness, the

void, emptiness—is perhaps to glimpse *why* power can create the most damaging deception in those called upon to wield it. However much we may mistrust and abhor power, we have come to regard it as one of the few inescapable constructs of our civilization from Alexander on, as, indeed, the single force that has made our civilization what it is. Yet if we follow Naipaul's line in *The Mimic Men* do we not confront an inherent falsity of that premise? Does power bring order, or simply an illusion of order—that is, chaos? And does the man who establishes order through power reveal only the chaos within himself? May we not be charged with a new metaphysics of power and order as it pertains to individuals and nations? At least should we not be compelled to view all these concepts in a new light as Singh does?

> It has happened in twenty places, twenty countries, islands, colonies, territories—these words with which we play, thinking they are interchangeable and that the use of a particular one alters the truth. I cannot see our predicament as unique. The newspapers even today spell out situations which, changing faces and landscapes, I can think myself into. They talk of the pace of postwar political change. It is not the pace of creation. Nor is it the pace of destruction, as some think. Both these things require time. The pace of events, as I see it, is no more than the pace of a chaos on which strict limits have been imposed. I speak of course of territories like Isabella, set adrift yet not altogether abandoned, where this controlled chaos approximates in the end, after the heady speeches and token deportations, to a continuing order. The chaos lies all within. (p. 23)

If in the end we are to see *The Mimic Men* as more than a grand tautological expansion of one man's yearning for and securing the "final emptiness," we must ourselves try to explore beyond Naipaul's insights into questions of order and chaos. His novel is of course only anticipatory of a perspective that time has not yet lent us. For we have as yet mastered neither the patterns of colonial history nor the psyches of men "who have known grandeur beyond the football-pool dreams of [their] neighbors," who "made it," and who were changed and defeated in the making. We are still caught up, to echo Singh, in the "pace of a chaos." Like him, one must try to "impose order on one's history," but the act must come before falling into sublime and easy simplification. No doubt the strongest lure in a world of flux and complexity is for men to withdraw into their rooms, for nations to withdraw into their corners of the globe, and to discover "order, sequence, regularity" in isolation. Naipaul warns us, I think, away from an illusion so immanent, and so imminently destructive. For once we are no longer willing to contend against, but agree to surrender to Lawrence's idea and Singh's acceptance of "ordered chaos," we *are* the perfect mimic men. We can become nothing else. For our substance has dissolved into shadow, and that, alas, a static one.

11

England's Greatest Tourist and Tourist Attraction: Andrew Sinclair's *Gog, Magog* (1967, 1972)

PETER WOLFE

Gog (1967) roots Andrew Sinclair's soaring imagination, vast learning, and omniform style in the rich soil of English culture. "There's no psychological motivation in *Gog*," says Bernard Bergonzi, speaking of the book's panoramic scope. "Instead, it tries to substitute an incredibly rich evocation of the past."[1] Bergonzi is right. The time-warps, identity glides, and recurrences do give the novel a scope that transcends, yet includes, the enacted drama. No Jamesian, Sinclair does not steer his action toward an expansion of individual consciousness or to a superfine moral discrimination. Although he chooses details carefully, he worries less about balance and interrelatedness than about massiveness. The language, incidents, and characters making up the action fuse in a ganglion of Englishness. He channels his materials into a people's self-discovery and self-

---

1. Bernard Bergonzi, *The Situation of the Novel* (Pittsburgh: University of Pittsburgh Press, 1971), p. 78.

being. These materials are historical and mythical as well as contemporary.

Within Gog pulse the energies of the British folk. Whereas history records event, myth captures the essence of event, digging under a heap of accidents and misadventures to find the underlying pattern. *Gog* invokes these patterns, or archetypes, in different ways. They objectify images and situations that consitute the British spirit; they cohere as paradigms of British conduct. Gog's personal life mirrors and interlocks with English prehistory. A historian, Gog both researched the Gog-Magog myth and translated an anonymous Old Norse fragment, *The Gogwulf Edda*. His own essay, "The Concentration of Power in the Middle Ages," and a miracle play he watches, *Everyman in Albion*, re-create the novel's main tensions at another level. His dreams, the present-tense narration, and the numerous historical parallels all bring the action to a flame-tip of immediate experience. While Gog discovers his heritage, he also rediscovers himself. He walks from Edinburgh to London in order to know himself after a shipwreck blasts his wits. Inevitably, his geographical travels make up but one level of exploration. As he moves toward London, through a blockade of tempters and tormenters, he also moves backward in both his personal and national history. The past must be known before it can be controlled and shaped into the future. Thus Gog reviews his earlier research; he reads William Blake on the birth of Albion; he reacquaints himself with the Gog-Magog legends in Ezekiel and Revelation; he looks at a film script called *The Battle Of Hastings*, showing "THE ENGLISH CHAMPION, *GOGFRITH*, FIGHTING MORTUS," BASTARD AND ENGLISH RENEGADE. He is conscripted into a movie (chapter 16), which depicts the 1644 Battle of Marston Moor between the Roundheads and Cavaliers. To become whole, he has to live the historical events he had once studied. And the meanings of the past, he learns, are too complex to be compassed by one mode or technique.

Gog shows vividly how myth works in fiction. Not only time, but also different states of being swim and glide, stumble and lunge, into each other. All is one. Gog, for instance, is a unique

Englishman. But he also embodies English history, the English state, and the English public. Touch him in one place and the reverberations are endless.

Gainsaying both moral radicalism and political panaceas, Gog sees identity as inherited, organic process. This view of myth as a seedbed of ancient accumulated wisdom seated in everyday experience by-passes the need for evidence and proofs. The ancient folk memory of a people never dies. But it lives in people's hearts, not in recorded history. By relying on truth instead of on fact, the Druids were able to pit magic against the bronze and iron of England's early Roman invaders. Scawton Moor is the scene of the movie version of the Battle of Marston Moor, yet nobody complains. Although the Brutus Stone, dated 1185 B. C., may not be authentic, it has strengthened generations of English hearts.

But Sinclair does not give in to facile romanticism. His broad view of culture keeps him from overrating history and legend. All savior figures, driven by folk-memory, must suffer; all searches for the New Jerusalem fail. Myth can invent, reshape, and criticize itself simultaneously. In chapter 18, Gog eats fish and chips out of a newspaper called *The People*. The paper's articles on crime, sex, and gambling show him the wrongheadedness of his hopes for the British people. Sinclair not only makes his important point to the side of the chapter's main action; the openness of myth also establishes a relevance and authority he draws on later. "The Tarts' Dart Match" in chapter 21 describes some British prostitutes using Gog as a human dart board, to the drunken glee of some soldiers in an Exeter pub. The American GI's and Tommies, the classical allusions, and the developing picture of Gog as a British folk-hero all make the match a powerful symbol of British self-cruelty in the presence of American cash.

I

Sinclair did well to give the Gog story an epical frame. Epics have always lent both form and continuity to myth; moreover, since Fielding, they have supplied a major strain of British fiction. Like the *Iliad* and *Tom Jones*, *Gog* is a narrative of some length that describes the travels of its main character. It has geographical sweep, tracing a southward path from Edinburgh to London. It contains epic epithets: an ancient warrior is called "Brereton of the burning cauldron," and, to show the oneness of history, a modern-day spiv, or wide boy, is called "Maurice [Mowler] with the glib lips." A military garrison, a munitions depot, the military convoys that roll through the book, the film accounts of war from history—all these sources furnish the battle scenes belonging to the traditional epic. The hero's descent to the underworld comes in Gog's harrowing visits to various caves and pubs and, perhaps most spectacularly, in his short stay (chapter 10) in an underground armaments warehouse, whose evil he routs with some sticks of dynamite.

Then there is the convention of the epical hero who represents the life of his people and whose acts help found a civilization. Bergonzi conveys the force of these conventions in his statement that, in *Gog*, "a man seeks for his own identity from some mythological tradition." He also refers to "the almost obsessive quality of Sinclair's concern for the English past and his feeling for myth, which he sees as overtaking history."[2] Gog is not crushed by the weight of history; instead, he merges with history. He is searching for himself by walking the face of an England struggling to remake *it*self and to find *its* way after the end of World War II. The action takes place during the spring and summer of 1945—that is, from VE- to VJ-Day. Although the victories over Germany and Japan are stressed, neither England nor its embodiment, Gog, acts like a winner. Chapters 1 and 34, each beginning with much of the same diction and syntax, show Gog as a patient, immobilized and convalescing. Like England, he is worn out by the war. Also like England, he is recovering slowly. And his long, hard vigil mirrors his country's struggle.

His identification with the popular hero of prehistoric Britain prompts a look into one of the corollaries of myth and

---

2. *Ibid.*, p. 77.

tradition—legend. Now, legend protrays incidents common to a class or race, like marriage, famine, and war. Often a peasant will marry, suffer, and endure, his endurance symbolizing the continuance of his nation. The wayfaring Gog, enemy of dogma and authority, sides emotionally with the British peasantry and is even called a peasant several times by his wife. And rightly so. His hand carries a tattoo of a wheatsheaf and sickle, and, in chapter 7, mistaking a reaper for a destroyer of corn, he hits the reaper with an oaken lance. As he reels and lurches over the English landscape, his nation stumbles into the postwar era. Though the war is over, England has not eased back into the ways of peace. Soldiers, tanks, and guns are common sights; the rationing of both food and clothing goes on; English faces are pasty and pouched from too much starch. The black market thrives, especially in London, which is torn and cratered by German bombs.

In the prologue, a naked man, nearly seven feet tall, drifts to shore after his ship hits a mine off the Scottish coast. Though the giant-man, Gog, suggests a mythical sea god who climbs mysteriously from the sea to start a new dynasty, he is also a helpless baby: "Water and green bile spew out of the man's mouth, he gags horribly. . . . One of the soldiers [who finds him] thumps his back" like a doctor smacking a newborn's rump. When he tries to speak, he gags, cries, or disgorges seawater. Later, a gypsy tells him that he will have "much water to cross." Gog cannot escape water, the element of the unborn, any more than his island-nation can. The book contains numerous births, rebirths, and false dawns in the presence of water; Lazarus is mentioned several times in connection with Gog. And though the threat of drowning does not leave him for long, he never drowns. More often than not, water cleanses and revives him. Accordingly, England never sinks into the sea, although she must die an imperial death in order to come back as a commonwealth. Gog and his nation both need refurbishing. They are outsized and ungainly, disjointed and uncoordinated, basically decent but, trying to be too many things at once, self-destroying.

From the outset, Gog's name, size, and amnesia turn his

behavior, that is, the personal acts of a private English citizen, into scenes from English history: "Although he hears every word in the present, a quirk of his mind makes him feel that he is hearing words said long ago." Gog, first of all, is Dr. George Griffin, ex-amateur boxer, hiking enthusiast, University of Durham historian, and British Army Intelligence officer. Politically, Griffin, whose first name comes from England's patron saint, is an old-fashioned English liberal; he favors personal freedom and a government that respects individual privacy. The Labour Party has just been elected to power, and Griffin is walking to London to see if the people are really ruling there. Chapter 1, showing his escape from hospital, launches the theme of the near-helpless private person at odds with a large, powerful, uncaring bureaucracy.

His travels fuse Gog with several British folk-heroes. These fusions, carrying the force of his background in history, mental recovery, and dramatic context, are not arbitrary. He cannot forget his kinship to Gog, the mythical hero who was present at the founding of Albion and who will also be present at her end. A towering British oak, he often finds himself (like Gulliver) surrounded by fanatics or mean-minded runts, who either want to victimize him or use him as a scourge. His aimless roaming along the countryside recalls King Lear. His identification with outlaws like Robin Hood and Dick Turpin, and Oliver Twist asking for "More," broadens the base of his Englishness in the same way as his having a Catholic mother and Celtic father. But British tradition—many-sided as it is—does not explain him fully. *The Gogwulf Edda* shows him crucified on a cross of oak; his tilting at the reaper in chapter 7, while charting his psychic unreadiness, recalls Don Quixote; his homecoming to his wife, Marie, in Hampstead in chapter 34 raises comparisons with the Ulysses of both Homer and Joyce. Often, too, the perpetual journey he tramps in search of a lost Eden puts him close to American literary heroes, like Leatherstocking and Huck Finn, and the Walt Whitman of *Song of Myself*.

When Maire calls Gog a suffering saint, he disagrees: "No . . . just a man walking to London." His disagreement, like the mythical aura he generates, evokes a wide spectrum of moral response. That he is once called a "holy turd" makes him capable of anything, a polygon of drives. His is as free as a character in a realistic novel. Rather than hemming him in, his mythical furnishings lend him both form and resonance. And Sinclair keeps him human by denying him elevation. His last name is that of a mythical creature with the front parts of an eagle and the rear parts of a lion. Yet he is capable of stupidities. In 1931, he may have sired an illegitimate son, Arthur, with a "jellied Everest" called Rosie. He tears a young tree out of the ground in chapter 3, and chapter 19 shows him killing a bird for no reason. He also admits, in a later chapter, killing a barracks-mate on the suspicion that he was a spy. He has the ferocity of the legendary griffin without its grandeur. Like Chekhov, Sinclair will build to a climax, then devalue it. Gog looks forward to visiting holy places—York Minster, Glastonbury, and Stonehenge. Yet Sinclair avoids surrounding him with holiness. The famous Five Sisters Window at York turns out to be a paean to Magog, Gog's sworn enemy. The Glastonbury excursion lasts less than two pages and adds less to the chapter where it occurs (chapter 23) than a sadistic comic book, "Sweeny Gog: The Demon Barber of Secret Street." Stonehenge becomes the setting, not for spiritual uplift, but for a slapstick fight-to-the-death between religious fanatics.

Gog needs deflating. For an educated man he holds some silly views. His scheme to give back the land to the farmers makes little sense, and his hatred of farm machinery, a perversion of agrarianism, goes against efficiency. He is an emotional man of good will, without program or policy. Freedom he also views unrealistically. At the end of chapter 3 he meets a troupe of circus freaks, drooling, moaning, and gibbering. His attempt to free these "holy . . . simple ones" from the tyranny of their keeper-nurse fails. They resist freedom. Not everybody wants freedom; not everybody can handle it. Freedom is both a dubious and a difficult goal when men enslave themselves. Ironically, nobody welcomes bondage more heartily than Gog himself, self-appointed champion of the obscure and put-upon.

Maire calls him "the perfect victim" and "a born victim," adding, "I could search the world over and never find a man so
exquisitely torturable." A colleague, one Professor Miniver,
accuses him of harboring an "appetite for the impossible" and a
"nostalgia for the nonexistent." Gog would not deny any of
these charges. His admitted "passion for persecution" keeps
clouding his judgment. Underrating Maire's cruelty, he gives
her too much credit. He may also overrate and magnify the
wickedness of his half-brother, Magog. This paranoia, a logical
extension of his passion for persecution, uncovers threates
everywhere. He sees himself as the target of a conspiracy reaching from the upper classes (Maire) through government
(Magog) and higher education (Miniver) to the working class
(Maurice Mowler): "Gog looks about and each fold in the
ground wraps the body of a villain and each rock shields the
weapon of a murderer and each trunk shades a highwayman
and the very ground may be mined and the very clouds may
rain bombs."

When Magog finally comes into the book, he is more weak
than wicked; his long fight with Gog in the last chapter, one of
the book's weakest spots, stems from the passage in Revelation
20 that makes Gog and Magog forerunners of the end of the
world. Although Magog sleeps with Gog's wife and filches
funds from Gog's estate, he deprives Gog of nothing important;
Gog has little use for his marriage or his property. In fact, his
chief quarrel, perhaps his *only* quarrel, with Magog is political.
Magog's coincidence with the machine, imperialism, and cen-
tralized power does not call for such obsessive fear and hatred.
Gog invents much of his trouble. He stumbles and clowns; he
makes himself the butt of other people's jokes; his good-
natured attempts to please (i.e., "appease") everybody rain
doom on his head. His search for the New Jerusalem, landing
him in endless contradictions, brings only frustration. His colleague, Miniver, sums him up as inconsistent:

You've always wanted to preserve every stick and stone from
the past. You hate change in old things. You loathe new

buildings. You're the true reactionary, far more than me. The revolution you want is to turn the clock back to the golden age when all men were free and equal. Which was never. And never will be.[3]

Miniver's summary, the product of many years' acquaintance, has merit. Yet Gog is no mere ineffectual. In spite of his inconsistencies, misjudgments, and self-delusions, Magog's legions go to great lengths to break his journey. Their persistence bestows importance both on Gog and his trek. Whey they work so hard to crush his already bruised spirit, though, is a question that must wait the discussion of narrative strategies that touch on the development of the plot.

The itinerant Gog has no Sancha Panza, Leporello, or Partridge—no loyal, slow-witted retainer—accompanying him on his tramp. Instead of a squire, he has a series of tormenters or tempters who incarnate a side of his personality he must face and cope with before achieving wholeness. The first alter-ego he meets after leaving hospital is a military policeman lying unconscious, "his head cracked open by the clubs of other men." This encounter on Edinburgh's dark, ravaged streets is important: Sinclair has Gog leave the hospital unshod in order to include it. The MP's huge size parallels Gog's, and his unconsciousness in the middle of a large city looks back to Gog's sea-wracked helplessness in the prologue. Finally, the bare feet of Gog, enemy of the power structure, match the bare, bloody head of the policeman, the power structure's servant and protector. His putting on the MP's boots foreshadows playfully the practical steps Gog must take to convert his sentimental agrarian populism into political fact.

Just outside Edinburgh, Gog meets his next double, Wayland Merlin Blake Smith, alias the Bagman. A vagabond-prophet nicknamed the Wandering Jew by the police, Smith is another would-be savior. His name reflects his high ambitions.

---

3. Andrew Sinclair, *Gog* (New York: Avon Books, 1969), p. 141. Subsequent page references will be to this edition and found in parentheses following quoted extracts.

The name Wayland comes from the architect of the original Jerusalem, prehistoric London. Smith also imagines himself a reincarnation of the original Archdruid: "My mission on earth," he claims, is "to broadcast the coming of Israel again to this holy island," as he did in his earthly stay as William Blake. To forecast the end of the world and to proclaim the coming of the new Israel, he wants the BBC to give him its studios. At their first meeting in a derelict bus, Gog and the Bagman exchange bread and kippers wrapped in newspaper. Their symbolic trade of loaves and fishes helps create an apocalyptic tone, which Smith's later appearances, with their booming pulpit redundancies, both heighten and mock. Like most other saviors, Smith dies without reaching his goal. He invades the underground studios of the BBC near London's Strand and airs his end-of-the-world prophecies. But then, in a chaotic flash, a bolt of electricity charges through him and kills him.

Another spokesman of the holocaust is Evans the Latin. Like Gog, he sees enemy spies and informers everywhere. Like Gog's father, he is a Celt, teaches school for a living, and favors radical politics. But his plan to secede from England and form a Celtic Union — the true Albion — goes beyond the wildest fancies of both Gog and his father. Evans dies as he lives. Garbed as a Druid priest in chapter 1 (Gog goes to a pub called The Thistle), he meets Smith the Bagman at Stonehenge. A head-on meeting of two fanatics with similar philosophies must end in blood. Smith's stabbing Evans with a radio antenna shows the new overcoming the old without improving it, all within the religious frame supplied by the looming twilight pillars of Stonehenge.

A secular counterthrust to this holy war comes in with the Cockney profiteer, Maurice "Morrie" Mowler. Morrie first appears in chapter 1 preaching the creed of Marxism in a workingman's pub. He returns in chapter 5 as the leader of a sheep massacre. The two appearances are consistent. Morrie and his friends kill a hundred sheep to protest against food rationing ("I don't do it for the money. . . . I do it for the people, I do everythin' for the people."). The mass butchering, done in the name of democracy and freedom, makes him rich. Chapter 10 shows him much risen in the world; he has made a fortune peddling weapons and explosives, "all the etceteras of survival and destruction needed by the compleat soldier." Although he steals his ware from the British army, he sees himself as a rubbish collector and landscape artist rather than as a thief. The fortune he earns is merely a side effect of his public service:

> Look at this lot. I pick it up dirt cheap, the government practically gives it away. Now the war's over against the jerries, it's surplus. . . . I'm a preservationist, I am—I preserve what I can flog. I cart away the eyesores. Just to 'elp tidy up the place for peace and all. I don't charge 'em 'ardly nothin' for carriage. I must admit, I do cart away the junk by night sometimes, without askin' a by-your-leave, when the sentry's 'avin a kip on the side. But it's just to get rid of the eyesores. (p. 95)

Morrie is unstoppable. He next appears as "the greatest salesman of them all, Maurice the Supreme Wrangler." His high-pressure salesmanship in black-market hosiery, besides making him rich, leads to the peerage he gets in *Magog* (1972). His continuing insistence that his racketeering merely follows the example of his government is too modestly put. By thriving while his countrymen suffer, Sir Morrie Mowler of Bethnal Green proves himself a first-rate reconstructionist. And his philosophy of material self-interest outdoes the policies of Whitehall. He exploits people for profit without a grain of remorse. This easy adjustment to an economy created largely by American capital shows real wit. The prizes follow logically enough. Nor do they stop with money and public honor. Echoing Shaw's Alfred Doolittle and any number of rich businessmen in Henry James, Morrie uses money to break down British class insularity. He marries Merry, mother of Gog and Magog, and then becomes Magog's business partner. By the end of *Magog*, he is enmeshed with the British power structure.

A more spectacular plunderer than Morrie Mowler is the

satyrlike Crook, whom Gog meets in chapter 11. Animist and primitive, Crook stands as a rural counterpart to the Cockney spiv. His resemblance to a horse calls to mind the natural enmity between the griffin and the horse. His ability to make Gog act against principle objectifies Gog's base lust, weakness of will, and, it turns out, enslavement to Maire. Like the golden-eyed Maire, Crook has a tremendous animal fascination for Gog. Athletic, strong, and smoothly coordinated, his golden-haired body and brown, leather-wrapped legs do anything he asks. When he sees something he wants, he goes after it as ruthlessly as Maire, the novel's other arch-sensualist. The name of this killer and tupper of sheep suggests a shepherd, but a shepherd gone wrong. And his horselike look recalls the horselike name (Maire-mare) of the novel's only other bisexual character and the only other character but one who has sex with Gog in the course of the book.

Chapter 12, where Crook dominates, takes place in a forest. Decay, both moral and physical, pervades the haunted wood. Crook snaps a ram's spine and eats the raw flesh. Then Gog, morally opposed to the killing of animals for food, tastes the raw meat and likes it. Gog follows Crook hopelessly through the chapter. Crook rapes a servant-girl in a forest litter of lice, rotting wood, and toadstools. Not content to degrade her ("I've 'ad 'er every way there is. An' some there isn't."), he also mars her with scratches, bruises, and welts. His association with rot and with greenery that jabs and scrapes gives the lie to Gog's naive Wordsworthian idealism. The countryside contains as much evil as Magog's metropolis. Nor is Crook the only evil woodlander. Gog, who calls the episode "his fall and degradation," also has sex both with the servant-girl and, in his sleep, with Crook. And the chapter includes "a carnival of coupling" in the Gothic fretwork of a summerhouse in which Maire and her lesbian chauffeur, Julia, play sadistic sex games. This rampaging lust, embodied by Crook yet heightened by Gog's share of madness, rules out England's countryside as a source of moral goodness and strength. The whiff of decay stays with us. Lacking the restraints and refinements of civilization, rural England threatens all who go there.

But Crook's danger, urgent as it is, occupies only one chapter. Maire, accompanied by Julia-Jules, follows Gog everywhere in her black limousine. Clad always in black and white, symbolizing her stark rapacity, Maire calls herself "a woman of my time." But her destructive boredom outdoes that of Hedda Gabler, T. S. Eliot's lady at the dressing table in *The Waste Land*, and Ford Madox Ford's Sylvia Tietjens (*Parade's End*). She cadges extra ration cards, trades on the black market, and cheats at every game she plays. An old friend says, "Maire never pays if she loses a bet," and Maire admits, "You can't beat me at games of chance because I never give anyone any." Her favorite pastime and weapon are sex; she enjoys sex and she enjoys withholding it. Though Gog tends to forgive her and yield to her, his heart knows that his search for selfhood excludes her. He says, "Maire. . . . Do you know the old English word for a woman was a mare? And you're a nightmare. Always springing on me as I sleep." He might have added that Maire sounds the same as *la mer*, the French word for the sea, source of life and universal female symbol. Gog's half-French wife is prime womanhood—destructive and treacherous, yet also fascinating and life-giving. But, sealike, she must be avoided in favor of the moors, downs, and limestone of the mainland. Her repeated demand that Gog ride to London with her in the Black Maria rather than walk invites at least two different readings: she craves his body, which explains her cruelty to him when resisted, or, on a larger scale, she represents the lure of a foreign tie that beckons England, a nation of joiners, but that, being foreign, must be rejected. The English Channel both joins and separates female France and John Bull. England's postwar problems are largely internal. Giving into Maire, symbolic protector of the unborn, would rob Gog of the independence and self-reliance needed to do his man's work.

II

Gog's struggles against Maire and the others all combine in his opposition to Magog, who not only lives with Marie but may also have fathered her twin daughters. Gog and Magog are obverses, temperamentally opposed but metaphysically linked, caught in an eternal battle but joined forever. Gog, the gentle giant, upholds traditional ideas of honor, friendship, and natural process in a world shot through with expediency. Magog represents selfish power and London, the hub of British policy-making. Gog's frontispiece map pictures London as the fanged red mouth of a carnivorous fish. Red is also, along with black, Magog's color and the symbol of British imperialism. (England's former colonies, like Australia, India, and Canada, still appear as red on most maps; the imperial rallying cry, "Paint the globe red!" describes the gory process by which England got and then controlled her colonies.)

England's color is white. William Blake colored Albion white in his prophetic books. There are also the white cliffs of Dover and the chalky subsoil of the downland. In the prologue, Gog rides up to the shingle on the backs of white-collared waves. The first word in chapter 1, describing his hospital room, is *White; Magog* ends with the massive rock concert of August 1970 on the Isle of Wight (White). But if whiteness gauges the English experience, then Magog's London must have a share. Sinclair mixes his colors beautifully: he combines Whitehall, the seat of government, with the red symbolism of Magog, Whitehall's most ambitious servant, in a triptych of which the blue of the surrounding sea both forms the missing panel and completes the Union Jack tricolor. This color symbolism carries into the political realities of the postwar world in *Magog:* in 1963 a backlash of British imperialism installs a black baby in the cradle of an old and prominent Leicestershire family. The event, crafted discreetly by Sinclair, evokes England's guilty past in Africa, the emergence of the Third World, and a haunting primitive retribution.

This weft of narrative threads shows how a good writer can intertwine his materials. For the color symbolism, like everything else in the duology, owes its life to the Gog-Magog opposition. This opposition returns in the Arab-Israeli War; in Maire's twins, Rosa and Josepha; and curiously, in the one-eyed heroes, Admiral Nelson and General Dyan. Gog's greatest fear is blindness. Unfortunately, the fear never leaves him for long. A gypsy he fights recalls Cyclops after God closes one of his eyes; like him, Magog can see out of only one eye at the start of *Magog*. Whatever this train of semi-blindness means, it does express Sinclair's situational social philosophy: nothing has a fixed value. To adopt blindness as a business policy invites ruin; yet turning a blind eye—overlooking human failings and making allowances for people—is the best policy to extend to one's family and friends. Gog must learn that power and personal salvation exist inversely.

This truth informs his relationship with his bastard half-brother. Magog tells Gog at a threatening moment, "Spare me, for you cannot live without me." His plea has merit. Gog does not so much need to destroy Magog as to restrain him: "Let Magog be," he says in chapter 11. "He is my servant. And he will be a good servant. Only as a master is he evil." This judgment defines Magog as the Jungian shadow, or devil, who must be indulged so that he can be known and controlled. Magog, though, called by his mother, "a pompous little ass on the make," resists controls. Yet even after he has done his worst, Gog sees him as a "mocking caricature of himself." The tie between the brothers never weakens. Both confess having failed to revive England after World War II; Gog's withdrawal to the wastes of northern Scotland brings no more promise than Magog's plunge into public life. Magog's quick deterioration after Gog's death surprises while it convinces.

The common story of Gog and Magog has deep roots in English history. London's Guildhall contains hugh effigies of the mythical giants, built in 1953 to replace the ones burned in a 1940 air-raid; these, installed in 1708, replaced the statues that burned in the Great Fire of 1666. Nearly all the accounts of their exploits stress the interdependence of the giants. The excavations of T. C. Lethbridge, a modern archaeologist, reveal Gogmagog, the wicked monster of Albion, as a composite being, fusing God, a sun god and "the force at the back of all things," with Magog, "the great Mother, the Earth Goddess."[4]

---

4. T. C. Lethbridge, *Gogmagog: The Buried Gods* (London: Routledge & Kegan Paul, 1957), pp. 166, 93.

The Bible (Ezekiel 38 and 39 and Revelation 20) makes them the evil precursors of the end of the earth. Ezekiel, though, omitting Magog, promises renewal. Although Gog carries out God's revenge against the wicked Israelites, his defeat seven years later restores the holy commonwealth. The *Recuyell of the Histories of Troy* presents Gog and Magog as the survivors of a race of giants. After their brothers and sisters fall in battle, they come to London (Troynovant or New Troy) to serve as gatekeepers at the royal palace of Brut(e), grandson of Aeneas and founder of London. Geoffrey of Monmouth's *History of the Kings of Britain* (1:16) also links the myth to the reign of Brut. Enfleshing the brothers in one skin, it portrays Gogmagog as an evil giant who gets thrown off a Cornish cliff by one of Brut's generals.

Sinclair's portrait of the half-brothers retains their Englishness and their violent, apocalyptic aura. Like Shakespeare's bastards, Magog is wily and treacherous. Born in 1919, out of the waste and bloodshed of World War II, he grew up in the home of his adoptive parents, the wealthy Pononsbys of Leicestershire. Whereas Gog fights and suffers alone, Magnus Pononsby works through helpers and takes many forms. A radio broadcast warns of the cancerous spread of his power:

> Magog . . . ? In London? He is here. Everywhere. He wants to kill me. To kill us. Daily. In the farm. In the factory. He is there. Magog is. In the plough that crushes your foot. In the lathe that takes off your thumb. . . . His machines can kill you as you tend them. (p. 151)

M stands for Machine, Murder, Metamorphosis (because of Magog's many masks), and (owing to Magog's city-base) Mammon. Aides like Maire, Morrie Mowler, and Professor Miniver also take Magog's initial. The alliterative phrase from *Magog*, "materials for a mediocre memorial to muddle and muck," signals things gone wrong. Suitably, the date is 1951, time of the Festival of Britain and of Magog's first big political gains. The festival thus aligns with Magog's career, a career that includes spiritual as well as secular power. Gog calls the

Durham Cathedral "Magog's house": "The whole shape of the cathedral is the one distorted initial of Magog." Gog finds Magog's handiwork and helpers everywhere. The symbolic struggle of Gog and Magog to restore Zion to Albion takes place in the last chapter. The novel, we recall, begins on VE-Day and ends on VJ-Day. The day the Allies defeat Japan also happens to be the day Gog and Magog have made a date for lunch in a London chophouse. The coincidence is planned. For London is sometimes Jerusalem, sometimes Sodom and Gomorrah. His homecoming in chapter 34 finds Gog lulled and indifferent—"a middle-aged rich man, who has burned his books so that he cannot even teach, who has forgotten nearly all he knows and is too tired and disengaged to care about a future that is nothing to him but the repetitions of the aimless moments." His blood needs freshening. What plucks him finally from his moral stupor is the lunch date with Magog. After several exchanges of insults, Gog overturns a table of food on Magog's elegant new suit. The combined fight and chase that follow confuse present time, chronicle, and myth. To execute the book's form and purpose, the moving battle carries into caves and tunnels, the Houses of Parliament, and Westminster Abbey. Gog and Magog race down London's sunny streets while newsboys announce Japan's overthrow and the end of the war. Most of the book's main characters come back briefly while the half-brothers roil and roughhouse through the city, take a tube train, and then turn up in the underground studios of the BBC.

The chase tallies well with the prophecy in Revelation, with the destruction of Hiroshima and Nagasaki, and also with Gog's former research project and obsession—the history of Gog and Magog from the founding of Albion to the death of England. England's leading public institutions rush in and out of view. After Gog and Magog land mysteriously on the porch of Somerset House, they appear in St. Stephen's Hall, where the Commons are commemorating the war's end. Meanwhile, Sinclair has broken the chase several times to give us a guided tour of the smashed cityscape, to describe a historic interior or two, and to survey a political career. These digressions, while undercutting suspense, link the preservation of Britain's values and institutions with the outcome of the half-brother's fight. The fight lifts Gog out of the bog of Parliamentary rhetoric and also out of his indifference. On the book's last page, he is standing at a crossroads deciding whether to go back to Maire or to take the Great North Road to the bleak, bitter north. The novel ends like Joyce's *Portrait,* Sillitoe's *Saturday Night and Sunday Morning,* and Fowles's *The Magus*—just when its main character chooses a plan of action and matching route of travel. Whatever he decides, his choice will rest on a new awareness of personal sanctity. If the new Israel is to come, it must take as its watchwords kindness, mercy, and the sacredness of the individual. Gog does not leave us without first scoring a private victory as great as the military one being celebrated throughout London:

> While the drunken people of London pad and roar like a great beast about Gog, he knows himself a man at last. . . . He knows that the Gog before the war is forever dead and gone. For he loves the people no longer, they are the mob and the rabble. He loves persons, perhaps, if he can find persons to love. Even his arch-enemy, Magnus and Magog, why, he's a man, he bleeds like any other, he must be saved like each victim. (p. 447)

Gog's revelation, persuasive both as rhetoric and as human insight, has a sour ring, artistically speaking. His rescue of Magog from the drunken, murderous Londoners does show the reveling townsfolk as "a great beast." But the idea of collective man's bestiality is not fresh enough to crown a long, complex novel, especially since Sinclair's setting-forth of the idea adds nothing to Shakespeare's, Dryden's, or Burke's.

Gog's recognition both of Magog as a fellow-sufferer and of his interdependence with Magog has no more force. Although the recognition does pierce a wall of mass hysteria, it merely tells Gog what he already knows. Besides, his habit of extending charity to oppressors like Maire and Magog has hurt, not helped, him in the past. What he needs is a strengthening of will, not a softening. His failure to convert recognition to resolve will permeate *Magog*. Gog feels uncomfortable in this sequel. He leaves the action for seventy-five to a hundred pages at a spell; none of his efforts touches anybody, least of all Magog, whom he now befriends; his suicide voyage into the North Sea is ludicrous.

III

Gog is a gusty book—crowded, violent, and repetitive; the Bagman and Evans the Latin both pop up everywhere with the same thundering prophecies. Sinclair has a bloody imagination. When his characters are not preaching chaos, they are brawling. Although the war is over, fighting is still the norm of British conduct; there are pub fights, sado-masochist sexual bouts, a vaudeville boxing match, and battle scenes from movies in addition to the long chase sequence at the end. Fights rage without the fighters knowing the issues, what side they are on, or the identity of the winners and losers.

Though calamity throngs the book, Sinclair's theme does not drown in a sea of gore. *Gog* has a craggy, jut-boned form, which, while lacking artistic finish, coheres around a recognizable structure: motive underlies event, and events depend on earlier ones. The end of chapter 18 marks the book's halfway point. In this chapter Gog breaks his pilgrimage to visit York Minster church. But the church materializes as Magog's temple—not so much a shrine dedicated to Magog as the embodiment of him. He mocks and perverts all the virtues celebrated in the Five Sisters Window—Love, Faith, Charity, Meekness, and Understanding. This expansion of Magog's power to the religious sphere lends Gog's pilgrimage metaphysical force and gives the second half of the novel a strong start. The chair of sudden reversals that follow continues to involve the reader. Gog steals Maire's car, but his triumph curdles immediately when he runs the car into a ditch. Maire and Julia, wearing hospital uniforms, then kidnap him at gunpoint. His meteoric career as boxing champion, Robin Hood, and Dick Turpin ends with his being driven south from York in a stolen ambulance. Called in the first paragraph of chapter 19 "the sprawling Gogling," he has reverted to the helpless, sea-wracked infant of the prologue. Sinclair's delaying most of the novel's exposition until this point, the first chapter of the second half, shows skill in narrative structuring. While giving the novel the look of starting over, the device, first, suggests a pattern of cyclical renewal and, next, reinforces the aims of Gog's quest. Everything and nothing have changed, but Gog will never be the same.

Rivaling this two-part structure is a three-part division that breaks at chapters 12 and 24. Chapter 12 is where Gog meets Crook, spies on Maire and Julia clawing each other, and watches an orgy of sado-masochism involving androgynes, hermaphodites, and transvestites of all ages. These events—a long dream—fuse Gog's own impulses with those of the English, once God's holy people. His nightmare passage through the rank wood of brute sensuality, a necessary step in his search for self-being, ends with his wearing a red tie, green sweater, and brown suit in place of the drab khaki drill he has stolen in chapter 1. Another nicety of narrative design comes in Gog's visit in chapter 13 to Durham Cathedral; his movement from rank carnality to spirit proves that the lesson of chapter 12 has taken hold. Chapter 24, repeating the forest setting of chapter 12, also collects, assimilates, and then redistributes several of the novel's main subjects.

Here, chance leads Gog to his mother, Merry, and her latest lover, a half-German, half-English hunting fanatic named Otto. Otto's love of hunting points up the sport's bloody cruelty. Interlacing his motifs adroitly, Sinclair shows British imperialism as the offspring of the national British mania for the hunt: "The vision of hunters with shotguns stalking the crust of the globe confuses in Gog's mind with the vision of the red area of the British empire spreading its stain over the same crust." England's blood-hunger for colonies, looking back thematically to Gog's eating of raw meat in chapter 12, peaks in a debate over the sporting nature of the hunt. Taking charge, Gog, the protector of natural growth, chases Otto to a derelict tower, which collapses on them both. The air again is rancid. But whereas the rankness of chapter 12 came from animal, vegetable, and moral decay; here in chapter 24 the rottenness comes from the tower. Less busy than its counterpart, chapter 24 has a wider thematic range. The tower incident recalls chapter 20, where Evans's library caves in on Gog, and looks ahead to the pursuit in chapter 36. Chapters 20 through 24 show Gog scrambling, fetuslike, out of caves of rubble and debris. His defiance of his mother's lover (*The Ascent of F6* is mentioned) shows a new readiness and toughness. Gog's aggressiveness strenghtens him. In the next chapter (chapter 25) "Gog discovers that he is becoming a new man. Without his noticing, his walk has hardened his body and is healing the dark wounds of his mind." A final structural masterstroke comes in the unstated tension Sinclair sets up between the rural settings of chapters 12 and 24 and the urban setting of chapter 36. Crawling or walking, in country or in town, Gog has acquired the grip to cope with any kind of problem.

This powerful inclusiveness is pitted by two flaws—a casual acceptance of the fantastic and a reliance upon contrivances to steer the plot. Just when hunger seizes Gog in chapter 3, a stranded knapsack of food turns up. In chapter 9 he eavesdrops on a conversation that slants the Gog-Magog legend to the ongoing action. Sinclair's tactic of channeling his legendary data through his hero, so that Gog lives and learns about his heritage at the same time, is a good one. And admittedly, the legendary data need to be made individual and dramatic if we are to feel their impact. What disturbs is the scene's lack of technique. Sinclair makes no concession to realism: the characters—the two speakers and the listening Gog—are too obviously posed, and the related information is too obviously unloaded for the reader's benefit.

Still more damaging is Sinclair's practice of explaining away Gog's adventures on the road as dreams or visions. Sinclair resorts to the practice, to begin with, because dreams allow for inclusiveness without discrediting the realistic story line. Gog passes into "a nightmare trance" at the start of chapter 5, where the sheep-butchering takes place. Sinclair then says of a forest elf who twice tries to kill Gog, "Perhaps he only existed in Gog's mind." The novel's danger sequences contain some of Sinclair's best effects. But his practice of calling them dreams blunts their thrust. Cut off from the realm of shareable experience, they lead to nothing and mean nothing. The reader feels most put upon at the start of chapter 34. The diction of the first page of this chapter, we have noticed, nearly matches that of chapter 1, except that Gog, instead of being hospitalized, is now resting in his Hampstead bedroom. Maire's saying that he was driven home from Edinburgh while unconscious means that the events of chapters 1 through 33 may have never happened. Sinclair's introducing this possibility undermines our faith so much that he never wins it back for the closing chapters.

Gog is an uneven book. If our imaginative commitment to the plot flags, our senses reel at the whirligigs and gyrations of the style. The craggy, thickly worked sentences of *Gog* make the book a moving feast of language, but the reader is overwhelmed, not entertained or instructed, by the verbal bombardment. Sinclair makes language do more than impart information, tell a story, and build a mood. Many passages from the duology are not novelistic. Rather than building a tight, consecutive narrative, Sinclair will often smuggle in details of British history, landscape, or society. These set pieces, besides celebrating England's heritage, give him the chance to display the glories of English prose. What they forfeit in narrative continuity they recover in beauty and power. A prose poem on the London docks, "the muddy ditch from where England had grown to Empire," with their iron cranes, weathered warehouses, and banging barges, lets Sinclair vent his stylistic powers to the full. His rich, ornate syntax moves freely from the city to the country, from the colloquial to the abstract, and from the literary to the conversational. Like Gog himself, the book's style is hewn out of English granite. Sinclair seems equally at home with Cockney argot, the clipped Northumbrian dialect, and the strong, simple cadences of the Bible. He responds freshly to the outdoors—to the play of light on landscape, the textured greenery, the sough of breezes through high grass. Like Whitman, he gives existence to dappled, waving, growing things by simply naming them:

> From the ridge of the Larriston Fells . . . only a hidden train disturbs the smooth contours of the flattened hills beyond with its poplar of smoke. The track winds on over the saddle of the fells between bile-green moss on quaking bogs. Fern crawls over the brown marsh on curling feet, sundew stretches up its sticky spades covered with hair to trap insects in its lime, and a single butterwort here and there holds up one purple flower on a long frail stalk. (p. 71)

Throughout, Sinclair's language keeps pace with his powers of observation. The image of a fox escaping his cage as a "red brush whisking into the nettles of a ditch" imbues Sinclair's lyricism with motion, delicacy of touch, and animal eagerness. But his prose can also generate both mass and humor. Chapter 13 begins with a 222-word, one-sentence description of a moving train. Gog's fight with the Mumping Mugger (another M-named character) in chapter 17 gives a panorama of British boxing; as the style takes on the idiom of the sporting journals of the past, Gog invokes comparisons with England's great ex-prizefighters. Late in the bout "Gog manages to darken his [opponent's] left peeper in a scientific manner," and, in the next round, "stops his [opponent's] career." The Joycean humor of the passage builds to a near-mythical inclusiveness. But it also fends off longwindedness. Sinclair has no patience with the longwinded, the stuffy, and the self-important. To maintain proper human balance, he will deflate the heroic and the grandiose with the mundane. The movie *The Battle of Hastings* ends thus:

> And so, the lovers rode off into the greenwood, where the beauteous Hilda would bear a son, named . . . (SUSPENSE) Robin Hood! And King William, now called the Conqueror,

rode to London Town to build a Mighty England for Robin's
Merrie Men!
SOUND OF SEVENTY PIECE STRING ORCHESTRA
PLAYING "HAPPY DAYS ARE HERE AGAIN."
THE END (p. 55)

Accordingly, a homey detail will puncture the booming oratory
of the Bagman and Evans the Latin. A few well-placed scraps
of language from modern advertising can give the lie to the
most urgent-end-of-the-world warning:

ALL THOSE WHO BELIEVE THAT THE ABOVE IS
THE REVEALED TRUTH WHICH IT SURELY IS
ARE REQUESTED TO SEND DONATIONS TO WAY-
LAND MERLIN BLAKE SMITH . . . NO CHEQUES
PLEASE. GIVE AND IT SHALL BE GIVEN UNTO
YOU. DON'T *YOU* WANT TO SEE JERUSALEM
BUILT IN ALBION'S SACRED LAND? DON'T
WAIT—SEND YOUR MITE OR MINT *NOW!* (p. 26)

The novel needs more of this verbal irony to act as a control.
Bergonzi's complaint, *"Gog* is radically undisciplined and very
prolix over large areas, and I dislike its dwelling on violence,"[5]
sums up the book's faults. At one point, Gog "begins squirm-
ing, worming, storming, stalking, walking, baulking, bucking,
mucking his way up the great pothole of red rubble above
him." The description shows bad taste. The parade of
participles—adding nothing to Gog's situation and failing to
present Gog more clearly—needs trimming. That Sinclair
happened to think of it, that it amused him, and that he could
not resist the joggling repetition—these reasons do not warrant
the passage's inclusion. Sinclair's prose may do what he asks of
it, but sometimes he asks the wrong things.

IV

Less robust, wildly artificial, and fantastic than its predecessor, *Magog* (1972) profits from the five years' interval between

---

5. Bergonzi, p. 78.

its publication and *Gog's*. The style has a new concision, clarity, and control. Its impact is not additive, as in *Gog*, but detonative, relying on the quick release of a sharp sensory image: Sinclair calls an Arabian dawn "as perfect as postage stamps," and then says of a loris, "Its little buttocks were two mute curves of abandoned hope." These metaphors have a new boldness and ease: Magog notes of Maire, "Her breasts were two hot puppies against his jacket. There was no backing from their teasing." Sinclair has also learned how to put his metaphors into verbs, one of the most effective and most difficult stylistic graces: "He [the manager of a Beirut hotel] was too fat and wore a red fez. Late nights had sooted the lids of his sunken eyes."

This stylistic growth is not paid for with a weakening of purpose. Sinclair is still concerned with his society's roots and with where his society is going. His subject is futility: the failure of the generation that came to power after World War II. His focus is Magog's London from 1945–1970—the worlds of politics and business and the upper-bohemian world of arts, letters, and higher education. The book's pattern is that of social comedy. Thus the language of *Magog* has more sting and snap than that of *Gog*, and the proportion of dialogue to narration runs higher.

The book opens with Magog, the youngest Assistant Secretary in the Ministry of Resources and Development, applying a slab of raw steak to the black eye he got in the closing chapter of *Gog*. It is still VJ-Day. He is living with Maire, and, though he has no delusions about her lies and betrayals, loves her hopelessly. Bright, dapper, and conniving as ever, he gets little joy from the race for power. He finds the arts of peace harder to master than those of war. He hears in the first chapter, "The war's over, Magog. You can't lie and call it the national interest any more." Life lacks cohesion: Europe has no leader; Britain's economy still sags; forced to decolonize, the nation has shrunk from Empire to Commonwealth; further national intimidation comes from being located midway between the U.S. and Russia, the world's two feuding nuclear powers. Like England, Magog never gets his bearings in the postwar world. The strain of living with Maire and the cut-and-thrust of negotiation both overwhelm him. His decisions haunt him. A good example of this comes in 1946: the wily bureaucrat does not know what to do with several large drums of nerve gas left over from the war. Finally dumped off the Irish coast, the drums decompose and leak their poison in 1970. The same waters that Magog poisons, Gog tries to farm. His sea farm on a loch makes him, not Magog, the hope of the future. Yet, as has been said, he does not fit into the novel's plot. Nor does his death convince dramatically. Sinclair surrounds his suicide voyage aboard the dinghy *Blake* with so many literary allusions that it defies belief as a human event.

Gog's not-belonging is the book's only major flaw. Anthony Thwaite carps when he calls *Magog* "a febrile, self-indulgent, opinionated, and finally rather squalidly boring fling at the picaresque, written in a variety of styles . . . none of which carry much conviction."[6] Avoiding mythical heights, *Magog* scales its effects down from those of *Gog;* its title character, while consistent with the Magog of the earlier book, comfortably sustains his assigned weight; with him in the narrative picture at all times, the story line moves well.

After dumping the surplus nerve gas, Magog illegally licenses Morrie Mowler to sell weapons to Israel. Although acquitted in a formal hearing, he leaves the Ministry to head the Film Productions Finance Guild. His answer to the problems crippling England's cinema industry, so expressive of his negativism, is to stop making movies:

The way to get the film industry back to health is to stop making films. Let other countries make films and lose their money. We will show the films they make and take our cut. . . . But no more films! By ruthless economy, we can save our cinemas.[7]

6. Anthony Thwaite, "The Great British Novel—as if there weren't lots of them," *New York Times* Book Review, 2 July 1972, p. 7.
7. Andrew Sinclair, *Magog* (New York: Harper & Row, 1972), p. 73. Subsequent page references will be to this edition and found in parentheses following quoted extracts.

Magog invests his salary as a film mogul in real estate. These investments work out well. Permit-fixing, the buying of material and machinery on the black market, and the heartless eviction of tenants earn him a fortune. "True creativity lay in mortar and bricks" is a creed he follows as he mars the face of London with ugly office blocks. As has been said, England tailspins during Magog's heyday. Sinclair records the impact of the Suez Crisis, the devaluation of the pound, decolonization, the death of "the people's man," Nye Bevan, in 1960, and, finally, the Christine Keeler-Profumo scandal. Frightened by England's ruin, Magog leaves the business world. He commissions a series of essays on British anthropology that he publishes as his own book and then uses as leverage to become Master of the College of Charles the Martyr, a new Cambridge college.

But his administrative talents do not adapt to Cambridge's pure air. The breaking of his academic career on a local political issue changes his life for good. Gog, we remember, has the courage, crotchets, and animal stupidity of the British peasant; we can love him and laugh at him simultaneously. Yet, in the mid-1960s, our hearts open to the sleek, power-grabbing Magog. A shadow-cabinet of tutors, resenting his manipulative politics, uses his daughter-niece's student radicalism to weaken his power within the college. The expression of normal human impulse, that is, his love for Josepha, costs him his high office. He sees that the scramble for money and power forbids the outgoings of love. But he also sees the emptiness of these prizes when they are not shared. A pathetic rascal, he has traded success for decency, faith, and love. "Bored and idle in the cage of every day," he comes to see everything he has valued and worked for go sour on him:

I have nothing. No love, no respect, no wife, no daughters, no sons, no ties with my brother or my mother, nothing at all. I have some money and less power, both of which I lose more of every year along with my hair and my health. I have no glory, no thanks, and thus no mercy on those who wish to take away the little I have. Why the hell don't you let me die away in peace? (p. 231)

But his salvation depends on his giving up more than money and power, hair and health. He must throw away everything, including his security and self-respect, for the promise of becoming human. In 1969, he nurses Rosa, Josepha's twin, back to health and then becomes her lover. This surrender to his starved lust uproots him from his society, his received ideas about incest, and, most important of all, from himself. After clutching at power for most of his fifty years, he gives in completely to Rosa, who ignores him, exploits him, and sleeps with other men. This conduct scourges him. But it also purifies him. While he comes to hate his crawling, cringing ways, he learns the value of powerlessness, even of nobodiness. He welcomes his moral degradation. The eminently human process by which victory and defeat trade places uncovers new corners in his psyche:

> For days on end, Magog could feel a humble pride in himself at his acceptance of every wrong that Rosa could do to him. This was a full expiation of his incest. Above all, this was the denial of his life of ambition and intrigue. Power had corrupted him, had perhaps corrupted him absolutely, but in that absolute corruption lay the birth of a strange purity. . . . It was merely unfortunate that the lusts of the body lasted longer than the mind wished them to last. Or perhaps these idiotic appetites that would not die provided the humiliations that led a man stumbling towards wisdom. (pp. 301–302)

The book's finale finds Magog in a situation resembling Gog's at the start of *Gog*. Surrounded by pullulating youth and jolted by wild, percussive music, he staggers semi-consciously through the August 1970 Isle of Wight rock concert. On an island, he becomes an island himself by virtue of his sadness, apartness from the audience, and self-estrangement. Neither Gog on his Scottish loch nor Magog on his Channel isle is at home in England. Yet each is resoundingly English. Outsiders both, they constitute the English experience. To be a lonely, stranded island is the English norm. The growing alienation of the champion of the people and of the urban technocrat occurs in an upside-down world. The shrewd, conniving Maire is outwitted several times by her children. A visit to a retired Anglo-African couple finds the couple, who later die violently, haunted by Africa. The red stain of Empire has fouled the British bloodstream: "That's the trouble," says the old Africa hand, speaking of the dark continent's revenge. "You think Blighty's where you want to be, but when you get home, you're still back in Africa. It's got a hold. . . . You know, sometimes I'm not sure who took over, our chaps or the blacks. I mean, once you've been there, everything's somehow Africa." The upshot of this primitive retribution, we have seen, includes the Pononsbys' adoption of Rosa's half-black child.

The structure of the novel contains this upside-downness. Scenes snap off; plans either misfire or recoil; Magog's first outgoing act costs him the only job he ever enjoyed. The novel recounts the overnight death of authority in 1968 France. Yet the champion of the resurgence symbolized by this student revolt is murdered at age twenty-two; her death, moreover, is introduced casually, in a dependent clause: "Magog never saw the gunman who killed Josepha." Josepha's twin, Rosa, overturns her possible identity as Magog's daughter to become his symbolic mother. But this creator of new life, unlike most mother figures, gives herself an abortion and then has her ovaries cut out.

These reversals stabilize in the Jerusalem paradigm: all the characters and institutions feel the pull of the Golden Age. The founding of Zion or the New Jerusalem gains voice in a radio broadcast on the novel's first page. The goal of the worldwide movement known as the Children's Crusade, which begins in 1968, is the founding of another Promised Land. One character, writing the same year, says, "Havana is already halfway to Jerusalem." The lure of the Holy Land is magnetic, and there are as many Holy Lands as there are dreamers who wish them into life. Whereas Zion only beckoned to zealots like Evans,

the Bagman, and Gog in *Gog*, in *Magog* it snares everybody.
Magog models the college he founds on the Dome of the Rock
of Jerusalem. Gog, having lost faith in starting a people's government, now searches for the New Jerusalem below the sea:

> Gog knew that Britain's way no longer lay on the surface of
> the waters. The rule of the air and of space was too costly,
> while the land was being taken back by those who lived
> upon it from the spoilers who had spread over the seas in
> their ships of wood and iron. The last empire, the third
> empire of Britain, could only be found in the maw of the
> ocean, with its sunken territories unmapped, unmined, un-
> tenanted, a drowned and weedy Atlantis of infinite food and
> riches, waiting for the first nation to lift up its treasures. (p.
> 126)

Even nations join the pilgrimage. England's fight for identity
in postwar Europe occurs alongside the birth-pangs of Israel.
Fellow questers for Zion, the two nations league politically,
militarily, and economically. The new Jewish state, further-
more, with its overseas markets, has already fallen into the
destructive pattern of imperial England. Magog, fearing that
Israel will overreach herself as England did, warns an Israeli
friend, "I don't want Israel to become a little British Empire.
. . . It's better than that. It's Zion, the Light of the World, or
should be." The warning is ignored. Israel's big European drug
combine reflects a corruption resembling not only that of Victorian England, when the moral need for decolonization first became vivid, but also that of early Britain, the first holy land on
earth before she sinned. But no matter. The moment Israel's
quest for blessedness stops, any number of nations will take her
place. The search for the lost Jerusalem is eternal, inevitable,
and, in the full range of ramifications, tragic.

Magog is more than a footnote to *Gog*. Its hard clarity lends
balance and variety to the Joycean excavations of *Gog*. At the
same time, the English question, the family drama, and the
expanded quest—all repeated from *Gog*—build a powerful unity. The *Gog/Magog* duology stands alongside the more serious
sequence novels to come out of postwar England.

12

The Four-Gaited Beast of the
Apocalypse: Doris Lessing's
The Four-Gated City (1969)

FREDERICK R. KARL

The classical experience of madness is born [in the 17th and 18th centuries]. The great threat that dawned on the horizon of the fifteenth century subsides, the disturbing powers that inhabit Bosch's painting have lost their violence. Forms remain, now transparent and docile, forming a cortège, the inevitable procession of reason. Madness has ceased to be—at the limits of the world, of man and death—an eschatological figure; the darkness has dispersed on which the eyes of madness were fixed and out of which the forms of the impossible were born. Oblivion falls upon the world navigated by the free slaves of the Ship of Fools. Madness will no longer proceed from a point within the world to a point beyond, on its strange voyage; it will never again be that fugitive and absolute limit. Behold it moored now, made fast among things and men. Retained and maintained. No longer a ship but a hospital. (p. 35)

Confinement was an institutional creation peculiar to the seventeenth century. It acquired from the first an importance that left it no rapport with imprisonment as practiced in the

Middle Ages. As an economic measure and a social precaution, it had the value of inventiveness. But in the history of unreason, it marked a decisive event: the moment when madness was perceived on the social horizon of poverty, of incapacity for work, of inability to integrate with the group; the moment when madness began to rank among the problems of the city. The new meanings assigned to poverty, the importance given to the obligation to work, and all the ethical values that are linked to labor, ultimately determined the experience of madness and inflected its course. (pp. 63–64)

The sensibility that informs Doris Lessing's *The Four-Gated City* (1969) finds some of its theoretical counterpart in these quotations from Michel Foucault's *Madness and Civilization* (1961, 1965). Not unusually, a novelist who tries to capture the sense of the 1950s and 60s as Doris Lessing does must come to terms with mad individuals, a mad society, a sick world. For in those two decades, even seen from the English point of view, the lines between health and sickness never seemed more blurred. Foucault's insights are especially valuable in that he views the history of madness within a thick social fabric in Western history. Comparably, Doris Lessing's long and ambitious novel (well over one-quarter of a million words) is an attempt to understand madness as part of a sociopolitical world and not simply in terms of the individual and his problems.

For those readers who have followed Lessing through the first four volumes of "The Children of Violence" series,[1] *The Four-Gated City,* the fifth and final volume of a twenty-year enterprise, appears unrelated. The earlier volumes were concerned with Martha Quest, with Martha's quest for political sanity, marital content, social equilibrium. She had questions about everything, and actively sought answers. Our image was of a woman struggling to assert herself, refusing the easy assumptions of her society about female roles and the expecta-

---

1. *Martha Quest* (1952), *A Proper Marriage* (1954), *A Ripple from the Storm* (1958), and *Landlocked* (1965).

tions of her male admirers. Moving from her provincial South African background through each new layer of society, Martha sought to confront the worst in man in order to discover the best. If the above description fits both the individual and historical matter of the first four volumes, the final volume appears to diverge radically, shifting from the external world of "mad" politics to an internal, individual world in which all resonances float within the human psyche. Collective insanity is now encapsulated in individual madness. Whereas before Martha's quest was for political and social values by which she could live, now her quest is for some personal way that shuts out and excludes the external world.

Early in the novel, Martha comes to the house of Mark Coldridge, a writer and scion of a well-known English family. His house is one of the four that appear repeatedly in the novel, each with its own kind of gate, four houses with four gates that are microcosms of English society, and, inevitably, of the world as Lessing envisages it. It is a society that follows the holocaust of the Second World War, and that immediately precedes the apocalyptic vision that ends our present notion of the world and the book. Yeats's rough beast has arrived; the 2,000-year cycle has entered a new phase.

Whereas once gates were entrances that one opened while seeking something or someone, they are now barriers that close off exits or prevent egress. The four bleak houses of England are the restaurant at the beginning, where Martha would be "Mattie" (a good fellow) and would be expected to lose herself in a dull marriage; second, the house of Mark Coldridge, a writer somewhat close to the center of power, but besieged by predatory journalists and a locus of madness, inactivity, frustration, as well as some kindness; third, Jack's house—literally, that Jack built—where girls go to be broken in for their future as prostitutes, where Jack sits like a spider catching them on the fly; and, finally, Paul's house—Paul is Mark's nephew, whose father has defected to Russia—where derelicts and misfits, sexual cripples and the maimed, as in some James Purdy story, congregate under Paul's protective wing.

Yet there is still another house, or at least another gate to another city that will not be consumed by the beast of the apocalypse. Having written a utopian novel while living in a dystopia, Mark offers the gospel of a mythical city that can be approached from four directions: "Great roads approached the city, from north and south, east and west" (p. 133).[2] This mythical, archetypal city lives in our imagination as once having existed, its four gates open to all who wished to live within the dream world of a perfect society. This four-gated city, evidently, could only exist in a golden age, an unattainable city in an unachievable time. Yet it is this city that Martha now strives for, amidst the Bosch-like images of madness and sterility that pervade the Coldridge household.

The connecting link to all the houses, to all the gates—real and imaginary—is Martha herself. At the opening of the novel, she arrives at the restaurant when she comes to postwar London—a continuation of the earlier *Landlocked*. She then seeks a job as a secretary, but accepts temporarily a post as Mark Coldridge's housekeeper. As the house becomes a walled-in medieval fortress that protects her against further action, even further thought, the job turns into a way of life; it becomes her destiny.

The house is Bosch's hell, Gregor Samsa's room, the Invisible Man's basement cell, but it is also a refuge. Perhaps a modern view of hell is no more than this, Sartre's *No Exit*, a place in which one loses himself, his will, his determination, and exchanges choice for a lair. Dostoevski pressed this option in the "Grand Inquisitor" scene, and the contemporary response is clear. Freedom, as Martha once quested after it in the stifling atmosphere of the white man's Africa, is not worth the struggle; we are, she appears to accept, all caught in a larger scheme anyway, and it is better to be besieged than to besiege. Using Mark's house as a base of operations—settling in for the rest of her useful years—Martha only occasionally ventures

---

2. Doris Lessing, *The Four-Gated City* (New York: Knopf, 1969). All subsequent references are to this edition.

out, to have casual sex with Jack and to continue the debasement of her former intentions. Or else she gravitates to Paul's house, a kind of live-in encounter group, in which the maimed attempt to support each other; all experience there is "tripping," hallucinatory.

Shut in, besieged, surrounded by madness, frustration, and sickness; experiencing inadequate, furtive sex; gated; with hyenalike journalists howling outside and jumping on whatever carrion is offered them; with nuclear bombs in production; with American madness symbolized by Korea and McCarthy never far; with marches and countermarches; with threats always looming—whether Russia, fission, or personal schizophrenia—in some fashion Martha has to put herself together. If she is enclosed in four houses, she is also Janusfaced: the softness of Mattie is the reverse of the questing Martha. The houses are both integrative and disintegrative, much as the notebooks in *The Golden Notebook* represent two opposing strains: those parts of Anna-Ella which can be consolidated and those pieces which defy stabilization.

The apocalyptic epilogue of *The Four-Gated City* represents, in some ways, the "golden notebook" section of that book. The content of both is seeking form. In geometry, the circle indicates perfection, completion. But Lessing utilizes not circles, but "fours": four notebooks, four gates or houses, four directions in a "four-gated" city, and epilogues or "golden" episodes. The "fours" indicate all directions, negate completion, baffle expansion, intensify the enclosed quest. There is no magic in four, unless as part of a utopian vision, the utopia that comes near the end of the novel along with apocalyptic destruction. And the content finally achieves a form that allows no exit, except through the apocalyptic vision of a new, technological world that ends the novel.

So it all seems. *The Four-Gated City* is, in several ways then, a curious finale to the "Children of Violence" series. It appears to cap the "enclosure" theme, so that Martha ends up, in Mark's house, as exhausted and otiose as the narrator in Proust or one of Beckett's dying gladiators. Up to this point, Martha, like

Anthony Powell's Nicholas Jenkins, had been involved in a *Bildungsroman*. Far more than Jenkins, however, Martha has rubbed her nose in the filth of events, the filth of unpleasant affairs and marriages. Observer more than participant, Jenkins moves easily in his own version of the dance of time. But while he waltzes or relaxes into old familiar motions, as appropriate to someone who glides through an established society, Martha contorts her body into the brittle shapes of modern dance, as befitting someone who must always create the society in which she is to move.

While we may resist Martha's "dance" as a form of surrender, she sees it as new phase in her development, a path to a new, different, and more intense kind of awareness. Her keying in to Lynda Coldridge for this new awareness is fraught with several ironies. Lynda would appear to be everything that Martha, previously, had resisted becoming. Out view of Lynda is of a woman too frail for life, too slender (both physically and psychologically) for the demands of wife, mother, bedmate, too mentally ravaged for any kind of existence except helplessness. Boarded in the basement of Mark's large house, Lynda has returned to a kind of womblike existence; she is at the end of the umbilical cord, gaining sustenance from what others can give her. Cared for by women who themselves either are incapable of handling "outside" lives or refuse such roles, Lynda appears a female Oblomov.

Possibly, for that very reason, *for* her otiosity, Lynda becomes attractive to Martha. All of Martha's former activity has now centered on simply "being." Previously, she had coiled her considerable energies toward becoming; she was always seeking new roles. She now substitutes being for becoming, and in matters of "being," Lynda has learned a great deal from her madness. She has learned, among other things, how to hear thinking, how to comprehend psychic forces, how to descend into a purity of line denied anyone who lives actively in the world.

There is the sense that in Lynda Martha has found the key to Mark's mythical, golden-age city. Since this idea is so antithetical to what Doris Lessing, through Martha Quest, has been getting at previously, we must attempt to understand in detail what she is saying before we can evaluate the idea in the novel in the series, and in terms of life itself. A little more than halfway through *The Four-Gated City*, Martha recognizes that she might be in love with Lynda: "If she was in love with Lynda, then it was with a part of herself she had never even been introduced to—even caught a glimpse of. This was the language of a schoolgirl crush! This unknown person in Martha adored Lynda, worshipped her, wished to wrap her long soft hair around her hands, said, Poor little child, poor little girl, why don't you let me look after you?" She then continues rather ironically, as the feeling reaches her understanding: "Well! said Martha, who would have thought it? I'm a Lesbian, and a schoolgirl Lesbian at that" (p. 352).

Martha's so-called Sapphism, however, is somewhat different from what is ordinarily associated with the word and the relationship. Her love for Lynda, such as it is, is the obverse of her love for Mark. Mark's activism, his man-of-the world character, originally attracted her to the house, as did his need for her services, as caretaker and bedmate. Her feeling for Lynda is for her inactivity, her inability, her helplessness. Mark and Lynda joined become one person, outer and inner. Martha is in love with both, for each suggests a side of herself. When she says she loves Lynda, she identifies with that part of Lynda which symbolizes the death of the flesh and the death of what we normally associate with life, replacing it with another kind of life that lies deep beneath the skin. Not fortuitously, Lynda wastes away physically: she has long since lost her breasts, and her buttocks gradually melt as she reaches toward skeletal proportions.

The death of the physical in her signals the birth of something else, and it is this quality that Martha loves; not even Lynda herself, but the fineness of psychic thought that Lynda is capable of revealing. We can say, then, that Martha is ready to be transformed, to become herself—not dead, not otiose—but a new person; prepared to head into new experiences on a psychic level unrevealed to all but a few such as Lynda, or the ever-present fortune-teller Rosa Mellendip and Jimmy Wood, the amoral scientist. If she tries to enter this world, Marth realizes, she must reject the other, represented by the madness outside the house and all those involved in that madness. By the end, the house itself is to be razed, and so decisions must be made. Mark allies himself with Rita Maynard, a figure from Martha's African past, and now seeks life in the external world as intensely as Martha seeks it internally.

Before we make any judgments in this area—before we determine whether Martha is intensifying her sense of life or simply deteriorating with age—we must seek further "external" images, to see whether a journey within is escape or survival of a sort. *The Four-Gated City* begins with suffocation and strangulation. The key images in the first pages—indicative of the book's entire range—are of grime, globules of wet, browny-gray textures, oilcloth with spilled sugar, gritty smears, grease, thumb marks. All these images are attached to both houses and city. Possibly the chief scenic effect of the book, as befitting Lessing's continued descent into a fiercely populated hell (her next book would be called *Briefing for a Descent into Hell*, 1971), is either Bosch's "Garden of Earthly Delights" or his "Last Judgment," In both paintings, as in Lessing's novel, enclosed space is a mixture of sacred and profane, of realism and fantasy, of the loving and the obscene, of large vision and carping detail, of panorama and locale.

Still "outside," the symbol of breakdown in social morality and in humanity itself is Jimmy Wood, a mild-mannered scientist and writer of space fiction who is a human computer of sorts. Jimmy represents the bland forces of military, science, and government which, with velvet glove, offer salvation while they are missing a human dimension: "It was as if Jimmy had been born with one of the compartments of the human mind developed to its furthest possibility, but this was at the cost to

everything else." Jimmy specifically has been designing
machines that can tamper with the human mind, making im-
provements on existing machines that destroy part of the
human brain by electric charges. In addition, he has developed
on government request machines to destroy the brains of
dangerous persons, who would then vanish without protest.
Further, Jimmy has worked on and perfected a machine for
"stimulating, artificially, the capacities of telepathy, 'second
sight,' etc." So that the machine will always have fuel, it is
necessary for governments or the military to have on hand a
"human bank" that the machine can utilize. Such a human
radio or telephone would provide an extension to the machine
and prove more flexible; after that, it is up to the military to
find a specific use.

Jimmy is by no means isolated on the outside. He is Mark's
partner in an enterprise that designs and makes machines—the
operation is itself covert. The point of their work together,
however, should not be lost. For the Mark who has preached
about the ideal city is the same man involved in designing and
manufacturing dehumanizing machines. His vision of a four-
gated city has little bearing on his work or life-style. Both he
and Jimmy are also writers. While Mark has written a utopian
book, Jimmy writes science fiction, in which machines kill off
those people who have "more senses than are considered normal." Mark only breaks with Jimmy when the latter's amorality
becomes apparent.

Thus, even though Martha feels intense sympathy for Mark,
her relationship with him, once examined, makes little sense,
for he represents something she has to purge from herself, that
"outside" world which negates personal choice or social morality. Despite his humanizing attitudes, Mark is attached to an
external system, from which he derives both money and satisfaction, that is part of the dehumanization of the entire outside
world. By sharing Mark's bed, Martha shares his interests; she
is an associate in almost the sense Jimmy Wood is a partner.

Martha more or less makes her final decision when she takes
a walk on a fine, sunny day, an idyllic day for the human spirit

to proliferate and become one with Nature. In a Swiftian turn-about, however, Martha has her vision, not of Wordsworthian divinity, but of human vileness and creature disgust:

> but then sounds came into her, they were vibrations of feet on pavement, and she looked down again at an extraordinary hideous creature who stood watching her, out of eyes that were like coloured lumps of gelatin that had fringes of hair about them and bands of hair above them, and which half protruded from a bumpy shape of pinkish putty, or doughlike substance. (p. 479)

Like Swift, she sees herself in their image; she is of their kind, and she cannot escape that:

> There they were, all soft like pale slugs, or dark slugs, with their limp flabby flesh, with hair sprouting from it, and the things like hooves on their feet, and wads or fells of hair on the tops of their heads . . . it was painful in a way she had never known pain, an affliction of shameful grief, to walk here today, among her own kind, looking at them as they were, seeing them, us, the human race, as visitors from a space ship might seem them, if he dropped into London, or into another city to report. (pp. 480–81)

People are shit: their guts are rotting, their bodily odor is appalling, their nervous systems and muscles are numbed by drugs, the air they breathe is polluted by fumes from industrialization, cigarettes, their own bowels. Even so, this is not so frightening as their behavior:

> that they walked and moved and went about their lives in a condition of sleepwalking: they were not aware of themselves, of other people, of what went on around them. Not even the young ones, though they seemed better than the old: a group of these might stand together looking at others passing; they stood with the masses of the pelt hanging around their faces, and the slits in their faces stretched in the sounds they made to communicate, or as they emitted a

series of loud noisy breaths which was a way of indicating surprise or a need to release tension. But even these did not listen to what the others said, or only in relation to the sounds they made themselves: each seemed locked in an invisible cage which prevented him from experiencing his fellow's thoughts, or lives, or needs. They were essentially isolated, shut in, enclosed inside their hideously defective bodies, behind their dreaming drugged eyes, above all, inside a net of wants and needs that made it impossible for them to think of anything else. (p. 481)

There is more here than disgust, more than an intellectual and physical turning away, more than alienation from one's self. There is the need to remake oneself entirely, in a new image, using different coordinates. Martha's vision is not only Swiftian, it is truly Bosch-like. In both *The Golden Notebook* and this novel, Lessing has spoken of being "in Bosch country." The various dreams of the former book were Bosch-like in nature, going beyond ordinary nightmare into visions of personal and societal Armaggedon, going even beyond that into primitive visions of degradation amidst extermination. "Bosch country [Martha asserts]. If I could paint, and I painted this, I would be a forger. Are forgers people who plug into Bosch country?" (p. 513).

Martha ascribes these views to her "self-hating" phase; but it is gradually this phase which, usurping all other possibilities, insists upon itself. In order to survive, she must seek an alternate life; and within this alternate life, Mark is insufficient, the wrong person in the wrong place. It is Lynda who can fulfill Martha's vision; or at least Martha can live within the gleams Lynda reflects. As she circles Lynda and finally decides to plug in, Martha sees her decision not as escape but as survival. She goes underground (Lynda lives in the basement), or, in another way, she goes into an enclosed place from which the outside world can be excluded.

From houses that had enclosed her, she now moves, first, to Lynda's basement apartment and, eventually, within Lynda's head where amidst her so-called madness extraordinary visions develop. Having rejected Mark's schizoid world, Martha in an excursion into a form of retrograde sanity now plumbs Lynda's schizophrenia, as an alternate experience far from the view of the external world. This movement, in the latter stages of the novel, is the culmination of the "enclosure" theme that Doris Lessing has pursued throughout the novel. Now she has gone further within, intensified.

The mad world within finds its shape and coherence from images of enclosure that run metaphorically through the entire book. Perhaps the closest we come to Lessing's sense of the 1960s is in Harold Pinter. At first, the two may seem dissimilar, and the coupling of their names bizarre. However, both the playwright and the novelist are heirs to a development in literature that has become insistent in the last fifty to sixty years. Since Kafka and Proust, there has developed what we may call a "literature of enclosure." It is a type of fiction in which breadth of space is of relatively little importance. Space exists not as extension but only as a volume to be enclosed in a room, or a house, or even in a city. Joyce's Dublin has this quality — as though the city were not open to the sky but were a series of enclosures of houses and bars and meeting places. Such a city conveys not the sense of something unfolding but of something accruing, like an internal growth that invisibly expands to tremendous size under cover of the flesh.

Kafka's use of rooms and houses is, of course, one of the prototypes of this kind of fiction. Another is, obviously, the room of Proust's Marcel, where he stifles in heat and frustration and self-hatred. A third is the cluttered rooms of Beckett's Murphy or Watt, who bitterly malign their fate and remain immobile. Such a development in literature may, at first, appear to be a direct response to the Freudian reliance on the regressive tendencies of the adult to return to the womb, that quasi-sacred place where needs are met without effort and without external threat. Such a response is certainly there, and it is questionable if such a literature would have developed, at least in this manner, without the influence of psychoanalytic thought. To follow this argument — which ultimately is not the major one—is to note that the room is the place in which one can dream, in which one can isolate himself as a consequence of neurosis or withdrawal symptoms, all as part of that desire to seek refuge from external onslaughts that are too much for the individual to withstand. All this is certain.

But a further argument exists for the preponderance of rooms and rooming houses in Pinter and Doris Lessing. I think we can say that the room or house signifies for them an entire culture, in particular England's shrinkage in the 60s from its postwar eminence to a minor "enclosed power." In *The Four-Gated City*, for example, Martha Quest has used Mark Coldridge's house as a way of settling her life and at the same time as an escape from a social and political world she cannot control. As a medieval family once hid behind drawbridge and moat, she hides behind the door, and this self-concealment is both a physical and psychological fact.

Since enclosure is so significant in Lessing's work, its features need detailed description: even though the room is a place of refuge, it is also the locale of one's descent into hell. Its physical desolation is indeed a counterpart of the character's psychological state. Further, the room serves as a tiny stage for those on a string in a puppet show. Enclosure fixes the limits of sexuality, threatens and reassures within bounds, freeing as it limits. As a consequence, the novel becomes personal, subjective, solipsistic, even when externals such as political events are of significance.

The room bottles up rage, leaves no escape for anger except when it is directed back into the self. The lair is itself a physical symbol of impotence—lack of choice, will, determination; identity is indistinguishable from one's furnishings. Clearly, the panoramic novel is snuffed out, adventure is lost; there is no struggle. The room or house is a battleground. The family relationship is symbiotic—Lessing discovered that fictionally before Laing publicized it psychoanalytically. In such a room, Eros becomes sex, spirit becomes physical, idea or theory becomes fact. Whereas space was once used for repetition of a holy act, the act of creation itself, now its repetition is one of staleness, of folding anxiety into neurosis. In the room, a dumb waiter serves as a feedline, or people are themselves "dumb waiters."

Finally, in the novel of enclosure, the room is the ultimate of the profane world, negating Mircea Eliade's idea of space as being sacred. The room is geometric space, not the infinite space that Eliade sees as central to a reliving of the cosmogony. "It follows that every construction or fabrication has the cosmogony as paradigmatic model. The creation of the world becomes the archetype of every human gesture, whatever its plan of reference may be. We have already seen that settling in a territory reiterates the cosmogony. Now that the cosmogonic value of the Center has become clear, we can still better understand why every human establishment repeats the creation of the world from a central point (the navel)" (*The Sacred and the Profane*, p. 45).

Keep in mind Lessing's "four-gated city" when Eliade writes: "On the most archaic levels of culture this possibility of transcendence is expressed by various images of an opening; here, in the sacred enclosure, communication with the gods is made possible; hence there must be a door to the world above by which the gods can descend to earth and man can symbolically ascend to heaven" (p. 26). When the room or house was sacred, one's conception of space was infinite, extending to the infinite space of the universe. Breathing in the air of this room, one could as it were breathe in something coexistent with the cosmos. Lessing and Pinter, like Beckett, provide rooms whose air is foul; space is not infinite, but geometric, and it signifies the final vestiges of the profane city.

Although images and metaphors proliferate in both parallel and varied directions, the lines of the novel are drawn. Before Martha decides to give herself over to inner experience—as a natural progression of her journey within—that inner world is presented as entrapment, loss of choice, loss of self and will. That is, the world within is claustrophobic. Once, however, Martha goes all the way in that inward journey toward Lynda and her mad form of sanity and insight, once she decides that, the inwardness is no longer claustrophobic, but a form of release and even freedom.

The novel is, really, a continuation of the journey we have come to expect from Martha Quest. But it is not a traditional quest, nor is she a traditional quester. Rather than going outward for her experience, she must learn to seek inward; rather than overcoming the traditional obstacles of temptation and virtue, she must overcome the temptations of will-lessness and loss of determination, as represented by Mark's house and Mark himself. Thus, she must come through the temptations of one kind of inwardness in order to reach the Promised Land of another kind, that represented by Lynda. Martha's disgust with humankind finds its resolution in her embracing those whom society considers mad, incapable, too weak to stand unsupported.

It is curious that in *Declaration* (1957) Lessing hardly prepared us for the sense of doom she sounds in her fiction of the next decade. In her essay there, she asserted her preference for the nineteenth-century realists — Stendhal, Balzac, Tolstoy, Dostoevski — who, despite their differences, stated their "faith in man himself." She said, further, that the writer must not plunge into despair, as Genet, Sartre, Camus, and Beckett have done. "The point of rest [for the writer] should be the writer's recognition of man, the responsible individual, voluntarily submitting his will to the collective, but never finally; and insisting on making his own personal and private judgements before every act of submission." Particularly ironic is her statement that "there is a new man about to be born . . . a man whose strength will not be gauged by the values of the mystique of suffering" (pp. 194, 191).

This statement is evidently part of Lessing's 1950s thought, when she was deep in the third volume of the "Children of Violence" series. And yet, as she rakes over the same 50s in the *Four-Gated City*, they are times of deep depression, quite different from Martha's attempts to struggle through as an individual in *A Ripple from the Storm*. In a sense, Lessing has rewritten her own feeling about the 50s from the vantage point of the late 60s. The rewriting of an earlier position, one already taken in the third volume of this same series, indicates how far her political intelligence has carried her. There are no longer any political solutions; solutions, such as they are, must be individual matters.

Even further, however, individual resolutions are impossible in the larger world; they can only take place—and not very satisfactorily even then—within that enclosed, inner sanctum of the Coldridge basement, within that rarified inner sanctum of Lynda's "mad" brain, which hears thoughts and, Cassandra-like, acts as seer. No Madame Sosostris, Lynda is the reincarnation of the Sybil of Cumae, although it is already too late for anyone to listen to her.

Once we have circled around to this, we can understand Martha's attachment to Lynda. The latter is simply the further extension of enclosure. Martha has been consistent with the imagery of her waking dreams and nightmares. She has burrowed underground and beneath, like Kafka's mole, in order to seek the furthest reaches of that subterranean sphere where mysterious things take place untainted by human will. Lynda is lair, refuge, partial solution, resolution of one's disgust with all that exists out there.

Lessing has taken us on a most difficult journey. She has wound and circled her way through the 1960s and offered something that is mainly unpalatable. Yet she has done her task with such intensity, with such honesty of intention and presentation, that the reader who rejects the "resolution" is hard pressed to find alternatives. Society as we know it, she asserts and demonstrates, has collapsed. The holocaust that informs the fifty-page Appendix of the book is not a radical break with what came before, but a logical extension of the earlier time's madness. Nerve gas, nuclear devices, the death of the West— these are geographical Final Judgments, the Day of Armageddon, but without even the sense of good and evil battling each other. The West has simply exhausted its possibilities, and other geopolitical areas—chiefly Africa and China—have asserted their claims for power.

Within the holocaust, Martha and Lynda (who had forewarning of the "accident" that ended the West) are surviving on an island off the northwest coast of Scotland, Robinson Crusoe-like, concerned almost solely with physical survival. Since radiation is a problem, many in the survival community die from undiagnosed diseases. Those who live, however, have decided to use the disaster as a way of finding an alternate existence. Unlike Crusoe, they will not leave their island. Some of the children born under these conditions have above-normal capacities, children who, like Lynda, "see" and "hear." Some of the children are subnormal, but they are treated with the others, not as social deviates or as isolatos. One boy in particular, however, a "brown" child, perhaps Moorish or Arab, Joseph by name, is unusual, extraordinary in his ability to comprehend. Joseph is to be sent to Francis Coldridge's settlement in Nairobi. Once there—we note ironically—Joseph is classified not as supernormal, but as subnormal, fit for third-grade school work. Joseph's talent as a seer is treated as a deviation; he is "mad."

The year is about 1997. The world is at peace. But forces are slowly shaping and reshaping toward another world comparable to the one exhausted and exterminated. One must search within, or go primitive, or seek isolated islands. In her next novel, *Briefing for a Descent into Hell*, Lessing has moved more deeply into private visions, into counterexperiences, into schizophrenia as an alternate experience.[3] None of this is witty,

---

3. In this later novel, she suggests that the schizophrenic life of one Charles Watkins, Cambridge classicist, is, for him, a chance to transform his drab, monotonous, ordinary life into something adventurous and meaningful. Found dazed on a Thames embankment in London, Watkins has entered his schizoid stage of seemingly aimless wandering among Keats's realms of gold. He has lost his memory and is, instead, refueling his brain, not with dead languages and dead experiences, but with a different kind of reality. In this condition, he sees himself as one of those sent by the Almighty to redeem the world—he has, as it were, been briefed for his descent into hell, the world in our time. Such a messianic mission in real-life terms would indicate madness. In his schizoid condition, it indicates a chance for him to reintegrate his personal desires with the ways of the world; in his state, such a vision is a form of superior knowledge.

But while he is moving toward some kind of final vision that will put his soul at peace with himself and the world, the world is trying to bring him back to its kind of

or even ironic. Perhaps because she was an outsider, Lessing
has always been earnest and has never traded on the English
traditions of social comedy, or muddling through. Both Anthony Powell and C. P. Snow, in their vastly different ways,
belong to that mode, as do most of the 1950s "Angries" writers.

In her rather grim, relentless manner, Lessing has tried to be
both panoramic (about racism, communism, bombism, all the
"ologies" and "isms") and subjective. Her length indicates as
much: *The Four-Gated City* runs one-quarter of a million words,
and her earlier book in the 60s, *The Golden Notebook*, is about as
long. And yet, with all her prolixity, she has burrowed within as
far as she can possibly go, certainly within the traditional novel
form. She is getting less personal, and she has destroyed the
objective world. There is always science fiction, but in that
mode those intense human relationships which are the strength
of her earlier work can have no outlet. There is also the type of
notation Norman O. Brown used in *Love's Body*, an attempt to
grapple with the fragmentation and disjointedness of human
experience through tying together quotations from literature,
philosophy, anthropology, psychoanalysis, et al., all toward a
personal journey into oneself to seek what is distinct, asocial,
potential.

The critic must not try to become Cassandra, however. What
is peculiar and generous about Doris Lessing and her work of
the last decade is that she is the sole English writer willing to
probe her mind and talent wherever they lead. Following the
contours of 1950s and 60s history and politics, she has refused
to stand still or resolve easily. Each book now is for her a new
start, an attempt to grapple with changes that occur more
swiftly than the writer can write. Now that her series is con-
cluded, she has been freed completely from the past. She is no
longer tied to Martha or her quest. The reader is left with a

reality. Working over him is a team of doctors who use modern drugs to restore his
memory, to make him a functioning human being. None of these modern cures
works, but when Watkins is subjected to electric shock, his schizoid state is wiped
clean, so to speak, and he returns to what he was: a rather drab academic figure
leading an ordinary tedious life.

dilemma: he wonders as he holds this considerable achievement in hand if still another novelist is succumbing to apocalyptic visions as a way of settling personal identity problems. Or else, he wonders, as he holds the same weighty book in hand, whether the novelist has any other choice but to attempt a breakthrough. Surely the old formulas are no longer viable. Surely politics has left the world of sanity. The old type of sex, the old relationships, the old politics, the old shibboleths — surely they are no longer possible.

And so, perhaps Lessing is serving the function reserved for the writer, which is to lead us, despite ourselves, into terrible areas of exploration. She refuses to play it safe, and she refuses to settle for any solutions. She will not accept personal sex, à la Norman Mailer, as a way of grasping reality; she will not settle for a declining society, à la Anthony Powell, as a way of defining exhaustion and depletion. Religion, politics, individual relationship do not suffice. Wherever she looks, she sees the beast and makes us experience it:

> And I saw a beast coming up out of the sea, having ten horns and seven heads, on his horns ten diadems, and upon his heads names of blasphemy. And the beast which I saw was like unto a leopard, and his feet were as the feet of a bear, and his mouth as the mouth of a lion: and the dragon gave him his power, and his throne, and great authority. (Revelation 13:1–2)

Biobibliographies of Authors

ANGUS WILSON (Frank Johnstone) was born on August 11, 1913, in Bexhill, Sussex, England, but spent most of his youth in South Africa. He attended Westminster School from 1927 to 1931, and read Medieval History at Merton College, Oxford, from which he was graduated (B.A.) in 1936. After taking his degree he worked variously as a tutor, secretary, restaurateur and social organizer, and in 1937 became a librarian at the British Museum until 1942 when he entered the Foreign Office. In 1947 he returned to the British Museum and was given the job of replacing over a quarter of a million volumes destroyed by bombings. In 1949 he was appointed Deputy Superintendant of the Reading Room, a post he held until 1955 when he resigned to become a full-time writer. Wilson has worked as a television critic, has lectured in over two dozen countries, and frequently contributes reviews and criticism to leading international periodicals. His books have won many prizes, and in 1972 he was made a Companion of the Royal Society of Literature, one of the highest marks of literary recognition in Great Britain.

NOVELS
Hemlock and After (1952)
Anglo-Saxon Attitudes (1956)
The Middle Age of Mrs. Eliot (1958)
The Old Men at the Zoo (1961)
Late Call (1965)
No Laughing Matter (1967)
As If by Magic (1973)

DORIS (May) LESSING was born on October 22, 1919, in Kermanshah, Persia, and moved with her family in 1924 to Southern Rhodesia, where she grew up on a large farm. She attended a convent school in Salisbury, later lived and worked there, and made an early and hasty marriage. Divorced from her first husband (Frank Charles Wisdom) in 1943, she married Gottfried Lessing two years later. Communist affiliations eventually made her *persona non grata* with the reactionary Rhodesian government, and in 1949 she was expelled from the country and prohibited from returning. She and her husband (from whom she is now also divorced) took up residence in London, where she began publishing almost immediately. Lessing, a recipient of several important literary prizes, has lectured extensively in many countries, and contributes short stories, criticism, and essays to many leading international periodicals.

NOVELS
The Grass is Singing (1950)
"Children of Violence" Sequence
  Martha Quest (1952)
  A Proper Marriage (1954)
  A Ripple from the Storm (1958)
  Landlocked (1965)
  The Four-Gated City (1969)
Retreat to Innocence (1953)
The Golden Notebook (1962)
Briefing for a Descent into Hell (1971)
The Summer Before the Dark (1973)

John ANTHONY BURGESS Wilson was born on February 25, 1917, in Manchester, England, where he was educated, being graduated (B.A.) from Manchester University in 1940. Entering the army upon graduation, he was assigned to the British Army Education Corps, and served for the next six years on Gibraltar. In the following thirteen years he held various and assorted teaching posts throughout England and Malaya, and devoted himself to musical composition, which he had studied at the university. Burgess wrote little until 1959, when a false diagnosis for a brain tumor set off a rush of literary activity that has proceeded uninterruptedly to the present time. In addition to being one of England's most prolific novelists, Burgess has written plays, verse, criticism, and hundreds of reviews, has lectured on and taught creative writing in leading American universities and colleges, and has written for the Broadway stage and television.

NOVELS

"The Malayan Trilogy" (American title: *The Long Day Wanes*) (1965)

> *Time for a Tiger* (1956)
> *The Enemy in the Blanket* (1958)
> *Beds in the East* (1959)

The Right to an Answer (1960)
The Doctor Is Sick (1960)
The Worm and the Ring (1961)
Devil of a State (1961)
One Hand Clapping (as Joseph Kell; 1961)
A Clockwork Orange (1962)
The Wanting Seed (1962)
Honey for the Bears (1963)
The "Enderby Trilogy"

> *Inside Mr. Enderby* (as Joseph Kell; 1963)
> *Enderby Outside* (1968)
> *The Clockwork Testament: or Enderby's End* (1975)

Nothing Like the Sun: A Story of Shakespeare's Love Life (1964)
The Eve of St. Venus (1964)
A Vision of Battlements (1965)
Tremor of Intent (1966)
MF (1971)
Napoleon Symphony (1973)

MALCOLM (Stanley) BRADBURY was born on September 7, 1932, in Sheffield, England. His early education was conducted at West Bridgford Grammar School, and in 1953 he was graduated B.A. with Honors from University College, Leicester. In 1955 he took his M.A. at Queen Mary College, London, and was awarded a Ph.D. in American Studies from the University of Manchester in 1963. He has taught both in the United States and in England, and has received numerous grants and fellowships. Though he has written only two novels, he is also known as a poet, playwright, and short-story writer. His critical writings have proved influential at home and abroad.

NOVELS
   Eating People Is Wrong (1959)
   Stepping Westward (1966)

KINGSLEY (William) AMIS was born on April 16, 1922, in London, and received his early education at City of London School. In 1947 he received his M.A. (First Class Honors in English) from St. John's College, Oxford, after having served three years in the Royal Corps of Signals, where he was promoted to lieutenant. Amis first came to the attention of the literary world as a precocious and brilliant poet of precise and witty verse, but became famous overnight with the publication of *Lucky Jim*, one of the first, and still perhaps the best of the novels written by "the angry young men." As well as being a poet and novelist, Amis is a promulgator of sci-fi and detective fiction, and under the pseudonym Robert Markham has written a James Bond adventure. Amis has won important literary awards, has taught creative writing at leading American and British universities, and contributes to such distinguished periodicals as the *Spectator, Encounter, New Statesman,* and *London Magazine.*

NOVELS
   Lucky Jim (1954)
   That Uncertain Feeling (1955)
   I Like It Here (1958)
   Take a Girl Like You (1960)
   One Fat Englishman (1963)
   The Egyptologists (with Robert Conquest; 1965)
   The Anti-Death League (1966)
   Colonel Sun: A James Bond Adventure (as Robert
       Markham; 1968)

I Want It Now (1968)
The Green Man (1969)
Girl, 20 (1971)
The Riverside Villas Murder (1973)
Ending Up (1974)

JOHN FOWLES was born on March 31, 1926, in Leigh-on-Sea, Essex, England, where he attended public school, excelling both as scholar and athlete, and eventually becoming head boy, a position of prestige and power for which he developed a confirmed distaste. After resigning his lieutenancy in the Royal Marines, he matriculated at New College, Oxford, where he was graduated in 1950 with a B.A. and with Honors in French. For the next thirteen years Fowles taught in France, Greece, and England, becoming head of the English Department at a small London college. Fiercely intellectual, and a recluse by nature, Fowles gave up teaching for full-time writing in 1963, and retired to Lyme Regis, Dorset, where he courts his two greatest avocations, nature and isolation. His first three novels, which have been commercial as well as critical successes, have all been filmed, to make Fowles's name something of a household word beyond literary circles.

NOVELS

The Collector (1958)
The Magus (1966)
The French Lieutenant's Woman (1969)
The Ebony Tower (1974)

MARGARET DRABBLE was born on June 5, 1939, Sheffield, Yorkshire, England, and is the sister of the distinguished critic and novelist A. S. Byatt. She was educated at the Mount School, York, and entered Newnham College, Cambridge, from which she was graduated (B.A.) with Honors in 1960. Drabble began writing novels after her brilliant undergraduate career at Cambridge, and after a short stint as an actress, during which time she lived in Stratford-on-Avon with her actor-husband, Clive Swift. Drabble now lives with her husband and three children in London. She has lectured in England and America, and is the recipient of important literary prizes. She is one of the first of the younger contemporary women novelists to champion the problems of women, and to try to define their ambiguous role in the modern world.

NOVELS

A Summer Bird-Cage (1963)
The Garrick Year (1965)
The Millstone (1965)
Jerusalem the Golden (1967)
The Waterfall (1969)
The Needle's Eye (1972)
Realms of Gold (1975)

NIGEL (Forbes) DENNIS was born on January 16, 1912, in Bletch-ingley, Surrey, England, but received his education abroad, first at the Plumtree School in Southern Rhodesia, and then at the Olden-waldschule in Austria. From 1935 to 1936 he served as secretary to the National Board of Review of Motion Pictures in New York, and from 1937 to 1938 he was an assistant editor and book reviewer on the *New Republic*, a post he resigned to become, until 1959, staff book reviewer for *Time Magazine*. Since 1960 he has lived in London as drama critic and joint editor of *Encounter* (1967–1970) and as staff book reviewer for the *Sunday Telegraph*, a position he still holds. Dennis has written only three novels, but the high quality of their style and their uncompromising intelligence have been enough to make him one of the most respected and influential novelists of his generation. In addition, he has written plays, verse, and criticism, and been awarded coveted literary prizes. In 1966 he was made a Fellow of the Royal Society of Literature.

NOVELS

Boys and Girls Come Out to Play (1949; American
    edition: *Sea Change*)
Cards of Identity (1955)
A House in Order (1966)

ALAN SILLITOE was born in Nottingham, England, on March 4, 1928. He left school at the age of fourteen to work in a bicycle plant, and later worked at a plywood mill and as a capstan-lathe operator. From 1946 to 1949 he served with the Royal Air Force in Malaya as a radio operator, and began writing novels and short stories and poetry. Discharged from active service, he lived for six years on the island of Majorca, and returned to England in 1955 where he has, with few interruptions, lived ever since. His brilliant *Saturday Night and Sunday Morning*, for which he won the Author's Club Prize, and his subsequent novella, *The Loneliness of the Long Distance Runner*, for which he won the coveted Hawthornden Prize, rocketed him to spectacular recognition in a little over two years, and film adaptations of these two books (for which he wrote the scripts) became box-office hits. *The Ragman's Daughter*, a novella that he also turned into a screenplay, was also successfully filmed in 1970.

NOVELS
Saturday Night and Sunday Morning (1958)
The General (1960)
Key to the Door (1961)
The Death of William Posters (1965)
A Tree on Fire (1967)
A Start in Life (1970)
Travels in Nihilon (1971)
Raw Material (1972)

V(idiadhar) S(urajprasad) NAIPAUL, whose grandfather had come from India to the Caribbean as an indentured laborer, was born on August 17, 1932, in Trinidad. He completed his early education at Queen's Royal College in Port of Spain, and after two years of working in the capital, he emigrated to England, entering University College, Oxford, in 1950 and being graduated with Honors in English in 1954. Between 1954 and 1956 he married, and became an editor of "Caribbean Voices" for the British Broadcasting Company, London. Naipaul makes his official residence in London, though he is an inveterate itinerant, and his travels are responsible for much of his nonfiction. Naipaul has traveled in the West Indies and South

America, in India, Africa, and throughout the United States and Canada. He has been a frequent contributor to leading international periodicals, and has won countless literary prizes, among them the Booker and Hawthornden prizes.

NOVELS

The Mystic Masseur (1957)
The Suffrage of Elvira (1958)
Miguel Street (1959)
A House for Mr. Biswas (1961)
Mr. Stone and the Knights Companion (1963)
The Mimic Men (1967)
A Flag on the Island (1967)
In a Free State (1971)
Guerillas (1975)

ANDREW (Annandale) SINCLAIR was born in Oxford, England, on January 21, 1935, and educated at Eton College, Buckinghamshire, where he was a King's Scholar. After serving as an ensign in the Coldstream Guards, he entered Trinity College, Cambridge, and was graduated with a double first in History in 1958. In 1963 he received a Ph.D. from Churchill College, Cambridge. After a very brief teaching career in the United States and in England, he became managing director of Lorrimer Publishing Ltd., London, a post he has held since 1967. Since 1969 he has been a film director and screenwriter for Timon Films, London, and has written and directed *The Breaking of Bumbo* (after his own first novel), *Under Milk Wood*, and *Byron's Evil*. In addition to his novels and film scripts he has written plays, history, criticism, social commentary, and biography, and has done translations from the Greek, Spanish, and French. One of the most fertile minds in British literary circles, and of enormous energy, Sinclair was made a Fellow of the Royal Society of Literature in 1970.

NOVELS

The Breaking of Bumbo (1959)
My Friend Judas (1959)
The Project (1960)

The Hallelujah Bum (1963; American edition: *The Paradise Bum*)
The Raker (1964)
Gog (1967)
Magog (1972)

Notes on Contributors

ROBERT K. MORRIS, Professor of English at The City College of the City University of New York, is the author of *The Novels of Anthony Powell*, *The Consolations of Ambiguity*, *Continuance and Change*, and *Paradoxes of Order*, as well as a number of articles on contemporary British and American literature. He is also co-editor with Irving Malin of *The Achievement of William Styron*, and he reviews regularly for *The Nation*. He is presently completing a study of John Fowles.

PETER E. FIRCHOW, Professor of English and Comparative Literature at the University of Minnesota, is the author of *Friedrich Schlegel's "Lucinde" and the Fragments* (1971), *Aldous Huxley, Satirist and Novelist* (1972), and *The Writer's Place* (1974), as well as essays on various modern subjects.

MARTIN GREEN, Professor of English at Tufts University, is the author of *Mirror for Anglo-Saxons*, *Reappraisals*, *The Problem of Boston*, *Science and the Shabby Curate of Poetry*, *Yeats's Blessings on von Hügel*, *Cities of Light and Sons of the Morning*, and *The von Richtofen Sisters*. He has just finished a book on dandyism in England in the twentieth century called *Children of the Sun*.

FREDERICK R. KARL is Professor of English at The City College of the City University of New York and director of its graduate programs in English. He is the author of several studies of the novel: *An Age of Fiction: The Nineteenth Century British Novel*, *The Contemporary English Novel*, and *A Reader's Guide to Joseph Conrad;* as well as *The Quest*, a novel, and a critical study of C. P. Snow. He is also co-editor of several anthologies, including *The Existential Imagination*, *The Existential Mind*, *The Naked I*, *Short Fiction of the Masters*, and *The*

Shape of Fiction. A former Guggenheim Fellow and Fulbright lecturer in France, Professor Karl is currently editing the collected letters of Joseph Conrad, projected for ten volumes, and working on "literary Enclosure," a thematic analysis of certain motifs in the novel since Richardson.

JAMES W. LEE, Professor of English at North Texas State University, is the author of *John Braine* and *William Humphrey*, as well as a number of essays on modern British and American literature. He is a co-editor of *J. D. Salinger and the Critics, Poetry: A Thematic Approach,* and *Southwestern American Literature: A Bibliography.* He served from 1967 to 1975 as editor of the quarterly *Studies in the Novel.*

MARVIN MAGALANER is Professor of English at The John Jay College of the City University of New York. He has written extensively on James Joyce (*Time of Apprenticeship: The Fiction of Young James Joyce; Joyce: The Man, the Work, the Reputation* [with Richard M. Kain]), and he has edited three *James Joyce Miscellany* volumes. His latest work is entitled *The Fiction of Katherine Mansfield.*

IRVING MALIN is Professor of English at The City College of the City University of New York. He is the author of *William Faulkner: An Interpretation, New American Gothic, Jews and Americans, Saul Bellow's Fiction, Isaac Bashevis Singer,* and *Nathanael West's Novels.* He is the editor of six critical collections and the co-editor of three others. He reviews regularly for *Commonweal* and the *New Republic.*

BERNARD MCCABE is Chairman of the English Department at Tufts University. His essays on British and American fiction have appeared in various journals, and he reviews frequently for *Commonweal.*

ESTHER PETIX lives in Suffern, New York, and teaches in its school system. She is a student of British and American literature in general, and of Anthony Burgess in particular, about whom she has just completed a long critique.

ROBERT PHILLIPS, writer, editor and anthologist, is the author of *Inner Weather* (poems), *The Land of Lost Content* (short stories), *Aspects of Alice* (a critical anthology), *The Confessional Poets, Moonstruck* (an anthology of poetry about the moon), and *Denton Welch.* He has taught literature at Syracuse University and writing at The New School in New York City, and his essays and reviews have appeared in the *New York Times* Book Review, the *Saturday Review, Commonweal, Centennial Review,* and elsewhere. He is a former editor of the literary journal *Modern Poetry Studies* and a vice-president at Thompson-Koch Advertising in New York City.

BARBARA BELLOW WATSON is Professor of English and Director of the Women's Studies Program at The City College of the City University of New York. She is the author of *A Shavian Guide to the Intelligent Woman,* a study of Bernard Shaw's ideas concerning women (1964) that was republished by the Norton Library in 1972. Her articles on women's studies and literary criticism have appeared in various journals and collections, and her poems have appeared in the *New Yorker, Harper's, Kenyon Review,* and *Prairie Schooner.* She is editor of the Women's Studies volume in Harper & Row's *Studies in Language and Literature,* and a member of the Editorial Board of *The Shaw Review* and of the Advisory Board of the Feminist Press.

PETER WOLFE teaches at the University of Missouri—St. Louis. His books include *The Disciplined Heart: Iris Murdoch and her Novels; Mary Renault; Rebecca West: Artist and Thinker; Graham Greene the Entertainer;* and *John Fowles: Magus and Moralist.* Another book, on Ross Macdonald, will be published soon by Bowling Green State University Press. President in 1972 of the Modern Literature section of the Modern Language Association, Professor Wolfe has also reviewed for the *New York Times* Book Review, *Saturday Review, The Nation,* and the *New Republic.* His current project is a book-length study of Jean Rhys.